Antiracist Education

ANTIRACIST EDUCATION

FROM THEORY TO PRACTICE

Julie Kailin

ROWMAN & LITTLEFIELD PUBLISHERS, INC.
Lanham • Boulder • New York • Toronto • Oxford

ROWMAN & LITTLEFIELD PUBLISHERS, INC.

Published in the United States of America
by Rowman & Littlefield Publishers, Inc.
A wholly owned subsidary of The Rowman & Littlefield Publishing Group, Inc.
4501 Forbes Boulevard, Suite 200, Lanham, Maryland 20706
www.rowmanlittlefield.com

PO Box 317
Oxford
OX2 9RU, UK

British Library Cataloguing in Publication Information Available

Library of Congress Cataloging-in-Publication Data

Kailin, Julie, 1947–
    Antiracist education : from theory to practice / Julie Kailin.
        p. cm.
    Includes bibliographical references and index.
    ISBN 0-7425-1823-X (alk. paper) — ISBN 0-7425-1824-8 (pbk. : alk. paper)
        1. Multicultural education—United States. 2. Race relations—Study and
teaching—United States. 3. Racism—Study and teaching—United States. I. Title.
    LC1099.3 .K35 2002
    305.8'0071—dc21

                                                                    2001048520

Printed in the United States of America

∞™ The paper used in this publication meets the minimum requirements of American
National Standard for Information Sciences—Permanence of Paper for Printed Library
Materials, ANSI/NISO Z39.48-1992.

DEDICATED TO MY CHILDREN
Kimanzi and Syovata
AND MY GRANDCHILDREN
Yazmin, Nialah, Razia, and Emayu

Contents

Foreword

This remarkable book, beginning with the personal history of the author, reaches beyond the awareness of a sensitive Midwestern child into a public (and socioeconomic) space pervaded by racism in all its forms. Professor Kailin is an educator, the daughter of parents committed to social action; and her work throbs, not only with a profound sense of injustice, but the passion of someone insistent on a vision of possibility—of a social reality somehow transformed in public schools. Without sentimentality, without a glimmer of false hope or reassurance, Julie Kailin ushers us into classrooms infiltrated by words and practices that demean and insult children who are not white, children thought of as hopelessly "other" by presumably well-meaning teachers who know not what they do.

There are numerous sociological and historical studies of prejudice and racism on the shelves of educational institutions, most communicating in the abstract formulations of social science. We are, it is true, beginning to find qualitative studies of tracking, profiling, even a kind of "apartheid" in schools. This book bridges the distance ordinarily opening between observers and whatever human dramas they have selected out to see. Readers are brought into the midst of classroom life. Voices seldom heard become audible. Not only are we permitted to hear what is actually said in classrooms marked by "diversity," or officially "integrated" classrooms where discrimination is still experienced by children. We are given insights into things teachers say to each other or write in their journals. As significantly, Dr. Kailin has opportunities to look at children's journals, some with poignantly empty pages, some with accounts of being misunderstood or wholly ignored.

What might be described as innocence on the part of certain teachers, or blindness, or denial is explored at eloquent length in these pages. Like so many Americans, many of them have been reared in atmospheres characterized by racist thinking and behavior. When they hang pictures of Martin Luther King and other African American heroes in their classrooms, it does little to change the deep roots of racist attitudes. Moreover, as Dr. Kailin repeatedly makes clear, it is not just a matter of altering surface opinions or communicating what has turned out to be "politically correct." It is a matter of translating what has been learned about racism and its consequences into some kind of transformative, critically oriented action so that signal changes may eventually take place.

It is after her often dramatic presentation of racist attitudes and conventions that Dr. Kailin widens the scope of her study and connects it to some of the important contemporary studies of schools in their relationship to the free market, capitalist economy. The very structures of our society, she reminds us, make racism a taken-for-granted way of treating the "other" and looking at the world. Race, class, gender: all work together to perpetuate inequalities and an incapacity to compensate for—or repair—the social suffering due to injustice. Like Paulo Freire, Julie Kailin stresses the necessity for critical consciousness and for an ability to reflect upon the assumptions that underlie and perpetuate racism, "othering," racial profiling, and the rest.

The movement in this book from the personal to the public, the gradual emergence of images of a more humane and equitable future makes it something far more than just another account of a prevailing racism and the need for remedies. Dr. Kailin's views of antiracism and teaching to end racism derive their power, not only from her obvious scholarship in social history, curriculum, and inquiries into classroom life. It comes as well from her feeling of outrage at the way African American children are mistreated, deprived of the education they need in order to survive. Being the mother of Black children, Dr. Kailin knows from very personal experience the damage done to young hearts and minds. When these insights and feelings feed into a knowledgeable overview of approaches to multiculturalism (many of them ineffective and superficial), and what is thought of as school reform, we are offered a new pedagogy, perhaps a new "pedagogy of the oppressed."

Never taking refuge in old idealisms, never depending upon blank materialism, Dr. Kailin remains true to important political and economic theories of social structure and social change; but she never condemns those of us who are teachers to the helplessness induced by determinism. Critical consciousness, thinking about our own thinking, a rejection of thoughtlessness, and opening to those who are different from ourselves: these are what this writer works for in her teaching, and these are what are nurtured by this text. Readers cannot but become personally involved and engaged through their encounter with Dr. Kailin. We can help realize the hopes she arouses through our own deliberate action for decency, social justice, and—if we come together—ongoing change.

MAXINE GREENE
Teachers College, Columbia University

Preface

How I Write Myself into This Story

This book on antiracist education probably began before even I knew it, perhaps when I was nine or ten years old and our Brownie leader called my best friend, Irma, a "n——" when we came late to Brownie class one day. As Irma and I stood before her, dripping wet from the rain we had just escaped, Mrs. Z said nothing to me, directing her anger only at Irma. Irma called her a "cracker," and we both spontaneously walked out of Brownies that day, never to return. This was not without some regret, for we had been practicing for weeks, fantasizing what it would be like to march with the Brownies in the annual parade around the state capitol dressed in those lovely tan uniforms (which we knew we would never be able to afford). Our mothers, who were also close friends, complained to the principal, but he did nothing. After this incident, I never wanted to belong to the Brownies again, even though all the other white girls in my school belonged. That was one of the first consciously "political" choices I recall making. It was also the first time I had ever heard the term "cracker," and I thought it odd that Irma's retort was so mild for such an ominous word as n——. While I had never heard the word "cracker" before (or if I did, it had no meaning to me), the word n—— was one I heard frequently from many of the white kids in my neighborhood.

The neighborhood where I grew up in the fifties in Madison, Wisconsin, was integrated, with most of the city's Blacks, Italians, and Jews living there. But there were limits to the amount of real mixing that went on, and except for a few white people such as my family, I recall few examples of whites interacting socially with Blacks. Racism affected the cultural backdrop for most of the white families in my neighborhood, as elsewhere. I was reminded of this just lately when I happened upon a recently published and locally acclaimed cookbook from my old and now nonexistent neighborhood, destroyed in the sixties in the period of "urban renewal," or what some have termed "Negro removal." *The*

Greenbush Cookbook, written by some of the members of the Italian community, features several photographs of the "good old days" in the neighborhood, showing members of the Italian community organizations in Blackface, having a "good time." As a child, it was clear to me that most of the white kids in my neighborhood and school were actually being taught racist ideas in their homes and churches (which I occasionally visited) and in our schools. And if it wasn't always apparent to me at first, it was made very clear when I found myself, along with my Black friends, locked out of the white kids' houses as we were told we could not come in to play dolls with the other white girls, and when some of the white kids in my classes were not allowed to play at my house because "you know who" might be there.

I was very fortunate that my parents were antiracist activists and educated me by their example. My mother, Margaret Coogan Kailin, one of seventeen children from an Irish Catholic farm family, somehow rejected the dominant racial prejudices and stereotypes of the white culture of her upbringing. In the late 1940s and early 1950s, she was active in the Civil Rights Congress, one of the organizations that fought the genocidal wave of lynchings and executions of Black people who had been framed for crimes they did not commit.[1] During my childhood, my mother, together with a multiracial group of working-class women friends, formed the "Friendship Club," which met frequently, bringing together their families as they shared favorite dishes and swapped recipes. My mother was one of the few white members of the Mary McCleod Bethune Club, a local chapter of the National Colored Women's Clubs. Although I saw my mother as a quiet and sometimes painfully shy woman, at the same time, I knew her as brave and fearless when it came time to take a stand. I remember when she went to my elementary school library and found a copy of *Little Black Sambo*, she took it to the librarian and said "What is *this* doing here? I thought you said you were not going to buy this book again!" Then she went to the principal's office and there was a meeting. Even when they removed the book, it would somehow find its way back onto the shelves, and my mom would once again be back at the principal's office. I remember the mixed feelings I had when my mother did this, especially once when I happened to be in the library when she came in. On the one hand, I wanted to disappear because my mother was making a "scene," but on the other, I felt proud that she was doing the right thing.

I also remember how even fun times like music class were often tainted by racism. Racist songs like "Ole Black Joe" or "Swanee River" or other slavery-glorifying relics were often standards in music class. My mother objected to such songs because, she explained to me, they created the impression that Black people longed for the days of slavery. I sat quietly in the back of the class with some of my Black friends, who were also conscious that this music was not "theirs," and we did not move our lips.

I recently read Paulo Freire's account of coming into "consciousness" in his twenties when he realized that the Black help in his home was poorly treated.[2] In contrast to Freire's late awareness, my Black friends came to "consciousness" when they were small children, and I learned much from them at an early age. In the neighborhood where I grew up, Black children were usually conscious of racism and injustice by the time they were in kindergarten. I recall the knowing in their voices when they would comment about the "prejudiced" treatment they received from teachers, shopkeepers, neighborhood house workers, and welfare workers (from whom the television would have to be frantically hidden).

My Black friends and my mother were not the only influences in my developing an "antiracist" perspective at an early age. My father, Clarence Kailin, has always been devoted to antiracist causes. He fought as an antifascist in the Abraham Lincoln Battalion, one of the International Brigades of the Spanish Civil War (1936–39), a "premature antifascist," as FBI director J. Edgar Hoover was said to have put it. After returning from Spain, my father, like other veterans of that war, was considered *persona non grata* by the U.S. government. He was harassed by the FBI; his employers, friends, and neighbors were "visited" by them; and they made a point of interfering with any job opportunities.[3] For most of my childhood, my dad worked on and off as a free-lance janitor. When white men wearing suits came to our door, I knew they were not our friends.

My parents' activities in peace and civil-rights struggles often found their way into our home, such as the time in the early 1950s when our house became the strike headquarters for African American migrant farm workers who were being held hostage in Mazomanie, Wisconsin, having been brought up from the South to work the fields and pick the crops, and then denied return transport home unless they paid most of their meager earnings back to the owners who brought them there. It is little known that this strike actually resulted in the first farm labor contract in Wisconsin.[4] I recall hearing that the great writer and playwright Lorraine Hansberry sat in our living room at political meetings while she was a student at the University of Wisconsin, and a photo of singer, actor, and activist Paul Robeson graced the pages of our family picture album.

Though neither of my parents went to college, they both had and continue to have (both are still active in their mid-eighties) a great interest in and knowledge of African American history, civil rights, and labor history. If they occasionally had any extra dollars after the very basic living expenses, the only material things I recall ever seeing them acquire were books. Not clothes or furniture or cookies, but books such as Carter G. Woodson's 1933 *The Mis-education of the Negro*, which caused me to wonder, "But what about the mis-education of the white people?" There were other books of an antiracist or antifascist nature too, such as the works of W. E. B. Du Bois, Herbert Aptheker, Langston Hughes, Elizabeth Gurley Flynn, Charles Wesley, Lillian Hellman, Marx and

Engels, and many others. And there were books on revolutionary Irish history and poetry, Jewish history, and working-class history. Yet unlike many children of the Left, who rebelled against the "dogmatic" leftist ideas of their parents, I heard no dogmatic preaching or intellectualizing about these things from my parents, who were busy working at janitorial jobs most of the time.

My working-class upbringing also had an influence on my early politicization and class consciousness. It was certainly an "educational" experience for me when I had to go to work many evenings, along with my mother and brother or sister—usually unwillingly—with my father (who was very allergic to dust) to help him out on one of his several night jobs cleaning doctors' offices, car dealerships, country clubs, or taverns, when I would much rather have gone off somewhere and smoked cigarettes with my friends.

Later, like so many of my generation I was influenced by the popular struggles of the sixties and worked for school integration with the late Father James Groppi (with whom I was arrested). I also went down South and worked on a civil-rights project in the Appalachian mountains of Eastern Tennessee for antiracist activists Carl and Anne Braden, who headed the Southern Conference Educational Fund. We frequently had meetings at the Highlander Folk School. Being in the presence of such people as the Bradens, Reverend Fred Shuttlesworth, Ella Baker, and so many other heroes and "sheroes" at meetings at Highlander was every bit as inspiring as what I knew of those antifascist struggles of an earlier period. During my time in Appalachia, I lived down the road from Florence Reece, the wife of coal miner Sam Reece, one of the founders of the United Mine Workers of America, and visited frequently with her. Florence was famous for her song "Which Side Are You On?" which she penned in 1931 on her kitchen calendar as her house was besieged with gunfire from the mine owners' thugs. The song challenged the myth of neutrality where there is injustice. She still lived in the same small mountain cabin, despite the fact that her song had become one of the anthems of the labor and civil-rights movements.

The idea that education matters—and that antiracist and antifascist education matters—is not just philosophical for me, it is very personal. Often I begin my classes and workshops by discussing the relationship of racism and fascism and talk about my own personal background. Recently, when talking to a group of teachers, I mentioned that my father fought with the International Brigades against fascism in the Spanish Civil War. I was met with some rather blank stares as well as puzzled expressions, for many of them thought I meant the Spanish-American War of 1898. When I inquired how many of them had ever *heard* of the Spanish Civil War, only seven or eight of the fifty teachers said they had heard of it. This was difficult to believe—after all, this was not a terribly young group of teachers, the average age probably being in the mid-thirties to mid-forties—so I asked them again, "How many of you have *never* heard of the Spanish

Civil War?" The vast majority of the people in the room raised their hands. I asked them if they had ever heard of Hemingway or Orwell, and of course, most of them said they had. I reminded them that these writers had written against the backdrop of that war. But that literature had been carefully decontextualized for them, allowing them to know isolated figures of the "canon" without addressing the significance of the contexts in which these human dramas had been acted out. They had been robbed of their history. They had been robbed of their right to know.

As sad as is this ignorance among teachers, they are hardly alone in this historical "amnesia." These misrepresentations of our history affect everyone in our society, and the "amnesia" is particularly acute when it comes to issues of capitalism, slavery, and racism in American history and culture. The importance of facing our history should not be underestimated. If we don't understand our history, we can't understand the color divide that continues to undermine democracy. This is all part of an antiracist worldview—to reclaim that knowledge that has been submerged, marginalized, distorted, stolen, or hidden from all of us because of the race, class, gender bias, and political privilege of those who have the power to determine whose "knowledge" gets known.

I preface this book to acknowledge how my own lived experiences have generated my antiracist perspective. I write myself into this story, not as an objective observer or researcher, but as an admittedly partisan participant who mourns our loss of memory and who believes that there is a good deal of sense— and love—in the Marxist dictum: "The philosophers have only interpreted the world in various ways. The point, however, is to change it." Of course, this does not simply mean change for its own sake. The purpose of such change must be to build a more inclusive, democratic, and just society for all. That is the mission of antiracist education.

Acknowledgments

No book is ever really written by an individual, and my writing and research are the end product of many minds and experiences. I am indebted to many scholars, activists, and authors, too numerous to mention all, but whom I have acknowledged in the text or in the notes. In my research and practice, there is the influence of my parents, Margaret Coogan Kailin and Clarence Kailin, a veteran of the Abraham Lincoln Brigade in the Spanish Civil War. Their social and political activism from as long as I can remember forms a backdrop to my own thinking. I also hear the voices of my children, Kimanzi and Syovata Edari, who have helped me—or forced me—to try to see the world refracted through different lenses of time. I thank them all for inspiring me to write this book. I also thank those who read and provided helpful feedback on parts of this book at various stages of its development: Kenneth Zeichner, Gloria Ladson-Billings, Sally Soriano, Mary Layoun, William L. Tate, Kimberly Yang, Robert Tabachnick, and Nancy Scherr. I have presented pieces of this research at various conferences such as the American Education Research Association (AERA) annual conferences (since 1998); also at the American Educational Studies Association (AESA) annual conference in San Antonio in 1997; the International Conference on Critical Legal Studies at the Lancaster Law School in Lancaster, England; and the Conference on Nationalism, Identity and Minority Rights at the University of Bristol in 1999. I have benefited from the suggestions or questions raised by anonymous members of these audiences. I am also grateful to the several hundreds of teachers who have been willing to undertake the uncomfortable task of "unlearning" their racism. My lengthy discussions with them enabled me to untangle the threads of theory and practice, which helped me construct a basic framework for teaching against racism. I am also appreciative of my editor, Dean Birkenkamp, for his encouragement and constructive criticism, not to mention his patience when my manuscript was long delayed due to illness. And to Aziz, who is always there to help me keep a perspective of what matters and what does not.

Introduction

This book is a theoretical, historical, and ethnographic study of antiracist education. It is about theory and about practice, mine specifically, when I attempted to implement my ideas in real classrooms with real teachers. One can hardly talk about theory without eventually talking about practice, or vice versa, because one informs the other. The ideas and beliefs that influence our understanding about a particular problem, whether we are consciously aware of them or not, influence our practice and behavior. Conversely, our theoretical understandings of things may change or shift as we become engaged in real-life situations that either confirm or contradict our assumptions or experiences. It is my hope that the examination of historical background and the varying theoretical perspectives discussed in part 1 of this book will help the reader understand the assumptions that guided my research and practice described in part 2.

In the area of race relations, I found it essential to examine the historical background to the problem of racism in education before I could attempt to develop a framework from which to implement antiracist education with teachers. This was because I saw not only a profound lack of knowledge and understanding about racism among teachers, but also found this silence or confusion applied to the knowledge base and curricula in higher education among those who teach the teachers. Most discussions about racism still tend to focus on symptoms and descriptions of how things are or appear to be, and not why they are that way or whether they really have to be that way. As Ladson-Billings and Tate (1995) also argue, the salience of race and racism as a topic of scholarly inquiry continues to remain untheorized. Of course, when one considers the role of higher education and other institutions historically in maintaining the status quo, perhaps this is not surprising. Without addressing the historical and theoretical background to the problem of racism in society and education, it is difficult to be able to imagine possibilities for change. Therefore the organization of this book reflects my conscious decision to address the issue of antiracist education in an integrated and holistic fashion, as outlined below.

In the preface, I acknowledged the relevance of my points of departure from the perspective of a white woman who has been involved in "race relations" from early childhood as a child of progressive leftist civil-rights activists, and later on in life as a mother of children of color, as well as a researcher and student who has witnessed or experienced some of the problems addressed herein. In chapter 1, I discuss how I came to find teacher education as an avenue of opportunity for developing and "testing out" an antiracist pedagogy for teachers and my subsequent decision to conduct more systematic research on this topic. Here I also address the research methodology I employed and the kinds of data I collected in my work with teachers.

In chapter 2, I put this problem into historical context and examine some of the recent trends with regard to race in American education. In chapter 3, I discuss some of the recent critical scholarship on multiculturalism and antiracism and delineate how the two paradigms may differ in terms of the basic parameters of educational reform. In chapters 4 and 5, I put forth the argument for antiracist education and propose a curricular framework, as well as discuss the social conditions of teaching and some of the practical considerations and constraints for doing this work in the context of in-service teacher education.

Part 2 of this book, "Putting Theory into Practice," focuses on my experiences in implementing antiracist education among teachers. Chapter 6 begins with a profile of the city where I did this work, which, for purposes of anonymity, I call "Lakeview." Lakeview is a city known for its progressive tradition, and the school district is considered to be among the best in the nation. Yet despite its reputation for "tolerance" and "excellent" schools, the city has had a very poor track record when it comes to successfully educating children of color. In the context of this "liberal" environment, I examine the contradictory consciousness and the opinions and attitudes of the teachers in Lakeview regarding race-related issues in their schools. Chapters 7 and 8 narrate my efforts to "actualize" antiracist education for teachers. In chapter 7, I discuss the curriculum and the methodology I employed as I attempted to help teachers unravel and decode the impact of racism on our individual upbringings and lived experiences. In chapter 8, I explain how we contextualized these collective narratives—facing history *in* ourselves. In these last two chapters, I also examine how teachers responded to this critical antiracist pedagogy and how it affected their understanding of their roles and possibilities as teachers.

I have included portions of a previously published article that I revised for inclusion in this book: "How White Teachers Perceive the Problem of Racism in Their Schools: A Case Study in 'Liberal' Lakeview," *Teachers College Record* 100, no. 2 (Summer 1999), reprinted by permission of *Teachers College Record* and Blackwell Publishers.

CLARIFICATION OF TERMS

This book uses the term *race* in its socially constructed sense, since in biological terms there is only one race—the human race. In the United States, the socially constructed and imposed "racial" categories are usually based on differences such as skin color or other physical characteristics, but at different historical periods, they have also referred to language, religion, or ethnicity. Whereas the term *race* has been around for hundreds of years, the term *racism* has only recently come into more widespread usage in the English language. Most dictionaries before the 1960s did not include the term at all, and it did not appear in Webster's New International Dictionary until the 3rd edition in 1961. The standard dictionary definition of racism is "The belief that race accounts for differences in human character or ability and that a particular race is superior to others. Discrimination or prejudice based on race." This definition absolves most white people from any responsibility, for few whites, except overt white supremacists, would say that they believe there is an inborn superiority of one group over another.

Racial prejudice, or prejudgment, refers to judgments or opinions held before the facts are known and often in disregard of facts that contradict it. In the sphere of human relations, it is is often expressed in suspicion toward or hatred of other races, religions, or ethnicities and results in inaccurate and/or negative beliefs that espouse or support the superiority of one race over another, or the "normalcy" or rightness of one race. *Racial dominance* refers to the domination of the societal structures by one racial group, and the use of those structures to act on or support that group's racial prejudices and maintain group privilege.

It is the combination of racial prejudice together with racial dominance that constitutes *institutional racism*. In the United States, the form of racism that exists is white racism or white supremacy, because whites control the economic, social, and political institutions and use these institutions to maintain group dominance and white privilege. Wellman (1977/1993) talks about racism as a system of "culturally sanctioned beliefs which, regardless of the intentions involved, defend the advantages Whites have because of the subordinated positions of racial minorities" (p. xviii). This explanation illuminates how institutional racism becomes embedded without necessarily conscious intention, for one may avoid the possibility of institutional change or reorganization if it affects one's own perception of well-being or advantage.

As central as the problem of racism has been in American history and culture, the denial of racism as a systemic feature is the *modus operandi*. The terms *racism* and *race* are still resisted in the United States, and elaborate code words are constructed to avoid using the terms. Examples of such code words are "welfare mother," "drugs," the "inner city," "inner-city violence," "gangs," "urban," and "underclass." In school systems and in the educational literature, one may hear or read references to children of "low socioeconomic status," "children at risk," or "children with special needs" in reference usually to children of color. Here the emphasis is placed on the "deficiencies" of those groups, rather than on the fact that they are suffering from institutionalized racism and oppression in a capitalist system.

As Lani Guinier remarked in a radio interview, race is the issue that nobody wants to talk about. And yet, as with those interviewed for Studs Terkel's 1992 book, *Race: How Blacks and Whites Think and Feel*, it is also a topic that seems to be on everybody's mind. But since it is not socially acceptable to talk about race, because it makes people feel defensive or uncomfortable, the code language allows people to talk about it without ever using the word.

In this book, the term *Black* refers to people of African descent. But this term is also a social and political construct and has historically sometimes been used to describe non-Anglo-Saxon "whites," such as Jewish or Irish people, when they have been subject to domination and discrimination. It is also a political construct coming out of slavery and does not necessarily describe skin color, but rather a political reality within a racist context. Historically, in the United States, "one drop of Black blood" meant that one was classified as Black, or at least as "not white," the idea being that "one drop of Black blood" destroys the "purity" of a white person. The irony, however, is that a Black person who has any white ancestry cannot be considered white. On the other hand, white people who bake themselves in the sun of the Jamaican beaches until their skin becomes darker than the skin of some people of African descent are still considered white. *Black* may have a different meaning outside of the United States. In Great Britain, for example, the term refers not only to Africans, but to Indians, Asians, or anyone else who is not white. As a Kenyan friend who is Black once remarked to me, "I had no idea I was Black until I was twenty years old and came to the United States!"

The term *African American* refers specifically to people of African descent from the United States and thus does not include Africans or people of African descent living in or from Britain, the Caribbean, or elsewhere. For some Americans of African descent, Black is still the preferred term, while for others, it is African American. In this book, I sometimes use the terms Black and African American interchangeably. Often I use the term Black rather than African American when my intent is to show that it is because of this feature of not being white (and being of African descent) that one may be receiving discriminatory treatment. For example, a British Jamaican or a Ghanaian may be discriminated against or stopped by the police because he or she is Black, not because of his or her country of origin. This was horribly illustrated in the murder of Amidou Diallo, an immigrant from Guinea, Africa. On February 4, 1999, Diallo was shot at forty-one times by four police officers in New York City as he stood, unarmed, in the vestibule of his apartment building in the Bronx. The four officers were acquitted of all charges a year later.[1]

A note regarding the capitalization of Black is in order. Conventions in publishing dictate that if Black is capitalized, then white also must be capitalized. I disagree with this convention because I think it is a false comparison. Hence, I do not capitalize white, because it does not denote any particular ethnicity or nationality, but I do capitalize Black, because I use it interchangeably with African American and also because Black denotes an ethnicity describing peoples of African descent. One of the reasons why people of the African diaspora may call themselves Black rather than a specific ethnicity is because their true ethnicity was robbed from them during slavery, when all attempts were made to erase the history and identity of the African peoples. In this sense, the use of Black is more characteristic of nationality and thus not comparable to white, which refers more to skin color of no particular or specific national origin. Whites can and do refer to themselves by their ethnic heritages—Italian, Italian American, German, Irish, and so on. The capitalization of terms identifying people of color is important for legitimation and recognition, especially for those who have suffered racial or ethnic discrimination in a white supremacist context. It was an issue of debate when the designated term was "Negro" versus "negro" or "Colored" versus "colored." African Americans have always had to fight to name themselves and to have that name respected. As W. E. B. Du Bois argued, any term that is a proper noun should be capitalized. Obviously for Blacks of the African diaspora who have been robbed of their right to know their specific heritage, whatever designation they choose should be respected and capitalized as a proper noun.

Over the last several decades, there have been numerous transitions in the ethnic group names of those who have variously been called Native Americans, American Indians, or Indians. As Pewawardy (1999) argues, many people have wrestled with those choices as if there were no other choices, suggesting that the term Indigenous Peoples is the more accurate representation. Depending on the context, I use either Native American or Indigenous Peoples.

PART ONE

Historical and Theoretical Foundations
of Antiracist Education

CHAPTER ONE

Observations of Covert Racism in Schools

THIS BOOK BEGINS WITH THE PREMISE that good and often well-intentioned people may practice everyday racism without being aware of it. To some degree we are all victims of miseducation, especially as it concerns the political economy of racism. This became evident to me when my own children entered school and was reinforced later when I came to more systematically study teachers and classrooms. I was often struck by the teachers' seeming unconsciousness of their behavior when it came to issues of race. The fact that I was raised in a progressive activist family involved in the civil-rights and peace movements certainly influenced my perspective on education. What drew me to the study of race relations in education, however, was not some romantic "leftist" idealism, but the practical daily challenges I confronted as a mother raising two biracial children, who in this society are considered Black and who, from a political perspective, consider themselves Black.

My progressive background did not totally prepare me for the challenges my children would face in schools. From their early childhood in the 1970s, when I had to object to their nursery school teachers teaching them racist nursery rhymes and songs like "Ten Little Indians," through their high school years, I saw how they were often marginalized, ignored, feared or stereotyped in school. As I began to talk to other children of color and their families, I was disturbed by what they have to endure to get an education. As a white parent, I also became increasingly concerned about the superior or chauvinistic attitudes that some of their white classmates were exhibiting. Like many of the children of color and their parents that I talked with, I saw the covert or subtle manifestations of racism that subverted their education, much of it coming from the very

3

adults who were entrusted with their education and "enlightenment"—their administrators, counselors. and teachers. While this racism or racial insensitivity may have been due to deep-seated prejudices and stereotypes, I knew also that much of what was happening in the schools was unconscious and due to ignorance and a miseducation of educators. After all, how can one expect someone to see what they have been taught to "not see"?

My education continued throughout the 1990s, as I found myself further drawn to study the world of schools and teachers' work. As I observed teachers at work, I came to appreciate the complexities of the job and the multiple demands placed on teachers. Yet as a working-class woman and an activist in the teachers' union, while I strongly identified with teachers as workers, I continued to be concerned about the sort of "everyday" racial and cultural insensitivity that affects teaching and learning. Such insensitivity is not necessarily conscious or intentional, as I observed while working on an educational research project that was not directly related to the study of race.

On this project, I visited several elementary classrooms weekly for a school year and found myself caught in the web of contradictions of the problems of racism in education. In these classrooms, I often observed what Murray and Clark (1990) identified as the ways in which racism shows up and is felt by students of color in schools such as harsher sanctions being meted out to students of color; bias in the amount of encouragement students of color are given by the teacher as compared to white students; bias in curriculum materials; low expectations of students of color; and denial of racist incidents. This behavior was seen across the socioeconomic spectrum: It was not only the poor Black kids or those from one-parent families, presumably seen as "at risk," who were receiving a particular kind of treatment, but also the Black children of professors, lawyers, doctors, two-parent families and even other schoolteachers.

I felt myself torn as I observed teachers work. I sympathized with the demands that were made upon them as workers, sometimes as union activists, as mothers, as women. Such as the time when Mrs. A felt ill but would not take off from work because she was in the middle of an important project with the kids and did not want them to have a substitute teacher for fear it would throw them off track. Or when Mrs. B had a new child who was homeless come to her classroom, who obviously needed much orientation and individual attention. I sympathized as she tried to juggle his needs with those of twenty-seven other children. When the temperature climbed into the high nineties one week and I could hardly keep my head up to take my field notes, I saw how these teachers, who had to bring in their own fans from home, managed to keep things going despite their own exhaustion from the heat.

I came to appreciate all of these teachers for specific qualities and skills in nurturing and teaching children. All of them were quite different from each other and very different from me. Despite our pedagogical, political and personal differences, as a mother I felt some identification with all of them in one way or another—in their attempts to respond to many different children at one time while trying not to show the stress of such work—and admiration for anyone who is trying to teach children in this world fraught with a number of social problems beyond their immediate control, a world that often puts schools and teachers in competition with powerful institutions like the corporate media, which are more interested in influencing children for profit so that they may become consumers, rather than teaching them or enlightening them.

Yet my solidarity with some of them as teachers and as women was challenged by my increasing awareness, as the months passed, that there were certain patterns of behavior that contributed to the process of alienation of the Black children in particular. In subtle and sometimes not so subtle ways, I often saw that they were not as nurturing or supportive of the Black children as they were of the white children, even though they all considered themselves to be fair and open-minded. Sometimes I left my intensive three- or four-hour observations and note taking and fought tears until I could get home and have a good cry before I typed up my field notes. For what I had observed were those subtle, hidden injuries of racism, and I knew that without reeducation, it would be difficult for the teachers to believe that they were doing anything to endanger the education of Black children or other children of color—or of white children as well. In the following section, I shall discuss how racial insensitivity may insert itself into schools simply by doing "business as usual." Such insensitivity contributes to disparate outcomes in education for children of color.

OBSERVING GOOD TEACHERS DO BAD THINGS

Mrs. A

Mrs. A was a fourth-grade teacher. She had a gentle manner and seemed to have a conviction and a consciousness about the importance of being fair to all of her students. She was precise in her classroom planning and displayed the day's tasks on the board each morning, broken up into fifteen- to twenty-five-minute segments throughout the day. She managed the constant transitions from one assignment to another smoothly and was affectionate to all her twenty-seven students, of whom five or six were Black.

While I saw the same affection and guidance applied to everyone, one day in Mrs. A's class something happened that could be detrimental to the development of good race relations. Mrs. A was reading a story to the children, a high point of the morning for me for I enjoyed listening to her story-telling style as much as the children did. On this particular day, the book described a Native

American character with every conceivable stereotype—the drunken, slow, simple-minded Indian, the savage scalper, the kidnapper of white women. These passages went on for several minutes. Mrs. A did not flinch, but continued to read those passages in her lovely, lilting voice as though there were nothing unusual. The children sat spellbound, absorbing all they heard. While I do not think she believed the stereotypes, her passivity in countering them was disturbing to me. Here was a "teachable moment" that not only went unproblematized but, I fear, legitimated and added to the database of racist stereotypes that children learn through osmosis, or even through direct methods, in our culture.

Miss B

Miss B was a third-grade teacher of a class of about the same size and racial composition as that of Mrs. A, but her personality was quite different—sometimes rather frenetic. While her list was also displayed on her board each morning, her attempts to move from one task to another were less successful and often disturbing to both herself and the students. Sometimes the children were just beginning to get involved in something when her singsong voice instructed them that it was time to stop what they were doing and move on to the next task written on the blackboard. These transitions were rarely smooth, and she had to constantly nag at many of the children: "People! Let's keep on task! Let's keep on task!" I could see that this caused stress for the students as well as herself. Yet I could also see that she loved kids and had the ability to laugh at herself and her students when things didn't move along as smoothly as she wished.

Often in Miss B's classroom, I observed as she, with a perky and musical voice, interjected sharp warnings more frequently to the Black girls and boys: "Tasha! Did I hear you talking again?" In this case, I had been sitting at a table nearby, and my field notes and my memory indicated that it was quite the other way around. It was actually Lisa, a middle-class, impeccably dressed little blond-haired, blue-eyed girl, who had been demanding that Tasha give her an answer on the worksheet, just as at other times she had told Tasha to bring her something from across the room or do some other task for her. The teacher never "saw" Lisa's bossy and chauvinistic behavior and only reacted when she thought she had heard noise coming from Tasha. Tasha never defended herself.

Another typical incident in Miss B's classroom concerned Jason, a Black boy who, during journal-writing time while others in the class were busy writing, would sit with his elbows on the table, chin cupped in his hands, staring at the ceiling with an expression of hopelessness on his face. Frequently Miss B would come over to him and say, "Jason, get to work. You only have ten minutes left. . . . Jason, look at your journal, not at the ceiling. . . . Jason. . . ."

One day, as I observed this typical interaction with Jason, I stopped my note taking and went over and sat next to him. I chatted with him for a moment, asking him what he did after school the previous night. He had played with his cousin, he told me. After several more questions, Jason revealed that his cousin had come over the day before and spent the night, that he went to such-and-such a school, and so on, filling me in with little details about their friendship. I happened to have with me an African American pictorial history book, and Jason asked me about it. He began leafing through the pages. "Oh, I know him!" he said, pointing to Martin Luther King. "Oh, I seen her before!" as he saw pictures of Sojourner Truth and Harriet Tubman. When he found a picture of Frederick Douglass, whom he had not seen before, he asked me who it was. He was fascinated with Douglass's hairstyle and clothing, and we talked about the kind of suit he was wearing. I told him a bit about Frederick Douglass and about how slave owners had tried to prevent Black people from learning to read. I explained how Douglass and others had risked their lives simply to learn to read and write and to get an education. He seemed very excited at the drama of Douglass's story.

"Do you like to read and write?" I asked him.

"Yes."

"Well, then, why don't you write in your journal?"

"I don't got nuthin' to say," Jason told me.

"Oh, but I think you have a lot to say. You were just telling me such interesting things about what you and your cousin did last night. That would make a very good story for your journal."

I encouraged him to begin with one sentence, and after a little prodding and help with spelling, Jason was writing the story he'd told me about his cousin. Miss B came over and interrupted to tell Jason that journal time was over, and he had to get on to something else. I explained to her that he was in the middle of an important story and asked if he could have some more time. She agreed. Jason finished with a story of seven sentences, which he counted over and over, finding that he had even gone way over the minimum number of words required for the journal that day. His face beamed with pride. I looked in his journal and saw that this had been the first entry of more than one sentence for the entire first six months of the school year! After the class, Miss B came over to me and, with a mystified expression on her face, as if I had accomplished the impossible, said, "How *ever* did you ever get *him* to do *that*?"

This was a classroom in which the teacher had put pictures of African Americans on her walls—the usual picture of Martin Luther King, as well as famous sports figures and inventors. But this was not enough to "multiculturalize" her teaching, for she had not integrated her approach with the lived experiences of her students in the classroom, nor even with her own lived experience as a white person. She was probably not conscious of who she was as a white person any more than she was conscious about who Jason or Tasha were as third-grade Black children.

I do not believe that Miss B's behavior was conscious or intentional toward her students of color or her white students like Lisa, whom she often allowed to act in bossy and "superior" ways. One reason that she could not stop to give the kind of individualized attention I gave to Jason was that she did not have the time, with her day being so fragmented and management oriented. However, there was another reason much deeper than the faulty mechanics of teaching. This teacher, like most others, had not been socialized or given the tools to truly teach a multicultural reality, let alone to teach from an antiracist perspective. Though she put images of African Americans on the walls, how could she implement culturally relevant teaching if she had low expectations of her Black students, and if she did not know how to engage them in culturally meaningful or personal ways?

Ms. C

Not all of the teachers were so unaware of the danger of students of color being marginalized, however. Ms. C, a fifth-grade teacher, was often an inspiration to me. She was quite the opposite of the other teachers, as was her class in several respects. For one thing, the class was nearly evenly divided between Black and white children. This was in large part because she had requested those whom other teachers viewed as "troublemakers," most of whom "happened" to be Black. No child was marginalized or tokenized in her room. Ms. C was firmly against structure for its own sake, and on any given day, she might change her schedule or routine to fit the needs of the moment. With fifth-graders, she may have had more freedom to do that, since presumably they had already learned some of the essential skills, allowing her to be more flexible in building on those skills in more spontaneous ways. If a teachable moment, such as a controversial issue like abortion, rape, homelessness, discrimination or a shooting in the neighborhood, was brought up by the kids, Ms. C was likely to cancel a previously planned lesson and spend much of the morning problematizing, critically examining the subject, involving everyone in a discussion about their feelings or understandings about it and encouraging them to ask the big "Why?" questions—to think relationally.

While her classroom was not "disciplined" in the conventional sense, she tried to get her students to develop self-control for reasons other than fear of punishment. Collaboration and cooperation were required in most class activities, as she practiced what has been referred to as "culturally relevant" (Ladson-Billings, 1995) or "politically relevant" teaching (Beauboeuf-Lafontant, 1999). To some teachers in the school, her classroom was perceived as anarchistic—it was often loud and seemingly unstructured. But I saw students become involved and serious about their projects and very much engaged in critical, ethical thinking and debate.

This class was not without problems, however. For example, I became concerned about Latisha, a Black girl who was an intellectual leader of the class. Latisha, an extremely compassionate and conscientious child who took all that she did very seriously, was looked up to by the other children for her strong sense of justice. She was a great storyteller, too, and entertained her classmates with elaborate tales. She spent her journal time focused intently on her writing. But when I happened to examine her journal near the end of the school year, I found that she was way behind in her writing skills. As I perused her little notebook, I saw that she had progressed very little during the year with regard to basic punctuation and grammar. Latisha did not know when to use a period, comma or capital letter, and each story was a long, run-on sentence with few words spelled correctly. I examined some of her other written work and saw the same problem. I was worried that the teacher was so focused on "caring" for the children that she did not have the time to enforce the discipline of acquiring good academic skills. Yet I could not simply blame the teacher, who spent much time and attention on the moral and ethical development of her students, helping them deal with the controversial issues that they confronted in their lives. For the reality was that she had so many other things to do, with little extra help, that she simply didn't have enough *time* to give the children's academic work the individual attention they all deserved. I feared that next year, in a new middle school, Latisha might have some kind of "learning disability" label tacked onto her by a teacher who may have low expectations of poor or minority students, or who may not feel so affectionate toward her.

I observed such a situation later, while visiting a middle school where I was conducting a staff development class. As I was talking to one of the teachers in the hallway, a seventh-grade boy whom I had observed several years back in a fourth-grade class walked by. Upon recognizing him, I commented to the teacher, "Oh, isn't that James?" explaining that I remembered him from the fourth grade. "Yes," said the teacher. "That kid's really got problems. He's severely learning disabled, he's got ADD [attention deficit disorder] and he's going nowhere. It's sad."

Not only did I know that James was not learning disabled, but he actually had been one of the brightest children in the fourth grade, was a very good writer and had even been featured in the newspapers for some of his activities in the community! Of course, it is not only Black children who may be misinterpreted by their teachers in this age of pathologizing the behavior of children, but Black children and other children of color are bearing the brunt of the trend to label anyone who is not in total conformity with the classroom (Coles, 1988; Thomas, Dove, and Hodge, 1986). I felt strongly that this teacher believed that about James only because he could not *see* him. What he saw was a stereotype that clouded his vision, one probably supported by his professional peers and challenged only by those whom society wanted to remain silent.

As a mother of Black children, I recalled what it was like to have had to go to the school to convince the teacher that my daughter had indeed written the essay on which her teacher had scrawled, "Who wrote this?" I often wondered what might have happened if I had not had the time or the confidence to go to the school to intervene—or how I might have been treated if I weren't white. And I cannot forget about the stress involved in raising a Black son whom white society may view as a criminal while he is waiting for the bus or cleaning out his locker.

Mrs. D

Of course, one cannot view these problems in isolation from the larger structural context. Take, for example, the complex issues in another third-grade classroom I observed. This was a typical traditional, structured classroom in a middle-class neighborhood. In this class (which was not considered a "problem" class) already, by the third grade, I could see that the teacher, Mrs. D, was facing far greater challenges than just teaching her kids to read and write. For, as I came to know more about the children's lives in my long conversations with the teacher, I realized that there were deep and complex problems that affected both children of color and white children, both middle-class children and working-class children.

In this relatively small third-grade class of only twenty children, a third of them had some significant problems that could affect their learning, concentration, and socialization. The class included a Black girl who was homeless and never sure where she would be waking up the next morning; a Black boy who had no winter coat, who frequently came to school very ill with a high fever and whom the teacher told me she expected soon would be homeless; and a white girl who had been sexually abused since infancy and had just recently been adopted, who sometimes clung to the teacher like a vine for security. A middle-class white boy was having emotional and behavioral problems because his parents were going through a bad divorce. A white working-class boy had just moved with his mother, who was fleeing an abusive husband, to Lakeview from California. The boy's mother had just confided to the teacher that she was finding herself and her children living on the edge, fearing impending homelessness as she was exhausting the hospitality of her family, who had been giving them temporary shelter while the mother was trying to get back on her feet and working at a low-paying waitress job. And there was a Black boy whose single mother was working two jobs and doing everything she could in a conscious effort to save him from all that was stacked up against him in her poor neighborhood, where she feared leaving him alone.

Unlike Mrs. C, who was committed to confronting the social problems that affected her students, Mrs. D tried to ignore those problems and focused only on the academic. As we discussed these "new" problems that had entered into this middle-class teacher's life, Mrs. D told me:

> Sometimes Sabrina [the homeless girl] comes to school smelling, uh, very badly, but you know, there are all of these problems with several of the children—like Nate not having a coat—but I decided that I would not take it home with me, because it leads to burnout.

She told me about one teacher in her school who got "too involved":

> She tried very hard recently to help her children and to help their home lives as well as their school lives. She took their problems home with her. She literally burned out and had to take a long period of time off. I don't want that to happen to me, so I try to have an attitude about it, to say there are these problems—I can't do anything about it, worrying isn't going to help, and I'll do what I can in the classroom.

In so many ways, Mrs. D told me, her life was very different from that of many of the kids in her class. She told me that she led "an extremely stable life," that there had never been any divorce in her or her husband's family, that her husband was a successful businessman and that she had the luxury of not working if she so chose, though she still wanted to. She told me that she lived in "a very nice condo with marble floors and a carpeted kitchen," and that she knew that for many of the children who will increasingly be entering her classroom, she would be very distanced from their reality and they from hers. Mrs. D was resigned to the reality of the social problems that affected her classroom. By the end of the winter Nate still did not have a warm winter coat, and she had decided to emotionally distance herself and just focus on the job of teaching. She did what she felt she could do—and from what I saw, she did do a professional job with many of the tasks of teaching reading and writing. She was always "on task" and taught to all, although her teaching was not received by all. While she paid more attention to skills than Mrs. C had the time to, because her class was significantly smaller, she did not engage her students on a personal level. Inadvertently, and I believe unknowingly, she sustained stereotypes, such as in her unit on American Indians, which reinforced the idea that they no longer existed, that they were a used-to-be people. Or, when a poor Black mother came to pick up her son one day, Mrs. D. was disgusted with the way the woman was dressed—"far too fancy for someone who is so poor!" she commented to me as the mother left the school. Mrs. D did not see herself as playing a role in challenging the social conditions that had changed teaching for her. Yet she was not overtly a "bad" teacher. She had been educated in the conventional sense, and she could not teach what she did not know. Like many of her colleagues, she was culturally ignorant and divorced from the day-to-day realities of a racially and economically diverse student population.

The Larger Picture

As I began to juxtapose this relatively subtle racism with my experiences with my own children, I felt a sad validation that what I was feeling through my own children as they had faced similar challenges in school—and as I was struggling against their becoming totally alienated—was in fact a very systemic or structural phenomenon. And the grim statistics reinforced my personal "subjective" observations and experiences. For in Lakeview,[1] where I conducted the ethnographic study of antiracist education that I discuss in part two of this book, the Black students had a slightly better chance of dropping out or being pushed out than of graduating. Over half of the Black middle school students had already experienced being suspended from school, and Black children were four times more likely than white children to be judged and labeled "cognitively disabled" in a district in which there was not even one Black school psychologist. At the five high schools, there were only five African American teachers, with one high school employing none, and half of the elementary and middle schools had no African American teachers at all.[2] Unfortunately, this district was not an aberration—it was "normal." Indeed, nationwide, students of color do not fare much better and are effectively "colonized" in our schools, where over 90 percent of all teachers are white and where the low rates of success for students of color are similar to Lakeview's. This was not just a Lakeview thing. Nor was it only an education thing, for I knew what would happen to so many of those who were disfranchised from education, especially when I visited juvenile detention centers and found that 70 percent of the youth who were incarcerated there were Black, in a city in which Blacks constituted about 20 percent of the school population.

These examples of how "good" teachers may do things that are counterproductive to the education of both children of color and white children are actually more widespread than just a problem in Lakeview or any particular school district. It is those subtle forms of racism that we may not all "see," especially if we have been miseducated about the larger structural and historical contexts to the problem of these inequalities. And it is not only a problem of resurrecting the history of people of color. We must examine the effects of this cultural and historical ignorance on both white people and people of color alike. James Baldwin addressed this issue back in the 1960s in his essay "A Talk to Teachers": "If I am not what I have been told I am, then it means that *you're not what you thought you were either!*" (1963/1988, p. 8).

I cited these particular examples of teachers' covert racial and cultural insensitivity because they are not uncommon and may often be unintentional, and so some may consider them to be nonmalignant compared to the overt ways in which racism is imposed on children by teachers who consciously don't like them. But problems of marginalization do not emanate only from teachers' direct actions or individual attitudes. I saw many other ways in which the culture of the school reproduced racial and economic divisions. One was the removal of children from the classroom, who usually happened to be children of color, for much-needed special help with reading, leaving the classroom to the more privileged, usually mainly white students. I was concerned about how the white children were interpreting this. Another was the fact that the white-dominated PTA made many of the decisions about the school's social events, which were usually culturally exclusive or irrelevant to parents and students of color. Also of serious concern to me was the relatively new phenomenon of psychotropic drugs, which seemed to be disproportionately given to African American children. In the hallways at lunchtime, I was distressed to see so many Black children in line at the nurse's office, where kids were waiting to get medications such as Ritalin or other drugs used for so-called "attention deficit disorder."[3] The cumulative effects of these instances of exclusion or marginalization are serious, as children of color may experience such differential treatment repeatedly throughout their school years.

Most of the teachers I discussed above were not necessarily "bad" teachers, but they were unconscious or ignorant of the multidimensional ways in which white supremacy percolates and spreads throughout American culture. The examples I have referred to here, such as not challenging stereotypes, or studying Native Americans as historical relics, or having low expectations for Black students, are not unusual. Because white supremacy is such an inherent feature of our economic system and culture, like male supremacist attitudes or sexism, one must be educated to consciously recognize and counteract these biases in practice. It is not enough to not do bad things. We must become proactive, taking an antiracist stance to counteract these tendencies.

After observing classrooms, I was reminded of the complexity of doing anything different in schools, where there are such societal pressures and so very little time, where you have individual children's various academic and social needs to be met—difficult for an individual or even several teachers to meet. We cannot minimize the importance of examining teachers' working conditions, which have become much more stressful over the last several decades. The "deskilling" of teachers (Apple, 1988) has taken much of the decision making—but not the pressure—out of the hands of teachers. Given all the structural realities of life outside and inside the classroom, to talk about introducing changes, such as antiracist or critical multicultural education, might seem like a luxury no one wants to think about when kids are coming into the classroom with bruises, hunger or pneumonia, and the teacher barely even has time to go to the bathroom! Yet at the risk of oversimplifying, we should not ignore the structural relationship between the social and economic crises in society and the intensification of racial inequities that are reproduced in schools. Nor can we ignore the sometimes unconscious white chauvinistic attitudes that prevent us from uniting to fight those very problems of exploitation, inequality, and injustice.

The experience of observing those teachers reinforced my interest in looking more deeply into the possibilities for antiracist multicultural teacher education. While I saw the subtlety as well as the severity of the problem, I also saw in those teachers some hope and the possibility for change. For the reality is that teachers, like everyone else in our society, often carry within them a contradictory consciousness that must be identified, understood, and challenged before it can be changed. Each of us has some power to interrupt and challenge injustice. It became my goal (which I discuss in part two of this book) to help teachers find their points of power.

FINDING AN OPPORTUNITY TO TEACH CRITICAL RACE-RELATIONS EDUCATION FOR TEACHERS

My involvement with antiracist education for teachers began with a conversation with Sandra (pseudonym),[4] a middle-school teacher in Lakeview, which led to a unique opportunity to develop and teach a race-relations course and to study the perspectives of teachers. Lakeview, where I did this work, was considered a relatively enlightened and liberal town and school district, which for many years had offered various workshops and in-services on multicultural education. These workshops usually offered the liberal approach to diversity, focused on making people realize that "we are all human beings in this great melting pot" or, as popular posters in Lakeview proclaimed, "Everybody's ethnic!" so we should just "celebrate our diversity!"

Yet many teachers like Sandra found such generic multicultural approaches to be insufficient for dealing with the dynamics of the changing race and class demographics, or for understanding the racial attitudes in their schools. Sandra had heard me speak in a multicultural education class and approached me after class. She told me that the issue of racism that I was addressing was what she thought people in her changing middle school were *really* dealing with—and badly. It wasn't that the teachers in her school were worried or unprepared for the increasing numbers of multicultural kids who were coming to their school. In fact, she told me:

> We've had some professors' children from India and Korea, and most teachers just love them. They think they are darling and fascinating. It's the Black kids, especially the ones from Chicago, who are having problems. They [the teachers] don't treat those kids like they do the other international kids. That's for sure!

She arranged for me to conduct the school's fall in-service and put the issue of racism "on the table" for discussion. That first experience conducting a three-hour in-service was one in which I adopted a personal approach, with some theoretical analyses of my and my children's experiences. I cited the research literature that corroborated the experiences my own children had with their teachers—being marginalized, doubted, stereotyped. I was sharing my personal stories and trying to put these into a larger framework in which I identified the objective and subjective factors associated with racism in our society. The response was overall very positive. The school staff seemed to find it fascinating to listen to a white woman—like them (the entire staff was white)—who had Black children talk about racism (was I a curiosity? a freak?) without blaming them specifically. They invited me back, and this time my approach was less personal. I drew upon my background in African American history and showed them a slide show in which I tried to demonstrate how distorted our understanding of the past is and how certain traditions of blaming the victim from the early days of slavery had worked themselves into our culture and continued to affect current-day understandings of the issues. I addressed how this affected the ways in which teachers often interpreted and labeled the behaviors of Black children.

While many seemed fascinated at this historical background to the problem of racism, I was concerned about those who could weep for the past and idolize or idealize its dead heroes, yet feel a relative detachment or alienation from the living survivors and their kindred strivings for liberty. After the slide show, I turned the discussion to the present and, more importantly, their interpretation of it. I asked them to discuss any issues or incidents that they thought might be racist or at least indicate racial insensitivity in their school. A good number of their responses concerned discipline issues or reflected common stereotypes of African Americans, as these three examples indicate:

What do you do when you tell a Black kid who is wandering the halls to get to class and he refuses? I don't know what I should do. When a white kid is in the hall and I'm trying to make small talk in a nice way with him, so I can get him to get to class, I might say "Well, hi there, Joe, what did you do this weekend?" But if it's a Black kid, I don't know what to say, and they don't listen to me anyway, and if I say anything about getting to class, they just ignore me. So I don't even say anything. I actually practice reverse discrimination.

A group of Black kids became very angry and upset when we invited a new DJ from a radio station to speak to our kids. When the Black kids asked him why he didn't play Black music, he responded that it was because there is no market for it here. He told them, "We have to please our advertisers." The Black kids were very upset, and I didn't know what to do. I didn't want them to get mad. They felt it was racist. We had a hard time trying to get them to control their anger.

On conference days, we rarely have any Black parents who show up. We send notices home, we have refreshments and we are there for them, but they are not interested. Our staff is very hard-working and dedicated, but some of these parents obviously are not. This makes it very hard for the kids to get an education, if it is not reinforced at home.

From our discussion, it was clear they had little critical understanding of racism or of the cultural and historical backgrounds of their students. Many of them referred to the deteriorating climate in their school, which they felt had gotten out of hand now that the Black kids were being bused to *their* school. Some were more concerned about the Black students' anger than they were about the causes of this anger. Unfortunately, we had little time to deal meaningfully with these issues in a three-hour workshop. How could I help them understand their perceptions of and reactions to the African American students, and the students' reactions to them, in a vacuum? That was, after all, why I had tried to introduce them in a more systematic way to the social context, to the history of racism and its manifestations. I wanted them to be able to see some of the continuities of the criminalizing or blaming of the victim historically with what was happening today. Not only did they not know their Black students, but most had little knowledge of themselves as *whites* living in a country that was founded on and still influenced by a system of white supremacy. The assumptions that *those* kids were coming to *their* school exposed their own unexamined white privilege.

This experience reinforced my discomfort with the piecemeal workshop approach to race relations, which I feared may either pacify people or demoralize them. I had often heard people say that they had already addressed the issue of racism because they had an in-service or two on the subject: "Oh, we already covered the race thing here." Then, when racial problems persisted in their school, they could say, "We tried it, and it just doesn't work." I told Sandra I did not feel comfortable with such "hit-and-run" approaches, and she and several other teachers requested from the school district that I offer them a longer staff development class. This gave me the opportunity to develop a more critical course on race relations and diversity education that would not be confined by the inherent limitations of the multicultural "one-shot" approaches that most districts take (Sleeter, 1992). The course was also certified by the Lakeview school district for continuing education credits.

These personal and professional experiences all became the context out of which I was drawn to more systematically understand the perspectives of teachers and to study the possibilities for teachers to become proactive antiracist change agents. I knew this would not be simple, and I was confronted with several nagging questions: Is it really possible to counteract racism within the context of a system still influenced by (often hidden and covert) white supremacist assumptions, particularly since we are all affected by it? How can we theoretically, politically, or ideologically do anything different in the schools with regard to race relations, or other aspects of social inequality, without changing the larger society first? Can race-relations education be an avenue of opportunity for countering the miseducation of teachers? And how can this be done effectively with people who are also workers in schools—under what are often very stressful and demanding conditions?

NEEDS AND ASSUMPTIONS UNDERLYING ANTIRACIST PEDAGOGY

Because we are talking about the problems of white teachers teaching children of color, we should emphasize that these problems arise not simply because these are white people, but because within a racist context they have been educated and socialized toward a racial chauvinism or superiority that is reflected in their worldview and their teaching. There is not some mystical quality about white people *per se* that causes many of them to be ineffective teachers of Black children. Indeed, there are some white teachers who are successful teachers of children of color and who are able to help children realize academic excellence while allowing them to still identify positively with their own heritage and background. In one study of eight successful teachers of African American children, Ladson-Billings (1994) identified the qualities that contributed to positive educational outcomes. Among other things, these successful teachers managed to legitimate the students' real-life experiences as part of the official curriculum. They helped the students whose educational, economic, social, political, and cultural futures were most tenuous become the intellectual leaders of the classroom. Such teachers helped their students participate in a broad conception of literacy that incorporated both literature and orature. And such teachers took a stand politically and engaged in collective struggle against the status quo. These particular teachers were cognizant of themselves as political beings.

Unfortunately however, most teachers are not encouraged to be "political" and are often rewarded for conformity, not for questioning authority (Liston and Zeichner, 1991). While it is extremely important to identify the qualities of successful teachers, we must also address the problem of *how* teachers can be expected to have the necessary skills, knowledge, and experience to become such culturally relevant teachers or what Beauboeuf-Lafontant (1999) calls "politically relevant" teachers. Such qualities often come out of one's own particular life experience. Those effective teachers in Ladson-Billings's study were not necessarily of the same personality type or political outlook, but they shared the commonality of being able to incorporate approaches that recognized children's gifts even if they did not share the culture of the children.

We must also ask the critical question, What was it about those teachers that enabled them to bridge the cultural gap? What else distinguished them from many other teachers? In posing this question to Ladson-Billings, I learned that the successful teachers in her study had some previously enlightening or transformative experiences that may have contributed to their ability to be multiculturally responsive teachers.[5] While this theme was not the focus of her study, I believe that it is critical that this factor be considered. Is it realistic to expect white teachers, who have usually been socialized in segregated white contexts, to be able to incorporate a culturally relevant pedagogy, especially if they are working in institutions that have not given this much value? How can we expect teachers to teach what they do not know? This highlights my motivations for my own research in the sense that I wanted to see if antiracist teacher education could provide the beginning of such politically transformative experiences for teachers by engaging them in critical analyses of society and their own "whiteness," so that collectively we could develop the tools to confront the problems of racism and other forms of discrimination in schools.

The assumption underlying antiracist pedagogy for teachers is that it is necessary for them to confront racism in their backgrounds and their backyards in order to become conscious of how it is expressed in their teaching practice and their interactions with students of color, as well as with white students. The goal is not only to raise consciousness at the individual level, but to contextualize this knowledge politically and historically, at the institutional level, as well. It is also assumed that teachers are in a position to benefit from reflexive learning situations, in which they engage in a critical self-examination.

The issue of racism in teaching arises, among other things, in connection with whether teachers are able to identify with their students or whether they are affected by stereotypes with reference to the students of color. Such stereotypes may be confirmed in varying degrees by the selective interpretations of their encounters with the students of color. Such biased interpretations often constitute an elaborate scheme of defenses and rationalizations that perpetuate racism in education. The task of a teacher educator is one of understanding these "racist constructions" by decoding them. Thus if one asks, "Give an example of racism or racial insensitivity in your school," as I do in my classes, this is merely a prod to engage the teachers in discursive communication, in which the underlying "reality" may be unraveled through interpretative analysis.

This focus on teachers should not be interpreted as an assumption that teachers are any more biased than other white people in American society. Rather, institutionalized racism and the socially constructed category of "race" have shaped white peoples' consciousness just as surely as they have shaped people of color, but in a manner that has been largely undefined and unrecognized by whites, who, as members of the dominant group, often take their "whiteness" and the societal racial arrangements for granted. Indeed, as some of the recent critical scholars of race relations (Roediger, 1991; Marable, 1995; Frankenberg, 1993; Steinberg, 1995) argue, even white progressive or leftist scholars and activists, while recognizing the structural oppression of women in relation to men or the oppression of workers in relation to capital, are usually less discerning when it comes to understanding the persistence of racism. While they may recognize it as a serious social problem, they may not necessarily examine their own racial identity, seeing themselves as racially undefined or racially "neutral." But as Frankenberg (1993) reminds us, "Any system of differentiation shapes those on whom it bestows privilege as well as those it oppresses. White people are 'raced' just as men are 'gendered'" (p. xi).

Using Participant Observation Research to Understand the Perspectives of Teachers

The methodology that was most appropriate for the ethnographic aspect of this research, which I discuss in part two of this book, was participant observation with teachers. This particular methodology has a long tradition in the fields of sociology, anthropology, and education.[6] In participant observation, the researcher attempts to understand social reality from the point of view of the respondents/participants. Whatever the respondents reveal in the course of an extended interaction with the researcher is what constitutes data. These data typically consist of field notes in the form of the narratives of what was said by the respondents. This database is augmented by other data from the researchers' own observations as well as official documents. In sum, participant observation uses a triangulation of methods of data collection in an attempt to find out about the respondents' beliefs, perspectives, meanings, concerns, interests, and the like. These are the data that the researcher analyzes through interpretive reasoning. In this sense, participant observation as a qualitative method is at the opposite pole from procedures that test hypotheses drawn from quantitative data.

As a participant observer, it was important for me to understand the ways in which these teachers understood or made sense of their reality. I could "know" their world view by what they said they believed, but I also wanted to open a dialogue to challenge the contradictions between beliefs and behaviors. The opportunity to have extended, focused discussions, to share journal thoughts and classroom arguments, to observe as well as participate in their interactions with their fellow teachers helped me sort out some of the underlying logic of what made certain people "tick."

The data that I collected for this ethnographic study included field notes, which I wrote immediately after each class; teachers' characteristics and other statistics that highlighted the extent of racism in schools; the background characteristics of the different teachers who participated in my courses; simple counts of the number of times certain phenomena were observed; content analysis of transcribed taped data to isolate themes underlying that information; contrived observations, where I broke the class into discussion groups and encouraged them to discuss among themselves various topics pertaining to their own experiences with racism. I recorded specific sessions or group discussions (when the group agreed to being taped), from which I then isolated themes. I also analyzed reflective journal entries in which participants were asked to respond to issues discussed or articles read for the class, as well as their feelings or thoughts as they began to unravel and decode their own understandings or interpretations of issues through other experiences in their work or home life. This data also included "racial autobiographies," in which participants reflected on the influence of race or racism at various periods of their life; unstructured interviews with selected teachers; and open-ended questionnaires in which I asked teachers to respond to specific questions concerning their interpretation of racism in their school, as well as an exit questionnaire that asked for their evaluation of the class and its impact on them.

Because of my role as both a participant and an observer, I was often faced with the dilemma of how much information I could capture without either influencing it or losing it. That is, while I would have liked to have been able to sit in from the outside and record all that was happening, that was not possible, because this class was happening in me as well. I also did not want to be obtrusive. As we talked in class, I made a point of writing down key words and phrases or sentences, and then immediately tried to reconstruct our discussions when I left the class, sometimes in my car before I got home. Usually I carried a small tape recorder with me and talked into it as I drove home in order to capture the details and nuances. I did not want to consciously try to take down every word people said, nor did I want an outside person to observe and take field notes, because I feared this would inhibit the natural responses and conversations that took place in my class. I wanted the teachers to be able to communicate without feeling as though they were being analyzed or spied upon. I was conscious and sometimes self-conscious about my role as a participant as well as an observer and researcher. I was also quite conscious that I was not the only observer in the place, for the participants were also observing me quite closely as well, and often let me know so in class discussions or their journal entries. This was a reminder that teachers make judgments about the "judges" from the university, as well they should.

MY THEORETICAL PERSPECTIVE:
A STRUCTURAL OR CLASS ANALYSIS

My story of examining teachers' racial constructions and of doing antiracist teacher education is only part of this book. That narrative is nested in the context of a particular historical background and theoretical perspective of a structural or class analysis of racism. A structuralist perspective of racism is distinguished from an idealist perspective, which views the struggle against racism as one of combating stereotypes and attitudes that exist in the mind. While we want to combat racist thinking and stereotypes, the limitations of reducing racism to categorical thinking is that racism is not simply a product of a racist mind. This is a key aspect of the Marxist concept of social being, which argues that we are situated within a structural context that revolves around certain relations of production and around the super structural elements that are erected on the basis of those production relations, such as politics, ideology, the legal system, education, culture and other institutions. The social context of our being—that is, where one is situated in a structural context—may greatly affect and inform our social consciousness. However, this does not mean that there is simplistically a mechanistic relationship to how one will act or think in relation to where one is situated in the social structure. Yet our knowledge and perceptions are often influenced or informed by our material conditions of life. Informed by one's particular class and gender, or "race" location or lived experience, some may have a deeper knowledge or recognition of the reality of structural inequalities, or, as some of the recent feminist scholars argue, this lived experience may constitute an "epistemic privilege" or a knowledge based on experience. But experiencing oppression or discrimination does not mean that one automatically understands causality or has more empathy for the oppressed, particularly if racist and classist ideology is used to obscure relationships, keeping oppressed groups divided against one another.

On the other hand, one may be very conscious of the inequalities or injustices in society, yet it does not necessarily follow that all who *see* share an understanding about causality or possibility for change. For example, from some of the liberal perspectives of the recent years, such as Andrew Hacker's *Two Nations: Black and White, Separate, Hostile, Unequal* (1992), the ravages of racism are documented in great detail. Hacker debunks many of the racist myths regarding crime, welfare, employment opportunity, and such. Yet, as Roediger (1994) argues, Hacker's liberal approach offers no hope for change. Citing Hacker, who writes, "I wouldn't know where to begin" regarding any possibilities for change, Roediger critiques such a perspective for offering no vision of any counter strategy to abolish racism.

From a structuralist perspective of analyzing racial identities and attitudes as socially constructed, we must also invest in that analysis possibilities for their deconstruction and reconstruction. In these efforts, we must consider how race intersects with other aspects of our being, such as gender and class, in the formation of attitudes and behavior. In the case of examining racist assumptions and racial identities, the goal of antiracist pedagogy is to understand and enlighten the way people—in this case, primarily, though not exclusively, white people—think about race. As a strategy of change, the idea of a cognitive restructuring has limitations, of course. Presumably, we do antiracist pedagogy because we are trying to change people's understanding, thinking, and *behavior*—the idea being that if you provide people with the "true" knowledge of things, they will eventually recognize their racism and see that it is in their moral and self-interest to reject it.

However, it is not so simple and linear as finding the rational argument and convincing people of its "correctness," for racism is ultimately buttressed by material interests—class interests—and even perceived group interests, for that matter. For some people, it may actually seem like good practice to practice racism. It may also appear to be good practice for a white person to go on being racist because it preserves his or her job (or so he or she may think!). This person may even admit: "I don't have anything against this person (or group), but neither do I want to give up my job." That is the nature of capitalist society. One may ask oneself: What's it going to cost me if I maintain this antiracist position? Hence, a structural analysis of racism must recognize the contradictory consciousness and consequences that are often involved in the struggle for justice in an inherently competitive and unjust system.

WHO WILL TEACH THE TEACHERS?: REPRESENTATION AND TEACHER EDUCATION

While most certainly the structural dimensions of this problem are greater than education alone, education must be an important facet of the struggle against injustice. Yet a major impediment to progress remains the *de facto* segregation in the teaching force, in which the vast majority of all teachers are white. Some people may assume that the civil-rights movement succeeded in integrating professions like teaching, yet the percentage of teachers of color has actually been decreasing over the last several decades. For example, the percentage of African American teachers decreased from 10.1 percent in 1976 to approximately 7 percent in 1986 (Perkins, 1989). By 1994, there had been little improvement, and 86.6 percent of public elementary and secondary school teachers were white;

7.34 percent were Black; and 4.25 percent were Hispanic.[7] These percentages have been projected to decrease even further over the next decade (Kunjufu, 1985; American Council on Education, 1988).

Unfortunately, there has also been little success in increasing the percentages of people of color in teacher education programs. According to Perkins (1989), a 1987 study found that 91 percent of teacher education candidates were white, and of these, 76 percent female; 4.3 percent were Black; and 1.5 percent were Hispanic. Also, significantly, this study found that the majority of the white candidates said they preferred to teach in either a suburban or rural school district (Perkins, 1989). Other studies of teacher education students have found that many show an insensitivity or lack of empathy for people of color as well as a lack of understanding about racism (Moultry, 1989; King, 1991; Banks and McGee Banks, 1995), and many state that they do not want to teach in an inner-city or urban school, where most minority students are found. In the context of what the educational system is doing for and against the education of children of color, and white children as well, this means not only that major reforms in teacher education and recruitment will have to be undertaken so as to include and greatly increase the number of teachers of color, but also that the cultural ignorance and racial bias of those who are already teaching will have to be counteracted with a systematic retooling and reeducation.

But who will teach the teachers? Like public school teachers, teaching faculty in higher education are nearly 90 percent white people, the majority of whom have largely lived and been socialized to a segregated "white" middle-class experience.[8] If we look to the curriculum in most schools of education, we find that despite some offerings on "multicultural education," there is not often a critical analysis of the socioeconomic context. Further, courses on racism in education or race relations education are rarely offered and almost never required of preservice teachers (Sikula, Buttery, and Guyton, 1996). Nor will taking one course in multicultural education be sufficient. A critical multicultural perspective should be infused in the entire curriculum. To paraphrase W. E. B. Du Bois (1973), the problem does not start in the kindergarten, as is often assumed, but in the university, "the true founding stone of all education," where those who will carry out the functions of our society are trained to set the standards for all.

TEACHING AS A METAPHOR OF PRODUCTION IN THE ERA OF INTENSIFIED GLOBALIZATION

The problem of teaching "against the grain," and reeducating teachers to teach in a multicultural, multiracial world that is characterized by ever-increasing tensions and class divisions, is complex. Unfortunately, the schooling process is not often conducive to such change, and as Aronowitz and Giroux (1985) argue, frequently students are being schooled to *not think*—at least to not think analytically or relationally: "Part of the growing crisis in public education centers around the declining competence of students and others to effectively interrogate and communicate ideational content. In other words, in jeopardy is not merely the ability of students to be creative, but the very capacity for conceptual thought itself" (p. 24).[9]

Referring specifically to the training of prospective teachers, Zeichner (1983) sees most teacher education programs not as educating teachers for a critical analysis of the structural realities of education and society, but as

> a metaphor of "production," a view of teaching as an "applied science" and a view of the teacher as primarily an "executor" of the laws and principles of effective teaching. . . . [T]hat which they are to master is limited in scope (e.g., to a body of professional content knowledge and teaching skills) and is fully determined in advance by others often on the basis of research on teacher effectiveness. The prospective teacher is viewed primarily as a passive recipient of this professional knowledge and plays little part in determining the substance and direction of his or her preparation program. (p. 4)

Many of the critical theorists in education trace this crisis in creativity and critical thinking to the increasingly technicalized theories and methods of teaching, which value efficiency and management over reflective and critical conceptual thought. This antidemocratic and technocratic rationality has intensified particularly since the 1980s. As we enter a new millennium, there is the ever-increasing influence of corporate globalization with trade agreements like NAFTA and GATT or bodies like the WTO, the IMF and the World Bank, which are restructuring government and transferring enormous debt to the public sector for the benefit of large corporations. Such restructuring of governments erodes democracy, resulting in an ever-shrinking public sector and having a devastating impact on public education and other public services.[10] This hegemony has intensified since the early 1990s, with the collapse of most of the socialist world, leaving many to assume that capitalism is the only way, that there is no alternative to privatization of the public sector. We must beware of such an arrogant perspective that refuses to consider other alternatives. However, there is hope that more and more people are becoming concerned about this increasing privatization of power (or what is referred to as globalization), as evidenced by massive demonstrations since 1999 in Seattle, Montreal, and elsewhere.

"PESSIMISM OF THE INTELLECT, OPTIMISM OF THE WILL"

My encounters observing the daily life of teachers in Lakeview, and seeing the complexities and the stresses of teaching today, made it very clear that the burden of change cannot rest alone on teachers, whose work has become so "proletarianized" (Apple, 1988) and taken out of their control in a society fraught with social and economic problems. The stressful nature of teachers' work today might make one think that they could only become apathetic or feel futile about changing anything. Indeed, many of them are, and this is reflected in the high burnout rate among teachers compared with their peers of just thirty years ago (Spencer, 1986; Spring, 1994).

But there are many teachers who have not given up and do see themselves as agents of change. The stereotype of teachers as being only those who tend to be uncritical and accepting of the status quo must be challenged, especially in this current period, when teachers are becoming increasingly politicized and organized to protect the small gains they have won over the years (Apple, 1988). However, while their consciousness as a class—their working-class consciousness—has indeed been heightened, and while their awareness of the inequities in gender relations has intensified in a largely female profession still managed and controlled by men, unfortunately their consciousness about racism or white supremacy, and its impact on individuals and institutions such as education, has not been significantly altered or challenged. While some critical scholars have theorized about teaching as a "gendered" profession, one rarely hears of teaching as a "raced" profession. But it is a "raced" profession when nearly 90 percent of its members are white.

Given that a critical analysis of the social and political context of schooling has been largely ignored in preservice teacher education (Liston and Zeichner, 1991), it is not surprising that teachers are going into teaching shortchanged not only with regard to their understanding of race matters, but also regarding other class and gender issues. While some may attribute this lack of consciousness of the sociopolitical context to be characteristic of the *kinds* of people who choose to go into teaching, I think this would be an unfair characterization of teachers. Rather, I believe the lack of understanding of social and historical context is not peculiar to teachers, but is characteristic of American intellectual and popular culture in general, which Hofstadter (1963) characterized as the "anti-intellectual" tradition in America.

In any case, the "solution" or approach to implementing antiracist education for teachers is not, in the foreseeable future, likely to come from the very institutions of higher education that have heretofore smothered such discourse. This is why progressive activists and scholars in education must work to ensure that major reforms in higher education are implemented such that those who are professors in higher education mirror the demographics and the diverse perspectives of American society. For we should not forget, when we are talking about the problem of a white Eurocentric teaching force in our public schools, that there is the very same imbalance in higher education, where nearly 90 percent of the professors are white. We must challenge the standards and the curricula for teacher education such that they incorporate the life experiences of people of color, and working-class people in general, who may not arrive with the traditional or conventional "cultural capital" to fit into the dominant paradigm. We must develop and create critical programs in teacher education that are reconfigured along the lines of a decidedly social reconstructionist perspective. If we do not do this, *de facto* segregation in teaching will prevail, and teachers will be ill equipped to teach.

Despite this rather pessimistic-sounding outlook, I do believe there are possibilities to counteract the hegemony of the dominant discourse, for there are always points of power from which we can work, even within an inherently unjust system. A phrase coined by the French writer Romain Rolland,[11] "Pessimism of the intellect, optimism of the will," expresses the stance that I believe we must take in the long path toward countering the injustices of an embedded system. That is, we must be conscious of how dangerous the conditions are and face those dangers, but we must also share the optimism of what the possibilities have been and can be when people organize collectively for democratic social change. We must not allow cynicism and hopelessness to overtake us at every defeat, for there may be some things that we will not live to see changed. In fact, we may not even necessarily be able to recognize change, for as a process, change may not always be comprehended. Though certain things may not be changeable in our lifetime, as James Baldwin put it, "Not everything that is faced can be changed, but nothing can be changed until it is faced."

I found my point of power in the opportunity to develop continuing in-service and preservice education for teachers, which could help offer critical analyses of race, class, and gender inequality. My goal is not only for teachers to theorize about the issue of racism and the other inequities in education, but also to provide a lens through which we can picture ourselves as agents of democratic social change. However, in order to have the clarity of vision to be able to imagine possibilities for change, we must also look back historically to see how we got here if we are to choose a different path.

Despite the overwhelming structural constraints against change, we cannot afford to be defeatist about it. We have seen worse times, and unless we are organized and activated, we will see still worse times. I often think about a passage I came across in a dusty, old autobiography of an antifascist that I found in my parents' bookcase, written by Klaus Mann in 1942, when the world was torn asunder by fascism. Mann quotes a diary note by Franz Kafka: "Do not despair, not even at not despairing. When everything seems at a dead end, even then new forces draw up and march—and therein lies the significance of your being alive."

—◇◈◇—

In the next chapter, I put the problem into a historical context and examine some of the dominant trends with regard to race in American education. This includes the role of the academy—the institutions of higher learning—which historically have played a significant role in upholding or obscuring racist structures and theories. However, it is also important to remember that there has been resistance to such oppressive structures. Over the last half century, this resistance has been seen in the important influence of democratic grass-roots movements in challenging racial and economic inequalities, particularly since the 1960s, when the civil-rights movement, the free speech movement, the women's movement, and the popular movement against the war in Vietnam were all influential in refocusing the debates on the nature and scope of education.

CHAPTER TWO

A Historical and Theoretical Context to the Current Debates on Racism in Education

CAPITALISM, SLAVERY, AND RACISM

The term "race" was first used in 1735 when Carolus Linnaeus, the Swedish botanist, applied the term to describe physical differences in people in his book *Systems of Nature* (Gould, 1996). While Linnaeus's original classification system grouped humans with higher primates such as monkeys, it did not subdivide people until the second edition in 1740, when he separated humans into four geographic regions: the Americas (*americanus*), Europe (*europeaus*), Asia (*asiaticus*), and Africa (*afer*) (Gould, 1996). Linnaeus assigned qualities to these groups that placed whites at the top and Blacks at the bottom. Hence, *Homo sapiens europeaus* were described as "white, optimistic and muscular, gentle, active, very smart, inventive," while *Homo sapiens afer* were described as "black, slow, foolish, relaxed, crafty, indolent, negligent."

Slaveholders and colonizers appropriated the notion of "race" as a convenient marker of inferiority or superiority to justify the extreme brutalities of colonialism, slavery and genocide. They argued that the races were biologically different and that whites were racially superior to all non-white peoples, thus naturalizing white dominance and white supremacy. The form of slavery which existed in the United States was *chattel* slavery, which by definition meant that legally some people were treated as chattel, defined as "an article of personal, movable property." Chattel slavery was a permanent condition where people were treated not as human beings but as actual property to be bought and sold, disposed of at will, like chattel or things. Marx wrote of the historical links between chattel slavery and the rise of capitalism:

29

The discovery of gold and silver in America, the extirpation, enslavement and entombment in mines of the aboriginal population, the beginning of the conquest and looting of the East Indies, the turning of Africa into a warren for the commercial hunting of black-skins, signaled the rosy dawn of the era of capitalist production. (Marx, 1967, p. 751)

"SCIENTIFIC" RACISM AND THE ACADEMY

To justify the moral contradictions that the brutalities of slavery, exploitation, colonization, and genocide posed, racist ideologies were propagated by the ruling class. These ideological justifications were refined into "scientific" theories and applied to fields like medicine, education, and the humanities (Gossett, 1975; Gould, 1996). For most of U.S. history, up through the 1920s, the dominant paradigm was of the inherent biological inferiority of people of color. This perspective was made respectable by the academic establishment that promulgated racist ideology through scholarly publications such as the *American Sociological Review*, which wrote in 1903 that "slavery was the most humane and the most practical method ever devised for "bearing the white man's burden." (cited in Aptheker, 1978). Or, as written in this same journal in 1908, "It is only through the recognition that the average Negro is still a savage child of nature that the North and the South can be brought to unite in work to uplift the race" (*American Sociological Review*, p. 37). This view was reinforced by the most influential historians of the day, such as Ulrich Bonnell Phillips (1929) and William A. Dunning (1897), whose work dominated in the American historical profession through the 1930s. In their "magnolia" school of Southern history, slavery was portrayed as a benign, patriarchal institution, often described using such euphemisms as a "homestead," a "social settlement" and even a "chapel of ease" (Phillips, 1929). Employing the classic language of white supremacy, Phillips argued that as bad as slavery might have been, it was ultimately beneficial, having a great "civilizing" influence upon the Africans, whom he described as "notoriously primitive, uncouth, improvident and inconstant, merely because they were Negroes of their time; and by their slave status they were relieved from the pressure of want and debarred from any full-force incentive of gain" (p. 197).

BIOLOGICAL DETERMINISM

In the field of biology, doctrines of biological determinism argued that Blacks were a separate and inferior species, an argument that was invented to justify the atrocities of chattel slavery. The "sciences" of phrenology and craniometry were concocted to lend scientific language and legitimacy to the "rightness" of Black subordination and white supremacy (Gossett, 1975; Steinberg, 1995; Gould, 1996). According to this "science," the "cephalic index"—skull shape, brain size, and protrusions of the jaw and brow—determined intelligence (hence the origin of the terms "highbrow" and "lowbrow" to denote intellectually superior or upper-class knowledge and culture versus "vulgar" or "simplistic" working-class culture). However, such cephalic arguments were highly problematic, for there was much contradictory evidence when, in fact, the Africans' skull shape and size were often found to be closer to the supposed ideal than were many of the so-called Caucasian skulls. Yet those in the academy who subscribed to such beliefs nevertheless continued to support their own bogus theories in the total absence of any corroborating evidence (Steinberg, 1995). Despite the crisis of its own contradictions, the paradigm of biological determinism continued to be the dominant strain of "scientific" thought until the 1920s.

A PARADIGM SHIFT:
FROM BIOLOGICAL DETERMINISM TO "INTELLIGENCE" TESTING

By the early 1920s, the old overtly racist theories of the African peoples or Indigenous Peoples in the Americas as "nature's savage children" or "beasts" were less overtly expressed but were replaced with other insidious racist theories in the scientific community. The racist paradigm of biological determinism shifted only after a more convincing and seemingly more objective methodology was devised by certain influential members of the academy: the intelligence test. In the area of education, the intelligence test became the most formidable weapon for "proving" the inherent inferiority of people of color and the working class in general. Hidden behind the guise of objectivity, the intelligence test had the most far-reaching implications for perpetuating the respectability of racism. In effect, it kept working people divided against each other, by tracking some people into lower-paid jobs, keeping educational opportunity limited or circumscribed for certain groups, and maintaining extreme racial segregation in the labor market.

In the post–World War I period, there was a wave of labor and racial unrest and instability for capitalism, both domestically and internationally.[1] Along with the internal labor and racial discord at home, the socialist Russian Revolution of 1917 was the impetus for the "Red Scare" of 1919, which resulted in increased oppression and discrimination against foreigners, socialists, "labor agitators," Blacks, and Jews. In this xenophobic climate, fifteen states passed "English only" laws requiring that English be the only language of instruction in all schools, public or private, regardless of what languages immigrant children

spoke or understood. In the first ten months after World War I, white supremacist groups were on the rise, and the Ku Klux Klan made over two hundred public appearances throughout the country (Franklin, 1974). Organized and overt
racial terror increased, as membership in the Klan grew to some three million to
six million by 1923 (Gossett, 1975). The so-called Roaring Twenties were actually a time, as Gossett writes, when "racist theories achieved an importance and
respectability which they had not had in this country since before the Civil War"
(1975, p. 369).

The mob terror of the Klan was the backdrop for the more sophisticated and
"civilized" forms of control that continued to legitimate white supremacy. Much
of this legitimation came not from mobs in the streets, but from institutions of
higher learning, where scholars developed new theories of white racial superiority. Among the most damaging of those theories was the invention of the
Stanford-Binet scales of intelligence by Lewis Terman and his associates in 1916,
which claimed to demonstrate "scientifically" the racial superiority of so-called
Caucasians. As Gossett (1975) writes, "Intelligence testing was to give racist theorizing a new lease on life—in fact, in the minds of many to make race the crucial determinant of human progress or retrogression" (p. 364).

In 1923, Carl Campbell Brigham, one of the "fathers" of the Scholastic
Aptitude Test (SAT), wrote *A Study of American Intelligence*, in which he warned
about the problem of the "possibility of racial admixture . . . infinitely worse
than that faced by a European country today, for we are incorporating the
Negro into our racial stock, while all of Europe is relatively free of this taint"
(cited in Fish, 1993). Brigham went on to refine his theory with the creation of
the SAT in 1925, the grandfather of the model currently in use today to determine who is suitable material for college. Intelligence testing not only had the
effect of weeding out people of color from the ranks of those considered "able"
or "intelligent," but it was also a weeding mechanism used against many of the
recent immigrants and working-class and poor whites as well. As Miller (1994)
points out, such intelligence "research" was also used by anti-Semites such as
Harry Hamilton Laughlin, who presented his "research" to Congress in 1924,
which found "evidence" that 83 percent of Jewish immigrants were "feeble-
minded." Laughlin successfully lobbied to maintain restrictions on Jewish
immigration, which later prevented an escape route for Jews fleeing the Nazis
(Miller, 1994).

"Intelligence" testing was used to "scientifically" justify a range of class as
well as racial inequalities. The intelligence test shifted the focus from the physiological structures of the brain, or the so-called "cephalic index," which had
sought to prove which group had the biggest brain capacity. Now the new
emphasis was on the intelligence test as proof of the inherent inferiority of the

cultures of nonwhite and non–Anglo-Saxon peoples, who were portrayed as culturally "backward." This gave rise to theories of cultural deficiency to explain and justify the unequal status of people.

THE ASSIMILATIONIST PARADIGM AND THE "UNMELTABLE ETHNICS"

Biological references to race often included biological notions of ethnicity as well, to describe difference. At various periods, usually in the early years of their arrival to the United States, Italians, Jews, and the Irish, for example, were also referred to in racial terms as being inherently inferior or lacking in intelligence and capabilities, thus justifying their exploitation (Jacobson, 1998). Over time, however, unlike the situation for people of color, ultimately there would be hope for the "white" ethnics, the argument being that if one worked hard enough, one could eventually assimilate and have a piece of the pie. If one did not assimilate, it was argued that it was because he or she did not have the merit, was lazy, or did not adhere to the "Protestant ethic." The prospect of assimilation was the bargaining chip for those "white" immigrant groups, who, while also extremely exploited, were pitted against the lowest on the ladder, the African Americans, Indigenous Peoples, or other people of color (Roediger, 1991). For non-European, nonwhite ethnic groups, although they did the most difficult, dangerous, and backbreaking jobs, hard work rarely correlated with "success." Legal racial discrimination and occupational apartheid reinforced a segregated job market that did not allow people of color to climb the ladder and assimilate in the same way as even the most oppressed of the white European immigrants. To borrow Michael Novak's (1972) term, these were the "unmeltable ethnics."

Until the 1950s, the dominant paradigm in education for white people revolved around assimilation, namely, how the school system could bring immigrant children of European descent to shed off their "primordial" ethnic attachments and become "acceptable" Americans. This meant that, along with diluting and negating their customs, language, and ethnicity, new immigrants would have to assume a new identity in America, to see themselves not only as Americans, but as "white" Americans.[2] People of color were not welcomed into this possibility of assimilation, yet their presence was always a central backdrop to American educational opportunity for whites. As Theresa Perry (1993) writes, "The history of American education is a history of the denial of educational opportunity for African Americans, a history of continuous struggle by African Americans to be educated for first-class rather than for second-class citizenship" (p. 1).

THE MORE RECENT HISTORICAL CONTEXT:
THE INFLUENCE OF DEMOCRATIC GRASS-ROOTS MOVEMENTS

The assimilationist paradigm in American education prevailed until the 1950s, when there were significant ideological shifts in the debates regarding the scope and nature of American education. With regard to scope, this became the question of expanding educational opportunities to nonwhites, beginning with the landmark decision of *Brown v. Board of Education of Topeka* (1954), which was a culmination of sixteen years of school desegregation lawsuits that had been filed by the NAACP and several other civil-rights groups. The *Brown* decision struck down the "separate but equal" doctrine that had been legally sanctioned by the *Plessy v. Ferguson* case of 1896,[3] and barred the *de jure* segregation of students by race, ruling that separate schools were inherently unequal. This was the first time the U.S. government made a formal commitment to include Blacks in the promise of educational equity. By the 1960s, education became a centerpiece of racial justice. For most Americans, the majority of whom now had television in their homes, it was the first time they were able to witness the overt racism in both the North and the South, as television news brought images of the violence imposed on Black children who were attempting to integrate schools.

It is illuminating that the *Brown* decision came in the midst of the McCarthy era, one of the most reactionary and conservative periods in our recent history. For we should not forget that the deep freeze of cold war anticommunism and McCarthyism had induced a state of paralysis within educational institutions at all levels. During the fifties, many teachers feared becoming suspect if their words or ideas could be deemed subversive. In a witch hunt against "communist infiltrators" and "traitors," hundreds of teachers lost their jobs, many of whom never returned to teaching, and a few even lost their lives (Caute, 1978).[4] For many teachers, including some of those who were more liberal or leftist, expediency and caution often became their modes of approaching controversial subjects, as they feared making waves (Caute, 1978). It is no wonder that some have referred to the youth of the fifties as the "silent generation."

In such a climate of such intense conservative reaction and conformity, the *Brown* decision was a significant challenge to the reactionary status quo and helped open the door for the popular upsurge of the sixties, which took educational institutions to task, insisting on their public accountability in the struggles for economic and racial justice in American society. However, given the composition of educational institutions at all levels, with respect to gender, race, class, and political outlook, it was not evident that these institutions would take the initiative to improve themselves on their own. That initiative came instead from the grass-roots influence of the civil-rights movement, which also influenced the movement against the war in Vietnam, as well as the free speech movement and the women's movement of the sixties and seventies. These social movements were instrumental in refocusing the debates about democracy and education. Under the impact of popular pressure, universities were forced to hire scholars who were assumed to be sensitive to the issues affecting people of color, women, and working-class people in general.

By the mid-1960s, the repressive atmosphere of the cold war was giving way to the deepest challenges to the very structure, practices, and purposes of education that had ever occurred in this country (B. Aptheker, 1969; H. Aptheker, 1978). Many people were influenced by a number of other developments around the world, such as the socialist and anticolonial movements in Africa, Asia, and Latin America, which were challenging the U.S. ruling class politically, militarily, and ideologically. Also of importance, in the institutions of higher learning in the United States, there was a qualitative change in the character of the student body. Whereas before World War II there were less than two million college students, of whom about forty thousand were African Americans, by 1970, largely as a result of the GI Bill and the civil-rights movement, there were over seven million students, of whom five hundred thousand were African Americans. In addition, a larger percentage of all college students were from working-class origins.

During the period of the 1960s and 1970s, the question of the nature of American education was hotly debated. Many on the left were critical that the goals of education were merely to serve the capitalist labor market and reproduce existing relations of domination instead of fulfilling other, more democratic goals such as economic equity and social justice (Bowles and Gintis, 1976). Books like Paulo Freire's *Pedagogy of the Oppressed* (1970) gave voice to radical educational reformers, and some grass-roots groups like the Black Panther Party made a radical reeducation project one of their primary concerns. This reeducation involved practical as well as ideological concerns. In addition to ideological activities, the Black Panther Party argued that in order for children to receive a good education, they also needed adequate nutrition, and the group agitated for free breakfast programs for poor children, the forerunner to the current school breakfast programs today.

Of course, the debates over the purposes and the liberatory vision of education did not originate in the period of the sixties, nor with the Left or New Left intellectuals, but actually had a long historical tradition, particularly in the struggles of the African American people. Ever since the time of slavery, life-threatening struggles for literacy and education were fought by African Americans who viewed the purpose of education as liberatory. As Theresa Perry (1993) notes, historically the prevailing philosophies of Black education have not been geared to reproduce inequalities and domination over others, but rather to lead people toward what was considered their historic responsibility—to build a better, more just and decent society (Du Bois, 1973; Perry, 1993). Instilling the capitalist ethic and the cult of the individual were not viewed as the main goals of education among most African American organizations, which held more humanistic and collective aspirations of the good for the many, not just for one at the expense of the many. This idea was expressed in the African American women's club movement and the National Association of Colored Women, which chose as their motto "Lifting as we climb" (Davis, 1981). From the early years of the twentieth century, African American writers and scholars, such as Charles H. Wesley, W. E. B. Du Bois, Carter G. Woodson, Ida B. Wells, and others, challenged predominant representations and assumptions, and counteracted stereotypes. One example of this was Du Bois's *The Brownies Books* (cited in Aptheker, 1978), which critiqued the ideological content and representations in children's books and sought to provide African American children with a more critical political perspective, one that encouraged them to view themselves not as conformists to the status quo, but as change agents for a better, more just society.

From the period of the 1960s, African Americans and other people of color as well as progressive whites were at the forefront of the movements for social change and civil rights. They challenged American education to its core. But apart from the obvious inequality of educational opportunity, they also raised fundamental questions regarding the relevance of curricula, the racism and cultural bias inherent in standardized tests, and the behavior of white teachers toward students of color—all of which challenged the predominant cultural deficit theories and raised fundamental questions regarding the very nature of American education (see, for example, G. Boggs, 1970; Churchville, 1970; Clarke, 1970).

These debates were taking place at a time when America had experienced almost three decades of sustained economic growth and prosperity, beginning with the stimulative effects of World War II. The climate of optimism regarding the prospects for American capitalism stood in sharp contrast to the extreme conditions of poverty that disproportionately affected people of color. In the search for the answer to the riddle of "poverty amidst affluence," the "Great Society" reforms of President Johnson's administration—which were implemented because of the mounting pressure of mass social movements—addressed education as a centerpiece of the social policies aimed at mitigating conditions of minorities and the poor. While these "Great Society" reforms did not address the *causes* of poverty or of occupational and economic apartheid, they were nevertheless important because of the objective social conditions and the organized mass grass-roots civil-rights movement that won them; and importantly, they were significant measures for alleviating (though they did not have the possibility to eliminate) inequalities.

Education was seen as the critical tool for upward mobility. The strategy of addressing education as central was given formal expression in the human capital theory (Becker, 1964). From the perspective of human capital theorists, the low socioeconomic position of minorities was attributed to their low "investment in human capital," meaning that many of them were poor because they lacked education and marketable skills. With this diagnosis of poverty came a series of educational and manpower programs. School integration through busing was seen as a mechanism of affording minority schoolchildren an opportunity to go to better (i.e., better equipped and financed) schools in white areas. However, such an approach was inherently limited, because racial segregation in housing and employment were left intact. Moreover, although there had been a ruling against *de jure* segregation in the abstract, as Lipsitz (1998) points out, the *Brown* decision "provided no means for dismantling the structures that crafted advantages for white students out of the disadvantages of students of color" (pp. 33–34). Whites had a "possessive investment in whiteness," which resulted in their refusal to allow for successful school integration, a resistance that was helped along by white political leadership. As Lipsitz explains:

> Close to 70 percent of northern whites told pollsters that they supported the Johnson administration's efforts to desegregate the South in 1964, but when urban riots, fair-housing campaigns, and efforts to end de facto segregation reached their localities, a conservative counter subversive mobilization (made manifest in the Goldwater and Wallace campaigns for the presidency and in the efforts by Californians to repeal fair-housing laws) changed public opinion. By 1966, 53 percent of northern whites told pollsters that they felt that the government was pushing integration "too fast." Richard Nixon secured the key support of Strom Thurmond in the 1968 presidential campaign in return for a promise to lessen federal pressure for school desegregation. White southern voters consequently provided him with a crucial vote margin in a closely contested election. Nixon supervised the abandonment of the school desegregation guidelines issued in the 1964 Civil Rights Act, nominated opponents of busing to the Supreme Court, and in his 1972 reelection campaign urged Congress to pass legislation overturning court ordered busing. (1998, p. 35)

White resistance to school integration took various forms in northern cities, often including violent mobs of whites, as in places like Boston. In addition to white mobs, less overtly violent forms of resistance were also common, as in Milwaukee, for example, where in the early years of school desegregation, African American students in overcrowded schools in black neighborhoods were bused "intact" to white schools,[5] where they were placed in a classroom separately, with a separate lunchtime and recess, having no contact with the white students in the school.

WHITE BACKLASH AND THE CONSERVATIVE RESTORATION

The implementation of school desegregation programs and other "Great Society" reforms triggered a series of conflicts between Blacks and whites; conservatives and liberals; and Blacks who supported integration and those who opposed it in the name of self-determination. In turn, these debates, together with other issues such as the war in Vietnam and American imperialism, triggered a backlash. This backlash took the time-honored form of whipping up racist sentiments. Nixon argued that the movements for social change were not accepted by most Americans, who were, as he put it, the "silent majority." This myth of the "silent majority" swept Nixon and other conservative politicians into office. Once in office, the battle to control American education escalated, but this time, the conservatives rather than the liberals took to the offensive. In order to effect this transformation, new or revamped theories of characterizing minority conditions had to be generated. It was in this context that the "culture of poverty" thesis[6] gained currency as a strategy for dampening minority demands for social and economic justice. The argument was that even though you may offer good jobs, abolish slums and create good schools, the lower class will remain chronically unemployed, turn new housing into slums, squander welfare checks, and destroy their own schools because "those people" are suffering from a culture of poverty or "cultural deprivation" that causes their own poverty.

Such ideas were validated by academics such as Edward Banfield (1970) and Nathan Glazer and Daniel P. Moynihan (1963), who, working within Nixon's inner cabinet, articulated a position of "benign neglect"—in other words, that too much government intervention was actually hurting rather than helping the poor, and we should just leave the government out of it. The conditions of racially oppressed minorities and the poor were put squarely on their own shoulders. In addition, there was a white backlash in the form of the "new ethnicity" movement, which set the stage for a more reactionary usage of ethnicity, in which Black poverty, in particular, was attributed to cultural deficiency (Glazer and Moynihan, 1963). The *Bakke* decision became emblematic of this period, and affirmative action became construed by many whites as "affirmative discrimination" or "reverse discrimination."[7]

Unlike the earlier, more overtly racist theories, which had argued that Blacks were intellectually inferior to whites, academics like Glazer, Moynihan, and Banfield were more guarded and restrained, and rarely even made explicit reference to "race." Instead, cultural inferiority was substituted for genetic inferiority, the argument being that it was bad environmental influences that kept certain people at the bottom, such that they have become so "damaged," so ill affected that they have internalized a "culture of poverty." Hence, it was argued, it is a waste of money to give such people government aid or affirmative action, for it would only do further harm by making them become dependent and spoiled by too many "free rides."

These "blame the victim" arguments, as Ryan (1971) called them, had—and continue to have—a devastating impact on social policy, as seen in the destruction of job and educational training programs in the 1980s; the ending of welfare in the 1990s; and the further erosion of public education by diverting funding away from the public schools to school vouchers for private and religious education. The destruction of all these social programs have had the most deleterious consequences for people of color, yet the word "race" is not used in the formulation of these repressive policies. Ironically, while covert racism may be behind the heartless withdrawal of the social safety net, it is not only people of color who have been adversely affected. In actuality, in absolute numbers, the majority of the victims of these cutbacks in welfare and social services have been white people, since numerically there are more whites on welfare, more whites who are unemployed, homeless, on AFDC (Aid to Families with Dependent Children), and such. However, because the chances of being affected by these cutbacks have been far greater for people of color, whose groups are disproportionately most highly affected, these policies have had an extremely disparate impact on them.

"COLOR BLINDNESS" AND THE "NEW" RACISM OF THE 1980S

Because of the progressive mass movements of the 1960s and 1970s, by the 1980s crudely racist language was no longer acceptable in public discourse in a "democratic" society, and the language changed to obscure overtly racist sentiments. Antiracist civil-rights activist Anne Braden (1980) wrote about the new, more "civilized" expressions of old-fashioned racism:

> Most people now will claim that they believe all people should have equal rights. Even the Ku Klux Klan is saying that. When the Grand Kleagle of the Klan went to Cullman, Alabama, a few months ago, to hold a rally where a Black man was being framed on a criminal charge, he attracted a crowd of 3,000 white people—in an area, by the way, where there had not previously been an active Klan in forty years. And he was very careful to say that the Klan had not come to Cullman to oppose equal rights for Black people. What he said was: "Lately everybody has been looking out for Black people, and now somebody has to take care of the rights of white people—and that's why the Klan is in Cullman." That struck me when I heard about it—because to me it sounded exactly like what Alan Bakke was saying in California, and exactly like what Brian Weber is saying in Louisiana, and exactly like what all the people who talk about reverse discrimination are saying at the same time they swear they are for "equal rights for all people." (pp. 13–14)

By the early 1980s, the U.S. economy was undergoing a period of rapid de-industrialization, and economic conditions declined for all working people. Many whites found their economic security eroding, as factories moved out of their communities to other countries where there were no barriers to the limits of exploitation of the workers, such as labor unions or worker protections. In addition to decreasing job security, many social programs were eroding, such as the dismantling of HUD programs, which contributed to the loss of affordable housing. This, combined with the dismantling of the mental health care system during the Reagan administration, contributed to increased homelessness. Many whites whose economic security was threatened were prone to scapegoat and to identify with the sentiments of the "white man under siege" mentality that were being promoted by white supremacist groups like the Ku Klux Klan or the newly created National Association for the Advancement of White People. Despite the fact that there was an increase in poverty rates for racial minorities, some whites resented any special attention being paid to people of color, whom they thought were benefiting at their expense. Edari (1984) explains how this state of affairs led to increased ideological confusion:

> Here then lies the crux of the matter: what begins as a justified indignation in response to the economic crisis, is transformed into an "ethnic" instead of a class issue, and comparing "ethnic groups" leads to the conclusion that some have benefited at the expense of others! The capitalist class remains hidden in the "establishment" omnibus, while the focus on minorities becomes a way of concretizing issues for "public discussion" and galvanizing reactionary power blocs. (p. 12)

Viewing ethnicity as analogous to race was a denial of institutional racism and served to distract attention away from the oppression and exploitation by the white ruling class. As Winston (1977) argued:

> What determines the status of Black people in this country is not "common customs" but *common oppression*. If one equates "white ethnics" with Black and other oppressed minorities, the special struggle to remove the racist barriers facing the oppressed can be dispensed with. The concept of "ethnicity" sets an ideological atmosphere in which affirmative action programs for jobs and education of Blacks can be twisted into "racism in reverse." When one substitutes "ethnicity" for class, one projects race against race—instead of projecting struggles of the multi-racial, multi-national working class and the oppressed minorities against the white ruling class. (pp. 58–59)

With the focus on blaming the victim rather than on the system that had created inequalities, the social and economic gains that minorities had made as a result of the Great Society reforms of the sixties were quickly eroding. The goal of *Brown v. Board of Education* to create an integrated and equitable education for all children was undermined, and many urban public school systems actually became increasingly nonwhite. This was due not only to "white flight," but also to the decentralizing of the population and economic activities that not only increased segregation, but also contributed to the impoverishment of the central city populations. Associated with these changes was the constant fiscal crisis of the local units of government, which exacerbated the problem of financing education. By the time of Reagan's election in 1980, racial minorities in urban areas were living in depression-like conditions. The deterioration of these already depressed conditions came about partly as a result of the regressive policies beginning with the Nixon administration, which had turned back the clock on the progressive programs implemented in the sixties. Ironically, Reagan pointed to those very conditions as evidence of the failure of the liberal programs—a total misreading of history! At any rate, President Reagan carried the repressive policies initiated by Nixon and others to a new level. His administration articulated a policy of a "new federalism," which further reduced the educational resources coming from the federal government.

Influenced by right-wing groups such as the Heritage Foundation and the Bradley Foundation, federal education policy took a sharp turn to the right in the 1980s. The Heritage Foundation in its various publications[8] argued that all of the country's educational problems stemmed from the increased role that the federal government had played in funding the nation's schools, as well as the "vested interests" of the two major teachers' unions, the AFT and the NEA. Heritage also charged that the schools were dominated by "secular humanists" and called for an increased involvement of Christian fundamentalists in the schools. The group also advocated the total withdrawal of the federal government from the field of education and urged the eventual abolition of the Department of Education and of affirmative action (Pincus, 1983).

The very mandate under which Reagan had gotten elected had an undercurrent of racism supported by groups who packaged themselves with new labels such as the "New Right" and the "Moral Majority." The Reaganites exacerbated a "state of siege" mentality for many white people who were also suffering from increased unemployment and other social ills as a result of the deindustrialization of America. Rather than look at the structural causes of these problems, right-wing propagandists convinced many whites to blame the victims, arguing that affirmative action for minorities had taken away opportunities for whites. In response, more extremist racist white groups came out of the closet and began to mobilize white support openly—no longer under cover of white sheets and hoods—such as the skinheads and the National Association for the Advancement of White People, and self-proclaimed racist David Duke, a grand wizard of the Ku Klux Klan, managed to get elected to the Louisiana legislature.

From *de Jure* Segregation
to *de Facto* Segregation in Education

While the civil-rights struggles had addressed the problem of segregation by law, the struggle did not end there. *De jure* segregation was replaced by *de facto* segregation. As far as education was concerned, since the mid-seventies, school districts from coast to coast had been ordered to desegregate, often after intense legal battles led by such organizations as the NAACP. The primary method of school desegregation has been through busing, whereby children from *de facto* segregated schools have been moved to schools outside of their neighborhoods, while the system of *de facto* segregation in housing and employment has been left intact.

In essence, the crisis of the larger society was exported to the schools, with the burden falling particularly hard on African American and Latino students. By the mid 1980s in the majority of large urban areas, schools became primarily Black and Latino, as many whites pulled their children out of the public schools and put them in private or parochial schools or moved to white suburban areas. Many children of color were also bused to these suburban areas, but this did not necessarily indicate true integration, for even in cases where children of color were used to "desegregate" a school, within the culture of the school they were often segregated or marginalized. This often resulted in a school culture that, in some respects, increased tensions between students of color and white students, as students of color and their families found themselves left out of the fold of the culture and structural arrangements of those white schools in white neighborhoods where they were still not welcome to work or live. Despite court-ordered school desegregation, real school integration did not occur, and students of color found themselves marginalized and segregated within those "integrated" schools.[9]

While many well-intended efforts by Blacks and whites alike rested on the assumption that if people were encouraged to have contact with each other, their relations would improve, the essential issue of the underlying social class divisions and power differentials was not addressed. Nor was the critical issue of the need for race relations education for the teachers or for the students. Changing laws to protect people from racism and discrimination, while essential, would not be sufficient to change people's thinking and behavior. For laws alone do not change the racism that is imprinted in the culture that percolates into people's everyday interactions. The solution to addressing racism in education through the moving of bodies was inadequate to address the fundamental *causes* and effects of such segregation in the first place. It became clear that contact itself was not enough.[10]

While there was a focus on the issue of integrating students, the question of the role of teachers and their representation among the affected groups of students was not seriously addressed. The almost total domination of the teaching force by whites was rarely questioned in the dominant white culture. While many naively assumed that integration would also lead to a diverse teaching force, in many areas of the country white teachers actually displaced Black teachers out of the educational system during the period of school integration. For example, in the early years of school integration in the South, many Black teachers lost their jobs to white teachers, who were given preference in hiring, thereby increasing the apartheid-like relationship between Blacks and the whites in control (Perkins, 1989; Steel, 2001).

During the eight years of the Reagan administration, while there was a serious decline in federal support for education, there was also a confusing shower of rhetoric of "educational excellence," beginning with the report *A Nation at Risk* in 1983 (Warren, 1989). The atmosphere that promoted more blatant forms of white racism throughout American society, as evidenced by the resurgence of white power groups, was a problem that not only affected public education, but found expression in institutions of higher learning as well. By the 1990s, there had been numerous instances of overt racial bigotry on many college campuses, including some that had the reputation of being progressive or liberal. In 1989, for example, a University of Wisconsin fraternity conducted a "slave auction" in which some of their members dressed in blackface. While Blacks have been and continue to be the most frequent targets of these racist attacks, other racial minorities have also come under attack. Fraternity parties with such themes as "illegal aliens," in which frat members wore dark makeup and sombreros, were reported at numerous universities (Martinez, 1990). The National Institute Against Prejudice and Violence reported that in 1991, over 115 college campuses suffered from such incidents,[11] causing many campus officials to reflect upon the need for greater sensitivity and awareness.

Many universities that had been on the cutting edge of progressive social activism in the sixties and seventies found themselves caught within the fold of right-wing racist reaction in the eighties and nineties. Once again, old racist theories had been rescued from the dustbin of academia. Since the mid-1990s, there has been a resurrection of the ultrareactionary racism of earlier conservative scholars like Shockley and Jensen, who had argued in the 1970s that people of color (and particularly Blacks) were genetically inferior to whites. There was also the much-publicized revival of such arguments in the work of Richard Herrnstein and Charles Murray (1994), whose racist pseudoscientific theories received exceptional exposure from the corporate media. They claim in their book, *The Bell Curve: Intelligence and Class Structure in American Life*, the inferiority of Blacks and poor whites, who, they argue, are less successful because they are less intelligent, as indicated by their lower scores on standardized tests compared with those of middle-class whites. In addition to books like *The Bell Curve*, there is a new mythology of the "end of racism," the title of the book by D'Sousa (1995), who argues that we no longer have problems of racism, but rather of cultural deficiencies and disfunctionalism in Black culture, which people are rightfully reacting to.

As Miller (1994) explains, the resurrection of such racist theories does not come out of a vacuum. The funding for this research often comes from foundations like the Pioneer Fund, a New York City foundation that promotes genetics, arguing for the selective breeding of humans. According to Miller, the Pioneer Fund was actually founded during the Third Reich in 1937 and continues to support research measuring racial differences in intelligence. Another major sponsor of such research has been the Lynde and Harry Bradley Foundation, the country's leading right-wing funder of conservative causes. Such foundations have fueled the national attacks on affirmative action, public education and a wide range of social welfare programs, in particular Aid to Families with Dependent Children (Wilayto, 1997).

Also since the 1990s, we have seen increasing pressures to privatize education through school voucher plans. Underlying the move toward privatization in education is the myth of "individual choice." From the right-wing perspective, the aim is to avoid the arm of the State in saying who deserves an education or who one should have to go to school with. It is a move to avoid public scrutiny and to insulate certain people from public accountability. One might argue that actually, in one respect, until the *Brown v. Board of Education* decision in 1954, we essentially did have "private" education for whites in the United States, in the sense that the State funded education for whites at the expense of Blacks, Latinos, Indigenous Peoples, and other racial minorities.

However, the racial and class politics of public schools have become very complicated. Ironically, it has not only been those on the Right who have supported the idea of school vouchers. By the 1990s, the issue of privatization had become very complex, particularly regarding many communities of color, for whom the issue of privatization was a response to the problem of local control of their schools. Because of their negative experiences being resegregated in public schools, and because the teaching force remained overwhelmingly white even when children of color had become the majority in most urban school districts, many people felt "colonized," as their schools were lacking representative teachers or culturally relevant education. Some people of color in their attempts to reclaim their culture and education, opted for vouchers with the hopes that this would allow their children to get out of white-dominated schools. While many people were concerned that this would be a step backward toward segregation, from the perspective of some of the racially oppressed, however, especially in very segregated cities like Milwaukee, for example, many thought that community control was more important than arguing over segregation, since most of their children were already in segregated schools or found themselves marginalized and still segregated within "integrated" suburban schools.

The problem with such arguments for privatization, however, is that they do not take into account the reality of power relations and the question of *who* ultimately has the institutional power to share or withhold resources. The falsehood is that school voucher programs will provide poor minorities with educational opportunities usually available only to the wealthy. But the amount provided by the vouchers takes money out of the public fund and is hardly enough to provide quality education. Furthermore, money spent on vouchers is money taken out of the purse for public education, further deteriorating the already scarce resources for the vast majority of children who remain in public schools. In reality, "local control" of education has ultimately backfired and led to even more inferior schools for children of color, because those who control the economic resources and the decision-making bodies are still predominantly upper- and middle-class whites who have little interest in the education of the poor or the racially oppressed.[12]

FIFTY YEARS AFTER *BROWN*: STILL STRUGGLING AGAINST THE OFFICIAL RETURN TO SEPARATE AND UNEQUAL

At the turn of the new millennium, it is clear that school funding has become increasingly unequal for communities of color, and that there are still dual systems of education for children of color and white children. In Wisconsin, for example, a study of school funding policies (Barndt and McNally, 2001) reveals a huge gap between the resources provided to urban students of color and those for the predominantly white suburban students. In Milwaukee, where 50 percent of the states' students of color and 71 percent of the states' African American students live, since 1980, as the percentage of students of color rose in the Milwaukee Public Schools, funding per pupil plummeted compared to funding in overwhelmingly white suburban districts. From 1980 to 1998, the gap between school funding for urban students (students of color) and that for suburban students in Wisconsin had increased by 400 percent. The result is that nearly a half century after *Brown v. Board of Education*, separate and unequal school systems based on race are being reestablished in the Milwaukee area with state approval. This situation is not unique to Wisconsin. Barndt and McNally (2001) note that in the state of New York, a landmark school ruling in January 2001 declared that the state's school funding system violated federal civil-rights laws by causing an adverse and disparate impact on minority students, who received unequal funding in New York City, where more than 70 percent of the state's students of color live. Steel (2001) writes that according to New York justice Leland DeGrasse:

> The state financing system was depriving city students of the "sound basic education" required by the state Constitution and was violating U.S. Department of Education regulations implementing Title VI of the Federal Civil Rights Act of 1964 by disproportionately hurting minority students, proclaiming that "the amount of melanin in a student's skin," his or her country of national origin or amount of family wealth should not be inexorable determinants of academic success. (p. 27)

—◁◇◇▷—

Underlying these debates is the persistent but often unspoken or unrecognized issue of institutionalized racism in society and in education. In the search for a paradigm to explain and counteract the persistence of racism in education, many educators have located the discourse in the realm of the individual psychology of prejudice and racism, while others locate it within the structural contexts that breed racism in the individual. Many look at the very process of education that contributes to racist outcomes, and others are seeking answers in programs for reform and change in education. Multicultural education and antiracist education have been viewed as reforms that could be implemented within the educational system. It has been within this terrain of liberal and radical discourse that multicultural education as well as antiracist education are located. Although the discourse of antiracist education is less prominent in the United States, it is seen by many as an alternative to the predominant approaches to multicultural education for its critical focus on addressing the centrality of the problem of racism in American education. One of the features that distinguishes these two approaches to reform and change has to do with the possibilities that each envisions within the existing institutional arrangements. In the following chapter, I examine some of the similarities and distinctions between multicultural education and antiracist education.

CHAPTER THREE

Antiracist and Multicultural Education

similarities and distinctions

O NE OF THE RESULTS OF THE CIVIL-RIGHTS MOVEMENT was the recognition of the need to make the schools more culturally relevant and inclusive for all children. This was attempted through the introduction of various models of "multicultural education" and, to a lesser degree, what has been termed "antiracist education." In this chapter, I examine the major ideological distinctions that inform the multicultural and antiracist perspectives and discuss some of the variations and oppositions within each perspective, as neither is a monolithic movement.

MULTICULTURAL EDUCATION AS AN EDUCATIONAL REFORM

In order to clarify what is distinctive about multiculturalism, it is helpful to examine the broader context of the different perspectives of American society that have informed educators. Brandt (1986) has isolated three perspectives that have shaped state policies toward education: assimilationist, integrationist, and cultural pluralism. Although his research focuses on the United Kingdom, these perspectives are helpful for gaining an understanding of the current debates about racism in American education as well.

The Assimilationist Model

Until relatively recently, the assimilationist model has been the dominant paradigm in American education. This perspective viewed one of the aims of

American education to be the task of transforming the cultures of all immigrants so that they would merge imperceptibly into the mythical American "melting pot." Alba (1990) and other researchers (e.g., Novak, 1972) have demonstrated convincingly that assimilation did indeed occur for many European ethnics. However, there was a price to pay for such assimilation. For in the process of shedding their "primordial" ethnic attachments to become "acceptable" Americans, along with diluting or negating their customs, language and ethnicity, European immigrants would have to assume a new identity formed in opposition to, in not being people of color—they would have to agree with an identity of being "white."[1] Obviously, when it came to "race," or more specifically, nonwhite "races," the assimilationist model proved to be grossly inadequate. As Theresa Perry (1993) argues, while people of color were not welcomed into this possibility of assimilation, their presence was always a central backdrop to American educational opportunity for whites. The progressive movements and debates of the 1960s exposed the fallacy of the assimilationist model for people of color. Many people began to argue for new models of incorporating minorities through integration.

The Integrationist Model

The integrationist model has emphasized expanding the opportunity structure by allowing minorities, with the means, to "participate" in American society. While recognizing that cultural differences do exist, the onus is placed on minorities to fit into a white society, hence the strategy of busing minority students to "white" schools. Apart from the mixed success and the opposition from both Blacks and whites, this strategy left untouched the racism embedded in educational institutional practices, or in the job market, or in residential segregation. The resistance by many whites to allowing their children to share classrooms with Blacks precipitated a "white flight" from integrated schools. The flaunting of open racism, especially from the period of the Reagan era, showed that all was not well. The emphasis therefore came to be placed on cultural awareness and understanding which is expressed in the cultural pluralism model.

The Cultural Pluralism Model

The cultural pluralism model has a long history in American society. It is reaffirmed in the popular discourse that "ours is a nation of immigrants." This model advocates tolerance and understanding of differences. It calls for mutual accommodation in order to enhance productivity in the economy, the workplace, the schools, and other institutions. However, cultural pluralism has always had an implicit assumption that cultural difference was a temporary condition that would give way to assimilation. But differences of a fundamental nature have not been encouraged, especially when they advocate systemic changes, such as a more equitable redistribution of the wealth. Such differences have been met with repression by the State and, in the case of people of color, often violence, such as the assassination and imprisonment of many of the leaders of the civil-rights and Black liberation movements, or the bombing of an entire Philadelphia neighborhood in order to destroy the MOVE organization and its members.

While some people have applied the cultural pluralism model to racial minorities, such a practice has resulted in a number of problems. For if Blacks and other minorities are equated with other ethnic groups that migrated to America, why have they not generally followed the socioeconomic patterns and successes of the others? (Ogbu, 1978, 1994). For some, the answer to such a question has led to the "cultural deficit" or "culturally deprived" explanation of disadvantage.[2] That perspective argues that the poor develop a "culture of poverty" that leads to their own undoing, thereby blaming the victims of poverty rather than the conditions that create it. While culture may indeed be affected by material conditions of life and vice versa, it is not the culture *per se* that produces poverty, but the structural arrangements in a capitalist society that require levels of unemployment and exploitation as a means to control wages and maximize profits.

CULTURAL PLURALISM AND MULTICULTURAL EDUCATION

The cultural pluralism model of tolerance and understanding has been incorporated by many in the multicultural education movement. In this sense, there has been a paradigm shift, such that an element of "progressiveness" has been injected. This element has to do partly with the recognition of the legitimacy of certain heretofore marginalized cultural experiences. Thus, for example, Black English or Ebonics has come to be accorded greater legitimacy as a form of expression that derives from the Black experience.

But not all attempts at multicultural education seek to truly include those who have been marginalized, and frequently in many school districts, "multiculturalism" has been used as a catch-all term that can mean anything from having a "taco day" at school to incorporating all aspects of culture into the curriculum. The terminology of multiculturalism can be a deceptive slogan system, providing a common umbrella under which anyone can cover themselves while not necessarily having anything in common. While in its entirety multiculturalism is not a monolithic movement, by and large the perspectives are circumscribed within the liberal discourse. Multiculturalism incorporates many of the perspectives of those who are seeking the answers to the conditions of oppressed groups. It is for this reason that many of its adherents begin by positing the legitimacy of the different cultural legacies: "Let us respect each other's heritage" is the invocation. This dimension, however, is often divorced from the historical and structural context and causes of inequalities and, as Brandt (1986) argues, may in effect "depoliticize" various problems, hence problems of racism tend to be attributed to a lack of understanding. This level of articulation of problems manages to leave untouched the *structural* sources of racism.

In general, multiculturalism, as it has been conceptualized and incorporated by most educators, falls within the liberal reformist framework. This perspective does not challenge the institutional arrangements in a capitalist system or the economic roots of the historical development of racism and class exploitation. Thus, even though terms like "institutional racism" may be used, the class basis for this institutionalized racism is not necessarily addressed. An example of the liberal multicultural education perspective is that given by Bennett (1986):

> The focus of multicultural education is on cultural perspectives associated with diverse ethnic groups and nations, rather than on different classes, although it is recognized that ethnic minority perspectives are usually more prevalent at lower socioeconomic levels than among middle or upper income members of the group. (p. 290)

Nieto's (1996) conception of multicultural education is more explicitly anti-racist and calls for a commitment to activism:

> To be anti-racist means to work affirmatively to combat racism. It means making anti-racism and anti-discrimination an explicit part of the [multicultural] curriculum and teaching young people skills in confronting racism. It also means that students must not be isolated, alienated, or punished for naming it when they see it. If developing productive and critical citizens for a democratic society is one of the important goals of public education, anti-racist behaviors are helping to meet that objective. (p. 210)

Sleeter and Grant's (1988) conceptualization of multicultural education incorporates the language of class, gender, race, and disability. In their review of the predominant multicultural approaches, they distinguish five major perspectives, all of which identify themselves as multicultural education: teaching the exceptional and culturally different; the human-relations approach; the single group-studies approach; multicultural-education approach; and education that is multicultural and social reconstructionist. Except for the last approach, these perspectives fit within cultural pluralism model and do not offer a structural analysis of society. However, the last approach—education that is multicultural and social reconstructionist—comes closer to an antiracist perspective in that it looks at the socioeconomic framework of American society and recognizes class, race, and gender inequalities. Nevertheless, as McCarthy (1993) argues the focus is still on the role of attitudes in the transformation of racism.

While it is essential to examine the intersections of race, class, and gender, this may also become another slogan system if it does not critically examine the historical and structural context for the production of racism, capitalism, and patriarchy.

As I discussed in the previous chapter, there has been a great deal of resistance from whites at true inclusion of students of color. Hence, many school districts accepted the language of multicultural education in its most generic sense while avoiding dealing with the difficult issue of racism, which might implicate the role of whites in maintaining the inequalities that multicultural education is supposed to address. Anticipating the problem of marginalizing certain groups under the umbrella of multiculturalism, Banks (1981) warned against the tendency of lumping all of the problems of diverse groups together:

> School reform efforts should go beyond the level of generic multicultural education and focus on the unique problems that women, Blacks, youth and other cultural groups experience in American society. Many of the problems these groups have are unique and require specialized analyses and strategies. . . . Multicultural education is a politically popular concept because it is often interpreted to mean lumping the problems of ethnic minorities, women and other groups together. Public and school policies that are based primarily on lumping the problems of diverse groups together will prove ineffective and perhaps detrimental to all of the groups concerned. Because of the unique problems some ethnic and racial groups have in American society, school districts should implement multi-ethnic education to complement and strengthen multicultural education. These concepts are complementary but not interchangeable. (pp. 52–53)

Indeed, the attempt to subsume a broad array of groups under the same rubric targeted by a multicultural educational strategy is problematic for some advocates of antiracist education. Some argue that if the aim is to eradicate racism, that should be the focus, and they pose the question, Why is it that whenever the racially oppressed groups attempt to agitate for social justice in a racist society, the response from the powers that be tends to suddenly be conceived in terms of justice for all groups, leaving people of color—again—last on the list (Sivanandan, 1985)? This does not mean that struggles against other forms of oppression should be ignored, but if the issue of racism is to be tackled within a racist society, it will have to be addressed in such a way that it is not seen as just another feature of oppression or difference that in effect generalizes disadvantage. Many have viewed the strategy of generalizing disadvantage or oppression as a way of overlooking or avoiding the specific structural sources of racist oppression and exploitation, resulting in abstract solutions that ultimately prove to be ineffective. It is for this reason that some activists and scholars have taken the position of going back to race-specific remedies in dealing with the problems of racial injustice (Kunjufu, 1985). This is reflected, for example, in the notion of "Afrocentricity" as a pedagogical strategy as advocated by Molefi Asante (1987) and others.

RADICAL AND ANTIRACIST CRITIQUES OF MULTICULTURAL EDUCATION

Many have criticized the dominant approach to multicultural education as it has typically been implemented in schools. Frequently multiculturalism has simply become another slogan system which tends to tokenize the racially and economically oppressed. While it is important for educators to be aware of the need to develop multicultural "values and skills" one must also critically analyze the role of class and capitalism and the relations of domination in the social construction of difference along race, class, and gender. It is also problematic to collapse race, class, and gender as though they are identical. While one may be seeking unity between people of different racial or ethnic groups, it is problematic to collapse race and class or racism and "classism" as though class is just another identity. As Rosenthal puts it, the solution to racism is antiracist working-class unity, whereas the solution to class exploitation is not the unity of the working and capitalist classes, but the "conquest of political power by the working class."[3]

A number of antiracist critiques of multicultural education have come from the United Kingdom.[4] Troyna (1984), for example, argues that most multicultural approaches lead not to emancipation, but to containment, for they ignore the differential experiences of white students and students of color and the importance of labor-market processes as a determinant of life opportunities. Counterpoising nonclass multicultural approaches with an antiracist perspective, Troyna argues that antiracist education, on the other hand, "proceeds along a different trajectory to conventional multicultural education programmes insofar as it explicitly recognizes racism as the crucial determinant of the life chances of black youth" (p. 91). Likewise, Brandt (1986) critiques the inherent limitations and assumptions of the predominant multicultural perspectives:

> [These perspectives] tend to view society as consensual. Thus it is assumed that there is a broad agreement in society about what counts as knowledge, and the basis on which this knowledge is constructed—or at least what it was like until "they" came. "They" refers to the "ethnic minorities" who now live in British society. . . . The liberal argument therefore is to make *them* feel a part of *our* society and then we will return to harmony. . . . The problem with this approach is that it fails to acknowledge the stratification of British society along class, race and gender lines and the oppressive structures that maintain the status quo. (p. 114)

Similar to the antiracist critiques of multiculturalism in Britain, in the United States there have also been critical analyses of the dominant approaches to multiculturalism (e.g., McCarthy and Crichlow, 1993; Giroux, 1994; Marable, 1995; Steinberg, 1995; McLaren, 1997; Torres, 1998). Like their counterparts in Britain, many of the critics of the dominant models of multiculturalism in the United States argue that multicultural education has been appropriated and depoliticized, robbing it of its transformative emphasis, which derived out of its earlier focus on community control, a capitalist critique, and representation. McCarthy (1993) argues that typically, the multicultural education movement has been appropriated to focus on the debates over content, attitudes, and values. Publishers and schools of education, when they have incorporated multicultural education, have usually focused on the themes of cultural understanding, sensitivity training, and cross-cultural communication, leaving the critical, participatory, emancipatory, and transformative possibilities of a democratic multiculturalism out of the framework for discussion. Instead, as McCarthy argues, multicultural education has tended to emphasize

> a normative rhetoric that accepts the broad structural and cultural parameters and values of American society and the American way. Some multicultural educators tend to graft the theme of diversity onto the negotiated central concerns and values of this society—the values of possessive individualism, occupational mobility and status attainment—leaving completely untouched the very structural organization of capitalism in the United States. (1993, p. 290)

McCarthy (1993) identifies three different types of discourses, all of which fit within the framework of cultural pluralism: the discourse of cultural understanding and cultural relativism, such as the human-relations approach that emphasizes improving communication; the discourse of cultural competence; and the discourse of cultural emancipation. The third perspective suggests that a reformist multicultural curriculum can enhance the educational and economic success of minority youth if knowledge of minority history and achievements are included in the school curriculum, where, by including the student's language and culture, one enhances the possibilities for success. While indeed such culturally relevant pedagogy would seem to contribute to the possibilities for academic achievement, such perspectives, however, implicitly subscribe to the human capital theory—that once such an education is achieved, one will have access to economic opportunity. Such an approach may not be sufficient in an era of capitalist globalization and the attendant downsizing, plant closings, and shifting, shrinking economies.

Marable (1995) identifies four major interpretations of multiculturalism: *corporate multiculturalism, liberal multiculturalism, racial essentialism,* and *radi-*

cal democratic multiculturalism. Corporate multiculturalism seeks to appropriate diversity as a means of gaining entry so as to dominate minority markets. This approach ignores troubling concepts like racism or exploitation. *Liberal multiculturalism,* on the other hand, may examine race but not address the issue of power relations. As Marable argues:

> Liberal multiculturalism is broadly democratic as an intellectual approach for the deconstruction of the idea of race. But like corporate multiculturalism, it does not adequately or fully address the inequalities of power, resources and privilege which separate most Latinos, African-Americans and many Asian Americans from the great majority of white upper and middle class Americans. It does not adequately conceive of itself as a praxis, a theory which seeks to transform the reality of unequal power relations. It deliberately emphasizes aesthetics over economics, art over politics. It attempts to articulate the perceived interests of minority groups to increase their influence within the existing mainstream. In short liberal multiculturalism is "liberalism" within the framework of cultural diversity and pluralism. (pp. 120–21)

With the exception of the radical democratic or critical perspectives of multiculturalism, by and large the multicultural approaches to change that have been implemented are by their nature reformist, in that they leave unchallenged the structures that contributed to the problems in the first place. The major difference between most multicultural and antiracist perspectives has to do with the extent to which the changes advocated by each go beyond the existing institutional arrangements and the extent to which race and class are seen as central. In this respect, antiracism may be seen as a "nonreformist reform," as it is aimed at transforming existing structural arrangements. The focus of antiracist education is on the relations of domination rather than on difference alone, as in most conventional multicultural perspectives.

THE HISTORICAL CONTEXT OF ANTIRACIST EDUCATION

Among those who view racism as endemic (though not necessarily unique) to certain structural arrangements of capitalism, there has been an impetus to move beyond the metaphysical plane of "celebrating diversity" that characterizes the multicultural approaches that most schools employ. In the United Kingdom, Canada, Australia, and to a much lesser extent in the United States, this movement in education has been located in the discourse of antiracist education. In the United States, the discourse of antiracist education is often framed in terms of radical approaches to multiculturalism. Hence, McCarthy (1993) calls for a "critical emancipatory multiculturalism" and Marable (1995) argues for a "radical democratic multiculturalism." Although the theoretical debate appears to have received relatively more attention in Britain and Canada[5] than it has in the United States, where the term "antiracism" is rarely used,[6] it is important to note that the antiracist perspective outside of the United States is also still at a rather elementary stage of development, tending, as Troyna (1984) puts it, "to be more of a political slogan—symbolizing a detachment from the multicultural education philosophy and its emphasis on cultural pluralism—rather than a coherent and consensual mode of operation" (p. 91).

As Troyna and Williams (1986) explain, the antiracist perspective is a critique of the multiculturalists for

> defining the educational difficulties stemming from a multiracial society as problems resulting from the presence, per se, of black children. These include "underachievement," lack of motivation, indiscipline and alienation, low self-esteem, damaged personal identities, and cultural differences. Anti-racist theorists, on the other hand, define white racism as the main problem. This is said to manifest itself in racist ideologies, racialist practices and structural inequalities. From this perspective then, the alienation of black students, for example, is not pathological but a rational response to racism in the educational system. Anti-racists adhere to the view that racism is an integral feature of the educational system and that it manifests itself habitually in institutional forms. (p. 46)[7]

From the antiracist perspective, the historical context of antiracism is structural oppression in a capitalist society. Such oppression, especially racism, is not only reproduced in all the major institutions of a capitalist society, but is also reflected in the capitalist cultural hegemony in which the cultural heritages of the subordinated groups are rendered marginal, deviant or problematic. Whereas most multicultural perspectives look at the world from the "top down," in the sense of a liberal analysis that describes the symptoms of the problem, an antiracist perspective examines the root causes of inequality looking at the world from the perspective of those who are oppressed. Antiracist education is a recognition of the limits of the liberal reforms and argues for the need to go beyond the current policy approaches. Because of its focus on confronting the roots of oppression, antiracism can be an effective strategy for social movements that are trying to agitate for racial and economic justice.

SOME CENTRAL ELEMENTS OF ANTIRACIST PEDAGOGY

A central element of antiracist pedagogy is empowerment. In this case, education is viewed as a tool to critically analyze existing power relations and knowledge paradigms. This means that knowledge presented from mainstream perspectives has to be subjected to a critical analysis in order to reveal the existing relations of race and class domination. Beyond the deconstruction of existing knowledge paradigms is the process of the reconstitution of knowledge in order to provide an alternative world view that presumably is radically different from the current oppressive arrangements, and that does not inherently reproduce other forms of oppression in order to exist.

An example of this reconstruction of knowledge would be a revamping of the curriculum to make it culturally and politically relevant to the needs of youth from oppressed backgrounds—including white working-class students— and to make use of the lived experiences of these students as part of the living curriculum in the schools. In this sense, teachers are not simply mechanical devices through which knowledge is imparted: rather, they are also change agents who creatively interact with their students, learning from them as well as instructing them. In this process of the reconstitution of knowledge, the positive legacies of people of color and working-class people in general, who have been whitewashed through the packaging of knowledge in the conventional textbook market, are salvaged. This requires that we look for nontraditional sources in building an alternative curriculum, such as publishers like Third World Press, Transaction Books, Rethinking Schools, or African American Images Press, to name a few examples of the production of alternative counter-hegemonic knowledge.

Another distinguishing feature of antiracist pedagogy is the concept of oppositional pedagogy, which Brandt (1986) defines as follows:

> Oppositional pedagogy is a theory and practice that premises itself on the notion of schooling as repressive and as serving to maintain the power structure vis-à-vis the social and racial status quo of schooling as well as in the wider social structure. Schooling, therefore, is seen as principally serving the ends of the powerful in society by maintaining their position of power through ideological induction into dominant norms and values of society, thus helping to maintain the social/racial status quo. (p. 132)

Given the current lamentable status of the education of children of color in the United States, the United Kingdom, Canada, and elsewhere, the movement toward antiracist education has been a critical response to the resurgence of racism and the failure or subversion of the liberal "multicultural" reforms in education that were initiated in response to the popular struggles of the 1960s. The cultivation of this oppositional consciousness, which goes against the grain of the dominant institutions, often leads to labeling the advocates of such an antiracist strategy as outcasts or enemies of the "system." It is for this reason that the leaders of such antiracist or critical multicultural-education movements have to ground their aims in grass-roots support and engage not only in theorizing, but also in developing a praxis that seeks to confront and transform unequal power relations. The dimension of activism is central to antiracist education. As Dei (1996) argues, being antiracist is more than simply being nonracist. The former is proactive, whereas a nonracist stance does not automatically imply activism or taking an antiracist stand.

The language and terminologies of multiculturalism and antiracism are at once distinctive and at times overlapping. One may employ the language of one discourse while actually be engaging in the other discourse. As Brandt (1986) notes:

> Ideologies generate the vocabularies and language that express, delineate and structure not only *what* is thought about but *how* it is thought about. . . . The "bottom line" . . . has to do with the extent to which the approach acknowledges the notion of oppression, institutional racism through both structural and cultural means and the need to consciously combat racism in and through institutions. This approach also operates from a premise that education is a politically defined social process. The only question is *in whose interests*. (p. 120 [my emphasis])

TENDENCIES WITHIN THE ANTIRACISM MOVEMENT

While there are various tendencies in multicultural education, there are also divergent and contradictory tendencies in the antiracism movement. These include the Left-oriented movements, the Black nationalist movements, consciousness raising, which includes Race Awareness Training (RAT), and critical whiteness theory as well as critical race theory.

The Left-Oriented Movements

The Left-oriented movements recognize the fact that no fundamental change in the existing institutions can be effected without addressing the issue of class. Like multiculturalism, this perspective is concerned with cultural pluralism and inclusion, but it specifically sees the exclusion and the marginalization of people of color not as an aberration, but as a product of capitalist class relations. Racism as an ideology developed in order to justify and obscure the contradictions of capitalism, slavery, colonialism, and exploitation. But there has been a tension historically among some on the Left in the United States regarding the role of people of color and the analysis of race. Some have regarded the Left's advocacy of racial justice as opportunism—that people of color were being used by the leftists to further their own class agenda. With the advent of the cold war, some nonwhite movements, often under pressure from the FBI (O'Reilly, 1989), distanced themselves from Left-oriented movements. To some, class analysis was regarded as a "white" discourse and as such not a relevant tool of analysis for the Black condition. For others, the Left was seen as containing its own racial chauvinism among the white individuals within it, similar to mainstream politics, and was thus avoided for that reason rather than necessarily for ideological or philosophical disagreements.

However, on the other hand, there have been those in the African American liberation movement who have strongly identified themselves with Marxism, class analysis, or the Left and in fact were influential in Left discourse, such as many of the leaders of the Black Panther Party or individuals like Angela Davis. In some Left parties, such as the Communist Party USA (CPUSA), African Americans were in the forefront of the movement to centralize the struggle against racism. Such examples of these efforts would include Claude Lightfoot's (1977), "On the Centrality of the Struggle for African American Liberation," as well as the work of Henry Winston (1977) and Angela Davis (1981). They were continuing in the tradition of W. E. B. Du Bois, Paul Robeson, and William L. Patterson, as well as some of the white members of the CPUSA, such as the scholarship of Herbert Aptheker or Victor Perlo for example.[8] Other African American and Left organizations and formations in the 1970s also centralized the problem of racism from a Marxist perspective, such as the work of James and Grace Lee Boggs (Boggs and Boggs, 1970; J. Boggs, 1970).

Antiracism and Black Nationalist Movements

Among the Black Nationalist movements, there have been different tendencies as well, such as the revolutionary nationalists and the cultural nationalists. While the cultural nationalist movement centers around race, this discourse actually fits within the multicultural paradigm in the sense that it does not necessarily seek to fundamentally change the existing institutions, only the people in them. Such approaches include creating an alternative autonomous structure that would be instrumental in bringing racially oppressed groups to be on a par with the dominant groups. According to this perspective, the dimension of class is given a lower priority, and cultural self-determination within some alternative structural framework is held to be the ideal.[9] Where the Left-oriented movements have in mind the ideal of a multiracial socialist society, the cultural nationalist movement aims at building a culturally autonomous and insulated entity. However, it is important to note that some of its advocates argue for communalism or "African socialism."[10]

Among the cultural nationalist perspectives, there is the influence of Maulana Karenga and also of Molefi Asante (1987), who advocate a strategy of an Afrocentric education so as to inculcate into the young a sense of continuity and pride in their African heritage. This sort of Afrocentric perspective is what Marable (1995) terms a "racial essentialist" model of multiculturalism. Such a perspective provides an oppositional framework to Eurocentrism and draws upon the foundations of Black Nationalism, rejecting cultural assimilationist ideology. Yet although this perspective critiques Eurocentrism, as Marable (1995) argues, the weakness of the Afrocentric perspective is

> its general failure to integrate the insights of cultural difference drawn from the perspectives of gender, sexual orientation and class. It has no theory of power which goes beyond a racialized description of how whites, as a monolithic category, benefit materially, psychologically and politically from institutionalized racism. Thus rather than seeking allies to transform the political economy of capitalism across the boundaries of race, gender and class, most Afrocentrists approach the world as the main character in Ralph Ellison's classic novel *Invisible Man*; enclosed inside a windowless room filled with thousands of glowing light bulbs. (p. 123)

Though the Afrocentric perspective focuses on race and rejects Eurocentric constructions, McCarthy (1993) similarly argues that it still falls within the liberal discourse of multicultural education, for

> proponents such as Molefi Asante [1987] fail to offer any serious class analysis of American capitalism. Within this framework the emancipation of the minority individual is fulfilled when he or she becomes a good capitalist. It is the nonthreatening social centrality of the "good bourgeois life" for the minority poor that the multiculturalist ultimately seeks to promote. (p. 290)

On the other hand, the revolutionary Black Nationalist perspective, as exemplified in the work of Amiri Baraka, combines Black Nationalist politics with a Marxist perspective. According to this paradigm, the only solution to Black economic inequality would be a radical restructuring of the entire society, based not upon the conservative notions of "individual freedom," but upon the understanding that people are inherently social and need to work together to produce what we need to survive. Thus this socialist view stresses collectivism as opposed to individualism in this radical restructuring.

Race Awareness Training

An approach that falls between these two tendencies of the Left-oriented and the Black Nationalist perspectives is Race Awareness Training (RAT), which became popular after the Kerner Commission Report (1968) issued its findings that "what white Americans have never fully understood—but what the Negro can never forget—is that white society is deeply implicated in the ghetto. White institutions created it, white institutions maintain it and white society condones it" (p. 1).

While the Kerner Report connected racism with white institutions, it did not connect the institutions themselves with an exploitative white capitalist power structure. Similarly, the U.S. Commission on Civil Rights, in its analysis of racism, made the distinction between "overt racism" and "indirect institutional subordination" and stated that combating racism would require changing the behavior of whites, thus focusing on the psychology of the individual while ignoring the structural contexts that breed racism in the individual.

Following these reports, there a was new focus in the fields of education and psychology on the white psyche and white racism and the damaging effects that racism had on white people. This interest was partly in response to the concerns of many in the Black Power Movement who had rejected the missionary-like approach of some of the northern white people who had gone down south to work in the civil-rights movement. It was sometimes the case that whites who went south exhibited their own racial chauvinism toward those they were there to "help," leading Stokely Carmichael, one of the leaders of the Black Power movement, to tell white people that if they wanted to help, they should go home and "free their own people" (Hamilton and Carmichael, 1967).

In efforts to "educate their own people," various models were developed that identified themselves as antiracist approaches or race-awareness training. Typical among these approaches was the work of Bidol (1971) and Katz (1978), as well as some of the publications of the National Education Association (1973), which focused on race awareness training. The focus of this work was on the cognitive aspects of racism to help people to turn inward to explore their own attitudes and understandings of racism. This analysis recognized racism as being inherent in all of our institutional structures, an inescapable fact that affects all white people. Therefore, Bidol (1971) argued, "all whites are racists in the USA" by virtue of being born into a system that bestows "white skin privileges" on every white baby. Bidol, who worked in the area of race awareness training for educators (and who was at the time the superintendent of schools in Baldwin, Michigan), wrote:

> As whites in a racist society we have only two behaviors to choose from vis-à-vis the issue of racism. We can choose to be racist/racists—those who recognize the benefits accrued through being white and either consciously or unconsciously support institutional and cultural practices that perpetuate racism. Or we can choose to be anti-racist/racists—those who recognize the illegitimate privileges obtained by whiteness but strive to remove these institutionally and culturally racist benefits even while still receiving them. There really is no place in between. (p. 8)

Whites attended "race awareness" workshops designed to shock them into confronting their own racism or to see what it felt like to be discriminated against. Though some may have been propelled to action, for many this led to depression and hopelessness or guilt, and for others anger and reaction against their perception that they had now become the "victims" of racism. The guilt-ridden concept of "anti-racist/racists" has been criticized by Sivanandan (1985), for example, who writes that such an approach to race awareness training is a dangerous method for "rescuing racism from structural taint and interiorizing it within the white psyche and white behavior and formulating programmes for combating racism on that basis" (p. 17). Though race awareness training does view racism as a central problem in American society, and the rhetoric of anti-racism is employed, this method often renders racism classless and focuses on changing the individual consciousness, while the system that helps reproduce such a consciousness is not challenged.

The attention to race awareness should not be dismissed entirely, however. As I discuss further in part two of this book, which elaborates on my practice with primarily white teachers, race awareness, specifically whiteness awareness, is often a necessary first step of antiracist education for dealing with the cognitive aspects of racism. It is essential, however, that such awareness go beyond the self-obsessive stewing in guilt (which was often the result of race awareness training) to a critical analysis of the social construction of "difference" and white supremacy. One must examine the dialectical relationships between race, class, and gender in order to understand the dimensions of racism and exploitation in a capitalist system. Part of this process involves whites examining their own racial positioning in society, which is sometimes referred to as "whiteness theory" or "whiteness studies."

Whiteness Theory

There has also been an increased focus by some scholars on critical whiteness studies, which concentrates on revealing the privileging of whiteness or white privilege (e.g., McIntosh, 1989; Thompson, 1999). Here the focus is on exposing the taken-for-granted assumptions and rights that whites have (often at the expense of people of color) but are often unaware.[11] Because the research focus in fields like education and anthropology has traditionally been on an examination of the "other," as the dominant white culture sees it, whiteness theory focuses on making white cultural assumptions and privileges visible so that whites do not assume that their own position is neutral or "normal." Though it is on one hand consistent with the aims of multicultural education in the sense that it aims to enhance understanding and appreciation of all cultures, as Thompson (1999) notes:

> Because multicultural approaches are concerned with displacing white culture from its position of dominance, they usually do not focus on white culture as a distinctive culture or identity. Whiteness theory, on the other hand, focuses specif-

ically on whiteness as a cultural identity—*an identity that, to a considerable extent, is gained at the expense of people of color.* [my emphasis]

For educators, race awareness and whiteness theory have particular relevance, since most white teachers have not been educated about how the history of white supremacy has affected and continues to affect racial assumptions and norms that percolate throughout the culture of all institutions, including schools. Hence, it is important to incorporate into antiracist education for teachers strategies to help them deconstruct and confront the meaning of their own whiteness so as to reveal how this whiteness is reflected and reproduced in various practices and institutions in society.

However, the recent proliferation of writings about whiteness theory should also be critically interrogated (Thompson, 1999; Sheets, 2000). An awareness of the social construction of whiteness may be new to many whites, but it is hardly new to many people of color who have long observed the distortions of white culture. This is why Black activists in the sixties warned many whites in the civil-rights movement to stop focusing on "saving" Blacks in a paternalist manner and take on the responsibility of saving their fellow whites from their own racist indoctrination. While it is important that whites examine their taken-for-granted assumptions about themselves and the world about them, there is the danger, as Sheets (2000) warns, that whites may colonize identity politics and benefit from so doing, with a focus on whiteness studies becoming yet another instance of whites gaining cultural capital and recentering the discourse on race, once again resulting in avoiding paying attention to research that explores the seriousness of the effects of racism on people of color. Indeed, as the editors of a recent volume on "whiteness," *Off White: Readings on Race, Power, and Society*, acknowledge, there is the danger that "whiteness" studies could "surface as a new intellectual fetish, leaving questions of power, privilege, and race/ethnic political minorities behind as an intellectual 'fad' of the past" (Fine, Weis, Powell, and Mun Wong, 1997, p. xii). However, an examination of the social construction of whiteness is important because it problematizes the identity of those who historically have been writing about, analyzing, and dominating the "other."

Critical Race Theory

By the 1990s, some scholars (e.g., Bell, 1995; Delgado, 1995; Ladson-Billings and Tate, 1995; Tate, 1996; Solorzano, 1997) began to argue for the need for a "critical race theory" (CRT) in education.[12] Critical race theory evolved out of critical legal studies, which focused on how supposedly race-neutral laws perpetuate subordination. Critical race theorists recognize that racism is endemic to American history and culture. CRT challenges the dominant approaches to dealing with race and racism, such as color blindness or supposedly neutral meritocracy. Because race has always been such a critical factor in American history, tied to problems of property rights and structural inequality, critical race theory is an important analytical tool for understanding the persistence of inequities in American society and in education. As Solorzano (1997) argues, critical race theory also provides an analytical framework for challenging the persistent genetic and cultural deficit theories. Of course, the tenets of CRT are not "new," but are an offshoot of some of the earlier scholars, such as Du Bois and Aptheker. A critical theory of race was also evident in some social movements of the civil-rights era and falls within the antiracist framework that has been advocated since the early 1970s, as previously alluded to in the work of Angela Davis, Victor Perlo, and James and Grace Lee Boggs, to name a few.

CONCLUSION

This discussion of some of the distinctions between and within the multicultural and antiracist educational perspectives is not meant to pose them simplistically as rival paradigms. While the terminology varies, the radical critiques of multiculturalism are becoming more fully developed. However, unfortunately there is no indication that this has affected the implementation of multicultural education in real schools in the United States, where the approaches to multicultural education continue to be disturbingly superficial. But while one may reject the predominant multicultural models, which celebrate diversity in the abstract, we must also beware of the present reactionary political climate, in which multiculturalism is still threatened. Michele Wallace (1993), while expressing her mistrust of multiculturalism, reminds us of the need to defend it in times when *any* liberal thought is under attack:

> While multiculturalism's inclination toward unrestricted inclusiveness as opposed to hierarchical exclusiveness doesn't automatically lead to significant structural changes in existing aesthetic and critical priorities and institutional discourses of power, it could offer and thus far has offered more opportunities for critical discussion outside the dominant discourse, and dissent and debate within, than its present aesthetic and critical alternatives. These alternatives I see as: 1) a color blind cultural homogeneity that originates in liberal humanist ideology; 2) separatist aesthetics and politics such as "Afrocentrism"; and 3) racist/sexist aesthetics [of] cultural fascism. (p. 252)

The advice to protect multiculturalism is even more timely as we enter an era of intensified ultra-Right conservatism, especially with a revisiting of another Bush era in 2000, in which the hard-won gains of the civil-rights and women's movements, such as affirmative action, civil-rights legislation, and public education, to name a few, are seriously threatened. While indeed we must defend and promote multiculturalism, we must not allow the generic corporate models that "celebrate diversity" in the abstract, in order to win markets, to dominate the movement. The antiracist perspective is a response to the sorts of multicultural perspectives that negate and deny the role of capitalist structures in maintaining racial inequality in society. Multicultural education that is not antiracist is superficial and patronizing, accommodating rather than confronting racism. Because a critical antiracist multicultural perspective examines the structural roots of inequality, it can be an effective tool for helping people analyze and organize to counteract the problems of racism and other forms of inequality.

Yet this perspective cannot be applied simplistically nor dogmatically. If one has a commitment to antiracist education, one must take into account the complexities of the lives of those who will be implementing such an approach, as well as the intricacies of the institutions in which they work. We must examine teachers' lives and professions, as well as their historical positioning in society as (mainly) white people, and mostly women, largely from lower-middle-class or working-class backgrounds. This consideration of teachers as raced, classed, and gendered actors must be critically examined and incorporated into an antiracist multicultural strategy for teachers. In the next chapter, I examine the social context of teaching and the demographic, moral, and ethical imperatives that call for antiracist education.

CHAPTER FOUR

The Moral and Demographic Imperatives for Antiracist Education

ALTHOUGH THE CIVIL-RIGHTS MOVEMENT opened up the doors for a more multicultural approach in education, there has been a continual struggle to keep those doors open in the face of a white backlash. The intensification of overt racism and resistance to reforms such as school integration, affirmative action, and welfare rights, particularly since the Reagan-Bush era, raised anew the need to confront the problem of racism in American society in general and particularly in the educational process. By the 1980s, some school districts had begun to introduce in-service workshops on multicultural education to prepare teachers to teach increasingly racially and ethnically diverse student populations. However, the majority of these in-services have been superficial, one-shot efforts lasting one day or less (Sleeter, 1992). These responses fit within the liberal discourse of cultural pluralism, in which the goal was to sensitize teachers to teach "diverse learners." Such token approaches to learning about "other people's children," as Delpit (1988) puts it, or how to teach those with different "learning styles" have been encapsulated in slogans like "celebrate diversity!" or "celebrate difference!"

The piecemeal nature of the typical "multicultural" workshops, in terms of both their short duration and their superficial content, has not provided teachers with the educational insights needed to teach from a critical multicultural perspective and, in fact, have often resulted in increased intolerance (Zeichner and Hoeft, 1996). This is because they are "done to" participants without allowing for a meaningful engagement with the complexities of the problem. Such "hit-and-run" workshops are bound to fail, placing the burden unfairly on teachers to address the problems of individual and institutional racism that emanate from the larger society, without giving them the sufficient tools to understand the problem in their work in schools. The problem with such approaches to dealing with difference is that they ignore the centrality of racism and its class roots in American history and culture. This obscures the fact that ultimately the most different thing about us is the way we are treated. It is the focus on this differential *treatment* and the *reasons for it* that characterizes antiracist education.

THE DEMOGRAPHIC IMPERATIVE FOR ANTIRACIST EDUCATION

In addition to being a response to racial conflict in schools, efforts at multicultural education are also a recognition of a demographic imperative that is impacting on education at all levels. As numerous reports issued since the late 1980s indicated, the portrait of the United States has been changing. By the end of the twentieth century, we could expect to see a dramatic change in the racial demographics of American society and especially in the public schools, where students of color would comprise at least 40 percent of all children in public education, due in part to higher birth rates, but also to the flight of many whites into private education (Pallas, Natriello, and McGill, 1989; Rury, 1989). By the late 1980s, students of color already constituted a majority in most of the nation's largest urban school districts (American Council on Education, 1988). Yet despite increasing numbers of students of color in public schools, due to myriad factors associated with race and class oppression there are fewer "success" stories today than there were during the "Great Society" era of the sixties, with African American and Latino youth having a greater chance of going to prison than to college. In California, for example, by the late 1990s, Black males were five times more likely to be found in prisons than in one of the state colleges or universities.[1]

With the increasing numbers of students of color in public schools, many people assumed that there would naturally also be an increase in the numbers of teachers of color, but in actuality, the percentage of teachers of color has been decreasing since the 1980s. The percentage of African American teachers, for example, decreased from 10.1 percent in 1976 to approximately 7 percent in 1986 (Perkins, 1989). By 1996, there had been little improvement, and just 7.34 percent of public elementary and secondary teachers were Black; 86.6 percent were white; and 4.25 percent were Hispanic.[2]

As I discussed earlier, there are historical reasons for the small number of African Americans and other racial minorities in teaching. Within two years of the Brown decision, many African American teachers were fired and harassed and were not able to get jobs in the South. In the urban North, they were hired on a token basis and were not welcome in small cities and rural areas, leaving most African American children with fewer African American teachers than before (Perkins, 1989; Steel, 2001). While there was an increase in the number of teachers of color during the seventies as a result of the civil-rights movement and the Great Society reforms, this was short-lived. As America deindustrialized since the 1980s, economic options for people of color became even more constricted in a service economy. And as the costs of higher education skyrocketed, fewer people of color could afford to attend four-year colleges and were attending two-year colleges and trade schools. There has also been the problem of *de facto* racial tracking in "desegregated" schools, which has excluded many Latino and African American students from college prep courses for the path to higher education. Of the relative few who have made it to four-year institutions, other professions more lucrative than teaching have opened up for racial minorities. Also, of no small importance, as the economic options for people of color become even more constricted in a service economy, a larger percentage of people of color will be entering the military than the university. With a decreasing number of teachers of color in the schools as role models, we can also expect that fewer children of color will identify with the teaching profession and will not aspire to become teachers (Perkins, 1989).

THE MORAL IMPERATIVE FOR ANTIRACIST EDUCATION: WHEN WHITE TEACHERS ARE TEACHING CHILDREN OF COLOR BY DEFAULT

In the African American community, the treatment of Black children by white teachers has long been a central concern, especially after the *Brown v. Board of Education* decision, when many Black teachers were forced out of teaching. Historian John Henrik Clarke (1970), writing in the late sixties, expressed the sentiments of many African American parents and educators regarding the insensitivity of many of the white teachers who now were put in charge of their children's education:

> Many of the white teachers in the large educational systems in cities like New York, Detroit, Philadelphia, Chicago, Los Angeles, came to the system with the preconceived notions about the ability of the Black child to learn. Instead of teaching him they spend a lot of time convincing themselves that the children are unteachable. They do not bring their best teaching ability to these communities because they do not respect the children or the community well enough to do so. In addition to being poor teachers for the Black community, these teachers are not even good baby-sitters. (p. 224)

Such complaints continue to be heard from many parents and teachers of color who feel that their children are often stereotyped by white teachers who have low expectations of them and tend to ignore them until they do something like get into a fight, after which they are suspended, as typified in the following comments made by an African American teacher (as quoted in Spencer, 1986):

> There were a lot of discipline problems, and it's really bad to say but it's true, that the discipline problems were in the white teachers' rooms. There were some white persons there that felt this is the way the black people act, so they didn't see anything wrong with kids jumping up and down and climbing on the walls and walking across the window sills. They actually believed that this is how these people are supposed to act. (p. 134)

The problem of an unrepresentative teaching force has serious repercussions when it comes to the life chances of many students of color. It is serious enough that the present pool of teachers does not represent our multiracial, multicultural society, but we must also be concerned about what is happening in the preparation of future teachers. By the late 1980s according to Perkins (1989), as a study on student enrollment in teacher education programs found, 91 percent of teacher education candidates were white; 4.3 percent Black; and 1.5 percent Hispanic. The white candidates "overwhelmingly stated no desire to teach in an inner-city or urban school where most minority students are found. Eighty-four percent of the candidates surveyed said they preferred to teach in either a suburban or rural school district" (p. 347). Also, as numerous teacher educators have reported, most preservice teachers have a lack of empathy for people of color, as well as a lack of understanding about racism (e.g., Moultry, 1989; King, 1991; Haberman and Post, 1992; Banks and McGee Banks, 1995; Kailin, 1999). This indeed paints a dismal picture for children of color, for they likely will be taught by people who are teaching them by default—after all, there simply won't be enough of those "suburban" teaching positions to go around. This leaves a teaching force that is highly unrepresentative and divorced from the lives of the students they teach. Since the majority of teachers are white and still live in segregated neighborhoods far distanced from their students of color, antiracist multicultural education for teachers is imperative.

In addition to the lack of racial and ethnic representation in the teaching force, there is also a lack of representation among the theoreticians who devise educational policy. Perkins (1989) points out that the major think tanks such as the Holmes Group, assigned to analyze problems in education did not include any advisors or consultants from the historically Black colleges that produce nearly half of all African American teachers. Neither did they give serious attention to the need to incorporate *critical* multicultural education into teacher education. Beyond the problem of building a representative teaching force, which may take many years, the question is also, What must be done until that happens? As Ladson-Billings (1995) observes:

> In the two most prominent reports addressing the crises in teaching, *Teachers for Tomorrow's Schools* (Holmes Group, 1986) and *A Nation Prepared: Teachers for the 21st Century* (Carnegie Forum on Education and the Economy, 1986), these demographic changes and the need to address issues of equity and diversity received only cursory attention. . . . More interested in increasing the number of minorities entering the profession, the reform movement seems to have ignored the need for teachers, regardless of their racial, ethnic, or cultural background, to address the needs of all students (regardless of racial, ethnic or cultural background). (p. 747)

SCHOOLS: A PARADIGM OF THE PLANTATION?

With a teaching force that is already nearly 90 percent white, children of color will continue to find themselves in effect colonized in our schools, with rarely the opportunity to find mentors or to see in their teachers role models for their future selves. In many ways, schools are a paradigm of the plantation. By and large, African Americans and Latinos are found in the schools as janitors, food-service workers, teachers' aides, and occasionally as physical education teachers, counselors, or administrators, but rarely as teachers (Kunjufu, 1985). Of course, this does not mean that all white teachers act in "plantation ways." What it does speak to is the necessity of addressing the impact of such racial disparities on both whites and people of color.

Given the legacy of racism that permeates all aspects of American society, it is predictable that most white teachers will be affected by racism, or at least with an uncomfortable social distance that will make teaching—and learning—problematic. For children of color, this racism or social distance contributes to their alienation from school and from their teachers. It has often been observed that this alienation sets in by the fourth grade, when enthusiasm for school is replaced with apathy and passivity, or anger and rebellion, followed by a downward learning spiral. This is reflected in the inordinate numbers of children of color who are tracked into "special education" and given such problematic labels as "learning disabled" (LD) or "educably mentally retarded" (EMR) or other such designations, or in the 50 to 70 percent dropout and push-out rate nationwide for African American, Hispanic, and Native American youth.[3]

However, we should not focus only on the teacher or the school as the cause of this alienation, for within the socioeconomic context in which many children of color find themselves, there are actually few possibilities or role models for "success"—that is, few objective possibilities for becoming self-supporting workers in the labor market (Ogbu, 1978; Apple, 1982). There is also the subjective problem that many young people of color face when they do try to go after these scarce resources—that they will have to leave many of their peers behind or that they will be rejected by them or alienated from them (Fordham and Ogbu, 1986).

While ultimately we must proportionately increase the percentage of teachers of color to reflect the demographic makeup of the population, until such parity is achieved, the question is, What can teachers do now, given the structural limitations of this apartheid-like situation? For the reality is that if anything is going to be done within the confines of the school to address these racial disparities, it is going to require the major participation of teachers, who play a pivotal role in education.

The Social Context of Teaching and the Working Conditions of Teachers

While teachers do play a central role, this should not be construed as placing the burden of the reproduction of class, race, and gender inequality solely on teachers. Rather, we should examine the ways in which teachers may come to practice their "craft" in a manner that often unconsciously or unknowingly contributes to or reproduces different forms of inequality. By the same token, if we are trying to develop a counter hegemonic strategy, we must ask: How can teachers be transformed through a critical pedagogy into agents and allies of progressive social change? How can this be approached in a way that is not simply another safe multicultural celebration that ignores the dimensions of race, class and gender relations? How can we create a reform measure that is nonreformist? What would be some of the major parameters of such a reform? These questions are key issues that have to be addressed in the quest for antiracist educational reform, one that has the possibility to promote a *fundamental* change in theory and action about the existing relations of domination.

To reiterate, an antiracist perspective begins with the fundamental proposition that racism in our class-divided and gender-stratified society has been a critical agency of ideological reproduction of the relations of domination in American society. Since education as an institution plays such a key role in ideological reproduction, it is not surprising to find that racism has been an organic component of the American system of education. This has been shown empirically by such indicators as segregation in student distributions, admission rates, retention rates, graduation rates, and such. What must also be addressed are the ways in which the subtle aspects of racism are reflected in the curricula and in the teacher–student interactions that contribute to the above-mentioned outcomes. From this perspective, antiracist education may be described as a strategy of incorporating into the teaching practice a pedagogy that sensitizes teachers to the racist constructions of reality in their curricula and behavior. Before teachers can be in a position to overthrow the racist paradigm, they must first be able to see how their own reality is socially constructed (Berger and Luckmann, 1966) and how racism has affected that construction.

The socioeconomic background of teachers shows them likely to be white females drawn from the middle and lower-middle classes. The teaching force has become increasingly feminized, with 74 percent of all teachers being women in 1996, compared with 66 percent women ten years earlier. In elementary education, the gender gap is even more pronounced: In 1996, 86.6 percent of elementary teachers and 53 percent of secondary teachers were women.[4]

As the majority of teachers do not aspire to teach in "urban" schools, it is not surprising that, as Feitritzer (cited in Spencer, 1986) reported, over one-half of the teachers in the United States are dissatisfied with teaching and would not choose to enter teaching if they could do it over again. This compares with 11 percent who said they would not do so in 1963. Teacher burnout is not necessarily only related to urban problems, for as Spring (1994) points out, the suburban teacher may also be so affected in a profession where people are increasingly alienated from their labor, particularly when the psychic rewards of teaching are diminishing as teaching becomes increasingly technicized and standardized rather than an art deriving its rewards from the very process of teaching and learning.

The task of developing an antiracist pedagogy that will inspire or even gain the interest of people who may be demoralized is indeed challenging and highlights the need to incorporate the working conditions and experiences of the teachers into this pedagogy. In the United States, teachers are often not perceived or treated as professionals, but rather as quasi-professionals, as their professional work has increasingly become proletarianized (Apple, 1988). An antiracist approach to teacher education therefore must relate how class and gender affect the oppression of teachers with the class, race, and gender oppression of people of color.

Such a pedagogy must recognize the stress of the daily working lives of teachers who are expected to do damage control for all the social ills of society. The stress that they endure and the injustice of it both for them and for the students must be acknowledged. As the crises of society have been exported to the schools, it is expected that teachers should solve the problems of the larger society—not only the racial problems in a society that has refused residential integration or full employment, but all of the social problems of our society. Daily, teachers are expected to bring the hidden gifts out of our children—or at least to teach them—despite the increasing stresses that are affecting our children, who may have problems outside of school, such as divorce, drug or alcohol abuse, incest, family violence, addiction to television violence or video games, hyperactivity, depression, or reduced attention spans due to junk-food addictions or allergies (which they may even get at school from their lunches or breakfasts), unemployment, or homelessness. Most of these problems enter into the classrooms of most teachers at some time or other, even in staid, middle-class communities. Of course, we should not forget that teachers, like the students, may be burdened in their personal lives by some of these same social and economic problems as well. This does not even speak to the pedagogical problem of dealing with twenty to thirty or more individuals (and individualists) who may have very different levels of abilities, experiences, and interests.

In addition, the "de-skilling" of teachers (Apple, 1988) that has occurred over the last several decades has taken decision making (but not the pressure) out of the hands of teachers. Because of the multitude of tasks teachers are expected to perform, the day has been divided and subdivided into so many discrete parts that many teachers are constantly jumping from task to task. So are the students. For teachers, this contributes to a sensory overload. According to Joyce et al. (1976), teachers receive approximately one stimulus every eight seconds, second only to air traffic controllers in the amount of stimuli they receive.

Yet in spite of these realities of their working life and generally lower-middle-class background, ironically, the teaching style and attitudes that teachers bring into the classroom setting often reflect not that background, but rather an idealized middle-class group outlook that may not really even reflect their own actual life situation. Thus teachers may become conduits of ruling-class ideas. In social studies classes, for example, students may be taught about the importance of voting in a democratic society without discussion about the limits of democracy in a capitalist society where it takes millions of dollars even to run for an election, or where it is even questionable how or if the votes will be counted, as the U.S. presidential election of 2000 illustrates. Students learn that to be "free," one must be able to vote, but they do not learn that in a capitalist society, this alone will not fundamentally alter the system of power relations. Here is where the Gramscian notion of ideological hegemony finds its most concrete expression—for here are people who do not even really belong to the ruling class, yet may continue to reproduce those ideas that reinforce class, gender, and race relations of domination.

Thus teachers may become conduits of ruling-class ideas. However, we must be careful not to characterize teachers simplistically as mere transmitters of propaganda, for because they occupy a contradictory class location and may identify with the aspirations of the bourgeoisie in good economic times, in times of crisis they are forced to assume a perspective of the working class in its antagonistic relations with capital. This has become quite apparent in the recent attempts by the ruling class to impose on teachers, schools, and the teaching profession schemes and programs that are aimed at even greater control and bureaucratization of teachers—which many have resisted (Popkewitz, 1987). On this level, the "proletarianization" of teachers has often led to their higher consciousness of their status as workers.

HOW RACISM DISTORTS THE CLASS CONSCIOUSNESS OF TEACHERS

Yet racism may distort the class consciousness of teachers, as it does with other sectors of the working class. White teachers who may be concerned about issues of gender and class inequities don't necessarily feel empathy for their students of color, especially those who are economically dispossessed. Often they resent any efforts to pay special attention to racially oppressed minorities and feel that it is not their responsibility to go to any extra efforts. As many teachers are becoming increasingly alienated from their labor as the pressures and demands of their jobs increase, they may be more prone to scapegoat their "at-risk" or disfranchised students. Other factors, such as the increased focus on standardized testing, have also had the effect of replacing or negating teacher creativity, and as Michele Fine (1986) found, as teachers become pressured to focus on routinized testing, this correlates highly with derogatory attitudes toward the students. If students do not respond "properly"—i.e., do not perform well on tests—this reflects negatively on their teachers, who may be judged ineffective in their practice. These teachers may then resent the students who are not "learning," for this puts increased pressure on their ability to do their job. As teachers are forced to become further focused on "teaching to the test," they may be less inclined—indeed will have less *time*—to teach critical and creative thinking to their students. Hence, when it comes to encountering people who have differences of any kind that do not "fit" within the very limited universe of discourse, one can expect that the teacher may have an increasingly limited capacity to recognize the gifts and abilities that different people possess and may resent those who are not "familiar." Then it becomes easier to blame the victim and reinforce all of the old stereotypes, such as "those people don't value learning anyway."

An antiracist pedagogy, therefore, must consider the contradictory consciousness of teachers as classed and raced and gendered actors whose work has become increasingly proletarianized. These dynamics may lead to a very complex ideological perspective. Despite their own gender and class oppression, teachers (like other white people in American society) may not have the background knowledge or experiences that will enable them to transcend white racism. Even though they may have experienced class and gender discrimination or oppression, this does not necessarily prevent them from discriminating themselves—not only racially, but also on class and gender issues. Thus it is not uncommon, as Vanfossen (1979) has shown, that teachers may exhibit an individualistic bootstrap ideology that denies their own working-class origins and prevents them from having empathy with others—"I pulled myself up by my bootstraps, why can't you?"—making the goals of multicultural and antiracist education more difficult to achieve.

As people who have grown up in segregated environments, most white teachers have had very little contact with people of color before coming into the teaching profession, although they have usually been exposed through the popular culture to negative stereotypes of them. Once institutional racism puts a particular group in a situation of disadvantage, this is bound to generate some derivative negative consequences, such as high unemployment rates and poverty. These negative consequences may be used to refine and reinforce racist stereotypes that people have already been exposed to, such as disruptiveness or violence, and these are the categories that many people are likely to be carrying around in their minds. Of course, there is no evidence to suggest that most students of color indeed manifest these characteristics. However, these problems, when they do exist, may be end products of a very complex historical process that produces negative aspects (as well as positive, but these positive attributes cannot be recognized when the negative stereotypes have already clouded one's vision). As I found in my work with white teachers in Lakeview and elsewhere, often these negative stereotypes and expectations did serve to place the blame for racism on its victims. I elaborate on this in chapter 6, which discusses how many teachers *perceive* the problem of racism in their schools.

Thus far, this discussion has focused on the objective conditions that I believe make it imperative that antiracist education become an inherent part of both preservice and in-service teacher education. There is not only the demographic imperative for antiracist education for teachers who are now finding themselves teaching in "new" multicultural, multiracial environments, but there is also the moral imperative for antiracist education for those charged with the education and intellectual development of all our children in a society still so deeply segregated by race and scarred by racism.

Merely to name an approach "antiracist" does not necessarily explain it. As I discussed earlier, there are a variety of perspectives that may use the same label but may not really represent the same ideological framework or categories or units of analysis. In the next chapter, I elaborate on my perspective of a curricular framework for antiracist education.

CHAPTER FIVE

A Curricular Framework for Antiracist Education

WHILE MANY PEOPLE MAY UNDERSTANDABLY FEEL the urgency of dealing with the problem of racism and insist that "something is better than nothing," unfortunately this usually consists of the one-time "shotgun" approaches that I referred to in the previous chapter. Such efforts present the danger of creating a backlash by provoking questions with controversial material without giving people sufficient time to allow for digesting, theorizing, and discussing new or controversial ideas. Often what is billed as a "design for diversity" may become a design for disaster, with the typical "hit-and-run" approaches that are disrespectful of the emotional and ideological struggles that people often experience in the *process* of unlearning or rethinking or relearning.

It is necessary to employ a more holistic approach that takes into account the complexities of teachers' lives and professions, as well as their historical positioning in society as (mainly) white people. By virtue of their socializations as members of the dominant group, the very cognitive orientations, attitudes, beliefs, and opinions of teachers as social actors are often affected by racism. Therefore, an antiracist pedagogy for teachers must become a *process* that confronts two aspects of the same problem of racism in society. First, there is the institutional dimension of racism in terms of rules, procedures, and practices that are inherent in structures. Second, there is the subjective or individual dimension of racism that is reflected in the categories, attitudes, and opinions that are held by individuals.

In view of these two dimensions of institutionalized and individualized racism, this calls for a two-pronged strategy of antiracist education: to provide teachers with the knowledge that can lead them to reflect upon their own racial positioning and personal experience or exposure to racism and its origins; and to provide them with the larger societal and historical context of the nature and origins of racism. In this chapter I discuss some of the key issues that should be critically examined in antiracist teacher education. Such examination will aid in unraveling the individual and subjective dimensions of racism.

KEY ISSUES IN ANTIRACIST TEACHER EDUCATION

The White Racial Autobiography and the Social Construction of "Whiteness"

As I discussed in chapter 3, one of the more recent developments in the discourse on race and race relations has been an examination of the effects of racial hierarchies on the perpetrators rather than the victims. This examination of whiteness has taken a number of forms, from white awareness "training," in which white "guilt" is confronted, to whiteness studies that center on the social construction of the white identity. Despite my earlier stated concerns about the limitations of race awareness "training" and "whiteness studies" as once again centering white people, I believe there is a role that such curriculum can play when placed within the larger context of an ongoing program of race-relations education. It is important to incorporate into antiracist education for teachers strategies to help them deconstruct and confront the meaning of their own whiteness as a social construction and to examine how the privileging of whiteness is reflected and reproduced in various practices in schools and the larger society.

There are various strategies one can use to unveil the hidden dimensions of race and "whiteness." For example, one can use race-awareness exercises that allow people to interact on a small group basis to reflect upon and discuss their individual experiences concerning race, as well as other issues of diversity and difference, addressing such questions as: When was the first time you recall realizing the world wasn't just like you? When was the first time you remember being conscious of race? How many "minority" teachers have you had in your life? This process allows white people to see how race and racism pervade or affect their cultures as members of the dominant group. It also reveals the ways in which white supremacy surfaces without whites being conscious of it. The collaborative autobiographical aspect is important, because people may not remember details of their upbringing when it comes to race if they have been part of the dominant group and take their "color" for granted.

Frequently, white teachers report that it is the first time they have focused on these influences in their life and the first time they are talking about their own racial identity with their peers. Often it is only when one member of the group remembers an incident that it triggers similar memories in others. Many times it is the most significant things that we take for granted. In my experience teaching about racism, when I ask people to relate how many teachers of color they have had in their life, most are surprised to realize that they never had a single one. "I never even thought about it before!" is a common response.

In addition to collaborative group discussions about race, another effective strategy is to have teachers write a racial cultural autobiography in which they reflect in five-year segments (0 to 5 years, 5 to 10 years, etc.) upon their personal experience regarding their awareness of race and racial prejudice; feelings about their own race or about other racial groups; family, friends, movies, or books that affected them; and incidents that happened to them, historic events or experiences that made them aware of their own racial prejudice or of prejudice in their country. It is also important to ask them to reflect on what activities they have been involved in throughout their lives that may have supported or worked against racism.

It is helpful to write these experiences and memories and compare stories, because it allows people to see that what they have taken for granted as "normal" may actually have some racial or racist overtones. For example, the common themes of relocating when people of color moved into their neighborhood or the racist folklore that pervaded their childhood have often been forgotten or unexamined but may be revealed when writing and sharing their racial memories.

It is also important to note that these exercises are also meaningful for teachers of color, who have often reported to me that no one ever asked them about these things before, or that they had suppressed some of these racial memories or taken them for granted as normal. One African American teacher, for example, remarked that in reconstructing her racial autobiography, it occurred to her that throughout her childhood, although she had contact with white children, she had never once been allowed to play inside their homes. "I have no idea, no memory of what the insides of their houses even looked like! That's deep! And what makes it really deep is that until writing this autobiography, I had not thought that I should even be invited into their homes!" she remarked to me.

Naming White Privilege

Recognizing and naming white privilege is important for white people so that they can see how much of their personal freedom and how many of their choices are influenced by white-skin privilege. Relative freedom is dependent upon one's color in the United States and in fact may have been gained at the expense of people of color. McIntosh's (1989) work on white privilege, for example, spurs insightful thinking and discussion about issues like merit and privilege. It is a useful tool for giving teachers insight into how certain basic human rights may not be available to the people of color living in their own town, such as the right to walk down the street without fear of a racially motivated insult or attack; the right to "name" oneself; the right to be represented by a member of one's group; the right to be able to buy common items for personal care, such as hair care or beauty products; the right to get a home loan or to rent in an area that one can afford; or, as a parent, the right to come into the school and feel that it reflects your community and your people.

Definitions of Racism: Examine the Language of "Race"

It is important to talk about the language we often use when discussing "race," including the fallacy of actual races (Montagu, 1974) from a biological point of view and the development of the concept of race as a social construction that is not universal. As well, we should discuss the various related concepts and terminology frequently used, such as "institutional racism," "cultural racism," "internalized racism," "reverse racism," "reverse discrimination," "prejudice," "stereotyping," "discrimination," and "ethnocentrism." Having teachers form into small groups to create their own definitions before the discussion is useful to illustrate just how contradictory and complicated and often superficial are our own understandings of the language of race.

Examine the Social Background of Teachers: Intersections of Race, Class, and Gender

Because of the seeming "normalcy" of their backgrounds or the "rightness" of their whiteness, it is important that teachers examine the larger picture of the social background of teachers in America with regard to race, class, and gender. Many teachers, for example, are not aware of how few teachers of color there are, or the reasons for this, or even of the commonality of the class backgrounds of most teachers. It is also relevant to relate the history of people of color in education and to acknowledge the barriers discussed earlier that have kept many people of color from entering the teaching profession, so as to dispel the myth that "those people don't value education." Many people are not aware that we have been given a one-sided view from which to interpret reality—one that is largely a white, upper-class, male social construction that does not necessarily have the interests of the majority of whites at stake as working people, any more than it does the interests of oppressed racial groups. It is important that we understand how racism, sexism, and class privilege not only have marginalized people of color, but have cheated white people of their history as well. This is why it is important to allow teachers to bring their own histories into the discussion, for over two-thirds of their parents were from farm or working-class backgrounds (Spencer, 1986). Yet the history of the working class in general has been ignored or marginalized in the United States, and the texts teachers use in their classrooms do not represent their people either (Zinn, 1980; Loewen, 1995). Without a recognition of the bias and the gaps in their own education, there is likely to be more resistance to learning a new knowledge base. Teachers often ask, "Why didn't we learn this stuff in college or in our teacher education courses?" for there has been little opportunity for preservice teachers to get exposure to this material, as it has rarely been part of the teacher education curriculum.

Given that most teachers in the United States are white women, it is instructive to show some of the common links with gender and race exploitation in order to encourage an understanding of some of the common economic roots of these oppressions. A heightened awareness of this commonality can help enhance possibilities for empathy and solidarity, for we cannot assume that an awareness of gender oppression necessarily gives any heightened clarity of thought or empathy for the racially oppressed. Female teachers are not necessarily any less racist than male teachers.

Examine How Individual Racism Is Manifested in Teacher–Student Interactions and in the General Culture of the School

There are a number of ways in which the school culture and the quality of teacher–student interactions may reinforce racial inequities without conscious intent. Teachers are often unaware of how their expectations of student competency may be affected by unconscious stereotypes of racial, cultural, and linguistic differences. Historical distortions and stereotypes impact upon our assumptions and expectations of each other, even when we are not aware of those stereotypes. This is particularly critical for teachers and their expectations of students of color. Reflecting the prejudices of the dominant white culture, many white teachers have undervalued and underestimated the possibilities for achievement for students of color and often respond differently to them than they do to white students. There are also the subtle expressions of racism that should be identified, such as paternalism, tokenism, chauvinism, and "exotifying" people of color. Teachers should understand these concepts if they are to develop the critical insights necessary to examine their own practice. After they become aware of these subtle paternalistic behaviors, they can try being their own "ethnographers" by working together with a trusted colleague observing each other's practice. Do they find that they automatically consider their students of color "at risk"? Do they call on white students more frequently or with more enthusiasm? Do they avoid eye contact with Black students in the hallway? By becoming conscious of some of these tendencies, over time teachers may become more aware of their own assumptions and how they affect their practice.

Teachers should also question the kinds of inequalities that just seem to "happen," such as when the detention room happens to be all Black or when the advanced classes consistently happen to be all white. Teachers should also examine their school culture. Often, without conscious intent, the dominant white, middle-class culture automatically excludes others. This may show up in the selection of school events and celebrations. It is also important to talk about the danger of passivity and silence when encountering racism. As I elaborate in the next chapter on teachers' perceptions of racism, there are many teachers who witness colleagues making insensitive or racist references to students of color, and though they say it disturbs them, they maintain a dangerous silence and do not intervene.

Examine the Phenomenon of Labeling and the Tradition of Blaming the Victim

The misinterpretations about "others" are not new, and it is important to contextualize this problem historically. I have found it effective to relate the historical precedents from slavery of labeling Africans as being somehow mentally ill and having to explain their resistance to slavery with "new diseases"—such as Drapetomania, "the disease of wanting to run away"—that were "discovered" by the medical profession to explain resistance to slavery. Teachers should be encouraged to question the current labels that we assign children. Why is it we are looking to actuarial models like "at risk" to define a population? Why is it some people can be called mentally retarded when they have high performance in some areas?

In order for teachers to be able to deconstruct the state of race relations in the United States, we must acknowledge our history. Part of this self-examination involves an awareness of the tradition of blaming the victim. This is operative in how teachers may interpret the behavior of students to whom they are not accustomed, as being inherently problematic. These biased interpretations have contributed to extremely disproportionate and disparate tracking, whether formal or informal, leading to large numbers of children of color being tracked out and pushed out of school. An overview of this problem nationwide, with the shocking statistics on children of color in "educably mentally retarded" (EMR), "learning disabled" (LD), and "educationally disabled" (ED) classes, can drive the point home (Coles, 1988).

On the other hand, in the area of labeling and stereotyping, we should also critique the "positive" labels and stereotypes, which can also have negative implications. Even "good" labels or kinder stereotypes can have a negative effect on children. The myth of the "model minority" is one such example often applied to Asians. Teachers who perceive their Asian students as computer scientists and mathematicians short-change them as well. For those who are not mathematicians may be ignored as they also fall through the cracks, not to mention that those who indeed are more skilled in such areas as math will be offered one-dimensional possibilities, and their capabilities or interests in other areas will be ignored. Of course, we should not forget that many Asian students are encountering the same socioeconomic and cultural struggles as other students of color. As Nieto (1996) points out, the "model minority" stereotype has been used to assuage the guilt of some authorities who do little to help Asians or Pacific Americans with social or economic problems they may face when coming to the United States, under the assumption that "those people have such a strong culture that they can take care of their own and do not need our help."

Examine Covert Manifestations of Racism and Reactions to Racism

While overt racial epithets are seen as obviously unacceptable behavior, we cannot ignore the subtle and covert expressions of racism, such as through body language, voice tone, eye contact, or actual informal code words or phrases that are understood to refer to the "other." As I discuss in chapter 6, many teachers report hearing references to "those people from the apartments" or the "free and reduced hot lunchers," and other such racial codes, from some of their peers. These impact negatively on children of color as much as do overtly slanderous words, while also reinforcing a sense of racial superiority and entitlement among whites. At the same time, while body language and other subtle forms of behavior and language act as a form of power, so can the unempowered use these same forms to take back or negotiate power. Thus teachers should recognize that some mannerisms and behaviors among students may be a reaction or a resistance to racism. As Majors and Billson (1993) illustrate, certain mannerisms or stylistic behaviors, such as the "cool pose," are often interpreted by white teachers as threatening.

Examine the Perspectives of Students and Parents of Color

After interviewing students and their parents, Murray and Clark (1990) identified the ways in which racism is felt by students of color in schools, such as harsher sanctions; bias in the amount of encouragement students of color are given; bias in curriculum materials; low expectations of students of color; and denial of racist incidents. Sharing with teachers such research from students of color in other parts of the United States illustrates that this is a systemic problem and not simply the subjective reactions of "oversensitive" individuals in their school. It is important, when possible, to include panels of students who can give their viewpoints of what racism feels like. This should be done after there is some level of trust and recognition that there is a problem of racism in education. It should also be done with clear ground rules for discussion so that it is safe for the students.

As well, parents of color and parents of children of color should be invited to come and talk to teachers about their particular concerns or experiences.

Again, careful ground rules should be established ahead of time for both parents and teachers, indicating that this should be a time for honest expression and that everyone should be allowed to speak his or her piece without feeling responsible to respond or justify for the whole group. After everyone puts his or her issues "on the table," it is possible that some will want to form an ongoing parent group or parent–teacher group to see how concerns can be addressed.

Successful programs for parent involvement should also be studied. One such model is Parents Participating for Progress (PPP), developed by Trevor Gardner at the University of Eastern Michigan. This model shows the possibilities for the successful participation and leadership of parents who have been traditionally and historically alienated or excluded, or who have felt unwelcome to participate in the schools.

Examine Teachers' Perceptions of Racism and Its Causes

There needs to be honest discussion about how teachers are feeling vis-à-vis their students of color and how they perceive the causes of inequities in the school. Some of the most common frustrations that white teachers bring to the staff development class are a helpless feeling regarding discipline of many of their Black students and an inability to communicate with them. On the other hand, an oft-heard complaint from the African American teachers is that the white teachers refuse to relate to the African American students, and whenever there is any sort of problem, rather than trying to work it out and open up channels of communication, they automatically will send these students to the (usually) lone Black teacher, who is expected to be *the* specialist in dealing with all the problems of the African American students.

This highlights the importance of understanding how teachers perceive racism. Early in my classes, I give teachers anonymous questionnaires in which they give examples of racism in their schools. As I discuss at length in the following chapter, many blame the victims of racism rather than the causes. Other teachers may be conscious of racially insensitive behavior but do not feel that they have enough knowledge to explain it. They sometimes express a sense of relief, when I later read their perceptions aloud to the class, that other people are witnessing some of the same kinds of things all over the district. They just haven't been talking about it. Still other teachers may say that as far as they know, there is no racism at their school, and for them it is important to hear these perspectives from other teachers across the district.

Assess the Damaging Effects
That Racism Has on White Children

Many people believe that they are implementing multicultural or antiracist education to improve the education of children of color. Of course, this is a central concern and necessity, but we must not lose sight of the fact that white children are also seriously damaged by racism. Often teachers in mostly white schools or districts will state that they don't have a problem because "we don't have children of color." Hence, we must understand the ways in which racism damages the education of white children and their abilities to develop skills of critical and compassionate thinking. White children are damaged by racism when they become educated to indifference or intolerance. As Abraham Citron (1969) writes:

> White-centeredness is not the reality of [the white child's] world, but he is under the illusion that it is. It is thus impossible for him to deal accurately or adequately with the universe of human and social relationships. . . . Children who develop in this way are robbed of opportunities for emotional and intellectual growth, stunted in the basic development of the self, so that they cannot experience or accept humanity. This is a personality outcome in which it is quite possible to build into children a great feeling and compassion for animals and an unconscious fear and rejection of differing human beings. Such persons are by no means prepared to live and move with either appreciation or effectiveness in today's world. (pp. 14–16)

Sometimes teachers (and parents, too) unconsciously contribute to this outcome when, for example, they have the presumably "bright" white child "help" what they perceive is the "slower" child of color. Thus it is helpful to discuss how we can encourage children to work collaboratively and cooperatively in ways that don't reproduce relations of superiority and inferiority. It is also important that we learn to recognize and intervene when we see white children behave in ways that are arrogant or chauvinistic.

Learn about the Antiracist Tradition

As important as knowing about the roots and manifestations of racism is knowing about the existence of the antiracist tradition in America (Aptheker, 1992). This does not mean, of course, that there were abolitionists in all our family trees, but that there is a precedent—*there has always been* a group of white allies against racism (albeit a minority), and in unlearning racism, we can choose to follow in that tradition rather than the racist one. We can also study how antiracists have been treated in our texts—either as not having existed or as being lunatics, such as John Brown has been portrayed by most historians.[1]

Examine the Historical Roots of Institutionalized Racism

Thus far we have discussed the need to help teachers become conscious of the various ways in which individualized racism is expressed, but it is also important to provide the historical context of institutionalized racism. To contextualize the phenomenon of racism in the United States, we must examine how racism was the outcome and the ideological support for slavery, rather than the cause of slavery (Williams, 1966). Racism has been the most effective ideological weapon to divide and conquer and has affected all groups of people of color. For example, with regard to the genocide against the Native Americans, certain mythologies have been established to justify the Europeans' atrocities against the indigenous peoples, such as the myth of the Indian as "scalper," when this was really a practice begun by Europeans (Zinn, 1980; Weatherford, 1988). It is important to show how racism has been the ideological cover necessary for the perpetuation of class and gender oppression and the making of super profits (Perlo, 1975; Marable, 1983). Racism has also affected our everyday culture. We must also examine how racism has affected our language over time, such as in the negative connotations of the word "black" (Moore, 1985) and the various ways in which racism has affected our language in general.

While I have discussed the need for whites to examine the meaning of their own "whiteness," it is important to understand the historical context in which the concept of whiteness developed. Whiteness developed as as an identity that evolved for the European populations in their common oppression of the Native American and African peoples (Marable, 1983; Roediger, 1991).

Examine How Institutional Racism Is Manifested in the Larger Society

By presenting the "big picture," giving the objective statistics showing racial disparities and discrimination in all aspects of life involving the distribution and allocation of land, labor, capital, and the overall quality of life, one can illustrate how institutionalized racism is operationalized. This would include statistics on the economy showing the distribution of wealth, income, and education; comparative rates of employment and unemployment; the locations of various "minority" groups in the job market; the representation of people of color in government at all levels; the composition of racial minorities in the criminal "justice" system; the problem of policing and racial profiling; apartheid in housing and landownership, health care, and child care; environmental racism; and media ownership and control. This data might also be juxtaposed with the impact of male supremacy on women.

Examine Representations of People of Color in Texts, Curricular Materials, and the Media

This examination should include racism by omission as well as by commission. Materials should be examined for the perpetuation of racial stereotypes in covert ways, even in some materials that are inclusive of people of color. This includes gathering from children's literature and textbooks examples of representations of people of color, women, and other marginalized or oppressed groups and spending some time deconstructing them—especially those texts that are currently being used. Teachers should be encouraged to investigate materials in their own schools or classrooms and bring them to the group for sharing. In addition, the texts and media that inform or influence us that are not necessarily part of the formal school curriculum, such as newspapers, television, and items of popular culture, should also be examined for their treatment or representations.

Schools that are predominantly "minority" historically have often had a different curriculum than white schools because of the institutionalized packaging of knowledge, such that each group was assumed to have a particular educational need that was suitable for that group. This is how texts get "dumbed down" for children of color. An example is the reading method DISTAR, originally developed for retarded children and then used universally for Black children in Chicago, at the same time that in Evanston, an affluent white suburb of Chicago, this method was used only for children who were thought to be mentally retarded (Apple, 1988).

We should also recognize the significance of the positioning and juxtapositioning of texts in particular ways, resulting in certain hierarchical ordering of information such that the information about the privileged supersedes that of the unprivileged. Teachers often unwittingly perpetuate racism or other biases by using texts just because they are the ones for which there are multiple copies. This is a fairly common occurrence especially in ill-equipped schools. Thus we should brainstorm ways in which we might use those same texts against themselves by using them as a springboard for discussion and critical analysis in the classroom.

Often more influential than any textbook are the various media, which impact the culture of the school and the thinking of teachers and students in profound ways. The stereotypes may be bold or subtle and are introduced in often "enjoyable" ways, as through children's cartoons or situation comedy. How television has been employed to imprint race, class, and gender stereotypes—and to sell products—should be carefully examined.

Examine the Organization of Schools and the Deployment of Various Resources

The organization of schools and the kinds and availability of various resources may reveal covert racial bias. This may include both human and material resources, such as teachers and other personnel in schools and the roles that people of color play (or do not play), as shown by the statistics; the allocations of texts and other curricular materials that are part of the infrastructure of the school; and other supportive physical structures such as playgrounds, lunchrooms, athletic facilities, computer labs, and other places in which learning occurs. One might also draw some comparisons with sexism in the workplace: male bosses, female workers (usually male principals, female teachers).

How Schools Through the Neighborhood Ideology Came to Be Segregated

The financing of schools in the United States through the property tax has affected schools such that a district whose housing stock is declining would naturally have less financial resources to finance education (Kozol, 1991). In fact, this is how schools came to be caught in the larger dynamics of racism in society, such that residential segregation led to segregation in education. Thus the crisis in residential segregation has been exported to the schools—to the children and to the teachers to "solve" the social ill of racism in society by placing bodies in "desegregated" schools and then asking children to go right back out into the same racially segregated society.

It is important to discuss why, despite efforts at desegregation, real integration has not occurred. Even in "integrated" schools, there continues to be segregation that occurs in a *laissez-faire* sort of way, as seen in academic tracking as well as in other aspects of the school culture, such as in the lunchroom, in after-school activities, on the playground, in the seating arrangement of the classroom, in cultural and social events or extracurricular activities in the school. After teachers have been sensitized so that they can "see" this level of resegregation and the factors that contribute to it, they can conduct their own action research in their classrooms and schools to document whether this occurs and how they might devise strategies to work against activities or arrangements that inherently tend to marginalize certain groups.

Credentialism, Testing, and the Labor Market

Credentialism is a mechanism of mediation between the labor market and the school system. We must question what the credentialing process has to do with the output of good teachers. Are such credentials intrinsically necessary to the production of good teachers the way they are currently designed? Has it been shown that those who have gone through the credentialing process are the best teachers?[2] This, of course, is not an argument against teacher certification, but we should ask, What does this credentialing process require that makes teachers particularly suited to teach a racially, ethnically, linguistically, and economically diverse population? Likewise, what does this process require that enables teachers to teach in homogeneous school populations in a society marked by race and class divisions?

Credentialing may give the illusion of capability for some, while denying many would-be teachers of color from becoming teachers, such as certain pretests that may screen out people of color due to racial or cultural bias. Credentialism is a gatekeeping mechanism of artificially selecting those who presumably will be best able to work with children. Yet the results don't show much success in learning, so we must question whether it is the teaching and teacher training that are problematic. Given the state of education today and the lack of success in school of so many children, we need to rethink and critique the basis of credentialing. Such a critical analysis is important for teachers or administrators who may be serving on hiring and standards committees. By encouraging a critical analysis of the underpinnings of such processes, we should consider how we as individual agents of change must challenge our assumptions about standards and organize against their oppressive use.

In addition to the problem of credentialing of teachers is the problem of "credentialing" of students through the process of standardized educational testing upon which our educational system now heavily relies. Such testing has been shown to be arbitrary and biased and, as some have argued, is rooted in racist ideology (Fish, 1993). Standardized testing, historically as today, contributes to tracking and labeling. Further, the testing industry should also be seen for what it is—a multibillion-dollar industry for profit that has its own self-interest in maintaining itself. It is not only the children who pay, but the teachers as well, who are often under constant pressure to prepare their students for standardized tests thereby depriving them of their own opportunities for creative and innovative teaching. This is also unfair to teachers, because they are often judged by the success or failure of the performance of their students on standardized tests.

PUTTING THEORY INTO PRACTICE: ACTUALIZING AN ANTIRACIST PERSPECTIVE

Once we have increased our understanding and knowledge about racism, the next step is perhaps the most difficult and involves not only learning about and developing new curricula, but also examining how to do this in an environment that may not be supportive or may even be racist. This means we must develop strategies to put our newfound knowledge and theory to practice. This may include organizing support groups within the school and the district so that people can exchange curriculum, experiences, and such. It also means parental involvement, including meeting with parents of students of color, who have traditionally been left out of the schools, as well as networking with them and incorporating their expertise into the curriculum and the school culture. One might also develop projects such as an oral history project on people of color and working-class people in general in the local community, which will get students involved on a personal basis with the living histories in their own backyards that have been left out of their texts. Such projects can also create a valuable archival resource for the future.

In this process of organizing, it is important to get the involvement of not only students and parents, but also of community organizations, churches, trade unions, and such. It is also important to get the involvement of sympathetic white parents, as well as parents of color, by calling them or writing them and explaining what you are hoping to do and inviting their participation. Becoming an antiracist teacher means that one must help people develop strategies to organize against those policies that are repressive or restrictive. This could involve activities through the teachers' unions or through teachers' committees in the schools, and through developing community ties. It might also involve helping teachers develop action research projects with each other to identify and address some of the race-related problems they are confronting.

In trying to implement a new antiracist approach, it is important to also include the perspectives of working-class people in general, their histories, participation in democratic struggles, and contributions as a class. It is important to be careful about a white backlash, which may happen if people perceive that they are left out of the picture. By this I do not mean that we should include whites just to appease them, but to help people appreciate that racism has also negatively affected the quality of their lives. In the long run, it is really in the self-interest of all of us to work against racism.

CONSIDERATIONS FOR ANTIRACIST STAFF DEVELOPMENT

Clearly, antiracist staff development classes are a different problematic than, for example, updating one's knowledge of mathematics teaching or new developments in computers for education, for antiracism classes challenge or interrupt most white people's notions of their own racial identity and entitlement. This is a much more profound and fundamental questioning of one's own social reality than the realization that one has been teaching reading "wrong" all these years. This means we must take into account the kinds of backgrounds that teachers are likely to come from, as well as the kinds of working conditions teachers experience before they come to the class. Whether teachers from one school are meeting together at their school site, or whether they are meeting from schools districtwide at a central location, we must deal with and incorporate into our pedagogy the reality of the working day they have just left. Typically, teachers have just come from situations that are stressful to some degree—even for those who feel personally fulfilled by teaching. Given the realities of the social contexts of teaching, we must create an in-service model that does not feel like *more work*; rather, it should be structured such that it will have as relaxed an atmosphere as possible, and such that a sense of camaraderie and comfort can be developed among the people in the class. Of course, the issue of "comfort" in the case of race relations is contradictory when dealing with a topic that is inherently *un*-comfortable. In fact, many of the workshop models that have been used, such as the race-awareness-training approach that I discussed in chapter 3, may be specifically intended to make people feel uncomfortable. What one does with this disquietude, however, is key. To raise the level of discomfort and dissonance without also helping people understand a sociohistorical context for race, class, and gender oppression, as well as the *precedents for resistance* to oppression, can be counterproductive. Hence, it is important to incorporate a perspective that also looks at the possibilities of becoming antiracist change agents in the tradition of our great civil-rights leaders.

Because teachers presumably will be coming to this course after school and therefore are likely to be tired, it is also important to have an empathic approach, despite the restrictions of an institutional setting. It is helpful to have the classes in rooms other than classrooms if possible, with seating around tables rather than at individual desks—and never in rows of seats! Food is important for bringing people closer together, particularly considering that people will be tired and at a low ebb of energy. (In my classes, I always bring food to the first session, and thereafter teachers agree to a potluck, with two or three people bringing something to share with the group each week.)

◄◊◊►

In part 2, "Putting Theory into Practice," I discuss my ethnographic study in which I analyze my experiences implementing antiracist education with teachers in a place I call Lakeview, a highly rated school district with a liberal reputation. The next chapter begins by painting a profile of "liberal" Lakeview, where students of color had a better chance of dropping out or being "pushed out" of school than they had of graduating. I then focus on a contributing factor to this low success rate for the students of color, which was the problem of how the white teachers perceived students of color and how they comprehended the problem of racism in schools.

PART TWO

Putting Theory into Practice

"The most difficult thing about theory is about practice."
—Paulo Freire

CHAPTER SIX

The Hidden Dimensions
of Liberal Racism

*how white teachers perceive
the problem of racism in their schools*

P UTTING ANTIRACIST THEORY INTO PRACTICE means that one needs to carefully assess where people are in their particular milieu. One does not have
to be consciously or intentionally racist to perpetuate racial inequality. Often
people think it is those "hard-core" backward places or impoverished large
urban areas that have serious problems, while not recognizing the racism that is
in their own backyards. Even in seemingly "liberal" and enlightened environments, such as Lakeview, where I conducted this ethnographic study, racial
inequities persist in part because people in the dominant group have relative
white privilege and may not see or do not care to see some of the less obvious
signs of racial injustice, especially if it makes them uncomfortable or if they may
have to give something up. Because people don't see overt racism, they may
assume that "it doesn't happen here" or stereotype it as a "southern thing." The
subtlety and the persistence of this covert liberal racism were what compelled
me to do race relations work in Lakeview.[1]

A PROFILE OF LAKEVIEW:
SAVAGE INEQUALITIES IN THE LIBERAL TRADITION

Lakeview is a city mythified by many for its "progressive" past, especially as one
of the centers of resistance to the Vietnam War. It is a relatively middle-class city

located a few hours from several major Midwestern metropolitan areas. For years, it has enjoyed the reputation of being a tolerant and friendly place to live, and many have seen it as an ideal place to raise a family and enjoy the comforts of relative quiet, lots of green space, and many lakes, while being close enough to (while still far away enough from) large urban areas so as not to feel "isolated." The economy is tied to a large research university. National polls place the Lakeview schools among the best in the nation, and national surveys rate the city as "one of the most attractive places to live" in America.

The infrastructure in Lakeview is in good condition compared to those of other American cities. The air and water are clean by American standards. The schools are in good shape as well, largely newer buildings built since the 1960s, modern and airy, with lots of windows and light and well-kept grounds. Most of the older, hearty brick school buildings of yesterday were closed down in the sixties in the frenzy of urban renewal and urban sprawl. Some of these older schools, which enjoyed beautiful views on the city's lakes or other scenic areas, have been converted into high-income "yuppie" apartment buildings. They were replaced with larger school structures or complexes located on the periphery of the city, areas that today are closer to the center as the city continues to grow and sprawl in all directions.

There is poverty in Lakeview, but it is not always immediately recognizable. Much of the employment is in low-paying, nonbenefit, service-sector jobs. There is little heavy industry, and a good number of jobs require higher education. It is not unusual to have people with Ph.D.s driving cabs, and college students have a large share of the food service and other service jobs in town. While the state in which Lakeview is located boasts one of the lowest unemployment rates in the nation, in actuality, throughout the state as a whole as well as in Lakeview, African Americans have not shared in this "boom." Official Black state unemployment statistics are nearly 20 percent. Over half of the Black children in the state overall live in poverty. In Lakeview, one of three African American children lives in poverty, as do many of the Hmong who have settled there in significant numbers.

The demographics of the city have been changing since the mid-1980s, when increasing numbers of African Americans moved to Lakeview. Just as the Southeast Asians moved there to flee war zones, many of the African Americans recently came to Lakeview to escape the violence and poverty of some of the poorest and most dangerous housing projects in the nation. Many resembled war zones after the government's withdrawal of the federal job, housing, and education programs of the "Great Society" reforms of the sixties. The Lakeview media sometimes refer to the African Americans from these larger urban ghettos as "immigrants," despite the fact that their forebears were in this country long before most of the Northern European ethnics that dominate in the state ever arrived. The public myth has it that "these people come to Lakeview simply to collect more welfare." In actuality, these new residents are seeking some of the very same things others enjoy in Lakeview. The welfare they receive hardly pays for their rents, which are five times higher than in the depressed urban areas from which they came.

Unlike larger urban areas, Lakeview does not have obvious big-city crumbling ghettos. But the African Americans have been ghettoized in hastily built apartment complexes located in various parts of the city, or in some of the older complexes that were originally built in the sixties for middle-class people. The latter are no longer recognizable as those same buildings, however. There has been minimal upkeep, and in fact, when they were converted into public housing, they were stripped of any amenities such as air conditioners or landscaping and hedgerows. Upkeep and maintenance have been neglected and are no longer considered cost-effective by the landlords. In many of these ghettoized complexes, the unemployment rate is near 90 percent. Here the infrastructure is crumbling, but very few whites see these areas, as they are located in pockets of lower-income apartment buildings. While African Americans are not segregated to one or two parts of the town, as has happened in some larger urban areas, they are segregated nevertheless, even while spread about the city. Hence there is no voting block and not one area that is considered *the* Black community.

There are almost no Black-owned or -run businesses in Lakeview. There is a bar but no grocery or clothing stores owned or run by African Americans. With a few exceptions, attempts by Blacks to own or operate businesses in Lakeview have failed due to what some have charged is racist harassment, as their shops have been forced to close, often charged with minor code violations. There are several businesses owned by Asians, including a number of grocery stores, specialty shops, restaurants, and liquor stores. The Black churches are the only places in Lakeview that are totally controlled by African Americans.

Like elsewhere in the nation, racial profiling by the police is a persistent problem. Over the recent years, many Blacks have complained about their treatment by the Lakeview police. A Black man driving a car has a greater chance of being pulled over and questioned for the most minor or suspected violation than he would have even in a larger urban area. This seems to cut across class lines as well, as many middle-class Blacks report being under suspicion for "DWB"— Driving While Black. The mayor has appointed a task force to examine such charges, but most Blacks are highly skeptical of its value and feel that the choice of a white male with no history of civil-rights activism to lead such a task force is merely another ploy to obscure the issue and keep them "in line."

THE LAKEVIEW SCHOOLS

The Lakeview School District is a medium-size district of approximately fifty schools. There are some two thousand certificated teachers and 120 administrators in the district. Of these, 94 percent are white and 6 percent are people of color. At the five high schools, there are a total of five African American teachers, with one high school employing none. Nearly half of the middle schools and nearly half of the elementary schools have no African American teachers.

Like elsewhere in the country, issues like increasing violence, drug use, and racial incidents have affected the schools. Many of the middle and high schools have now hired security guards or policemen to work in them. Yet on the whole, compared to much of the country, the schools are still considered safe places, suitable for the children of the many professionals who locate here. Year after year, the school district is voted as among the best in the nation. At the same time, however, more frequently, many middle-class professionals have opted out of the public schools, sending their children to private schools. Many of the middle-class whites fear the "changing demographics," with the recent increase in numbers of African Americans to Lakeview from larger urban areas. They do not welcome these students in their neighborhoods and see them as pulling down the quality of education for their children.

Children of color (primarily African American, Mexican or Chicano, and Hmong) constitute approximately one-third of the student population. African American children make up the largest group of children of color, comprising 18 percent of the district's total student population of approximately twenty-five thousand. It is on this group that I focus in framing the picture of racism—not because the statistics of school failure affect only African Americans, but because from the perspectives of a large percentage of the teachers in Lakeview (as well as society at large), African Americans are perceived and treated as the most problematic group. As I elaborate later in this chapter, the majority of white teachers have almost universally framed the issue of racism in Black and white. This racial framing is reflected in the statistics of school failure, with the African American student having a slightly greater chance of dropping out or being pushed out than of graduating from the district. In a recent year in the late 1990s, for example, ninety-six African American students dropped out, while ninety-four graduated. That same year, African American students received 1,959 suspensions, while white students, who numbered nearly five times as many of the school population, were given 1,877 suspensions. By middle school, more than half of the Black children in Lakeview had already experienced being suspended from school.

African American students in the district are twice as likely as their white counterparts to be placed in "special education," with nearly 7 percent in "learning disabled" classes and 3 percent in the "emotionally disturbed" classes (compared to 3.49 and 1.51 percent, respectively, for white children). They are also four times more likely to be labeled "cognitively disabled" (2.73 percent of Black children, compared to 0.69 percent for white children). While these special education programs comprise 8 percent of the district's enrollment, this same population received 46 percent of all suspensions. The district employs 436 special education teachers, five of whom are African Americans. None of the thirty-five staff psychologists who are instrumental in assigning these designations to "special" programs is Black.

Compared to their white counterparts, for whom the average ninth-grade grade point average (GPA) is 2.55, the African American students' average GPA by the ninth grade is 1.19. Not only African Americans, but racial minorities in the district in general are underrepresented in all of the advanced classes. In three of the high schools in the 1990s, the physics and advanced chemistry classes were usually 100 percent white. As well, 100 percent of the students in the computer and robotics classes at the high schools were white.

Yet this is not the story of the dramatic material "savage inequalities" that Kozol (1991) writes about, where toilets leak through classroom ceilings. There are no inferior black schools versus white schools. The schools have been integrated through mandated busing since the early eighties. But the schooling and the treatment that the Black students receive are qualitatively different, and as in other districts throughout the nation, Black children have been resegregated in desegregated schools.

THE LIBERAL DENIAL OF RACISM

Overt racism is not seen as acceptable behavior in Lakeview. Cheerful posters abound urging people to "Celebrate Diversity!" or to be proud of their ethnicity: "Everybody's Ethnic!" Because Lakeview has for many years enjoyed the reputation of being a liberal city, and has indeed been among the places in the United States often on the cutting edge of progressive social movements, one may not expect to encounter much racism there. But while one may not always "see" the savage inequalities, the extreme disparities illustrate that the city and the schools are still affected by the institutionalized racism that adheres to structures when it is not consciously routed from them.

There is no discussion from the school district about this institutionalized racism that has impacted upon the problematic outcomes for students of color. The words "racism" and even "race" are rarely uttered in the public discourse. The language of reform in Lakeview is the language of liberal denial. Black children are referred to as "children at risk." A recent superintendent referred to them as "children of promise," at the same time that some of the programs to help them were being dismantled. In a savagely liberal way, race is always on the agenda but is never named. Recently, public discussions reached a crescendo over the racial makeup of the schools. Yet whites expressed this concern in such terms as having "too many children with special needs" or "too many free or reduced hot lunch kids" in one school, who are seen as draining the resources and lowering the academic performance of all. Those in the wealthy and middle-class neighborhoods have never embraced the presence of "too many" poor Black children being bused into their midst. Using the benign rhetoric of "back to neighborhood schools" and "community," they have been working to end the school desegregation efforts begun in the eighties, and some are moving out to the suburban school districts.

In recent surveys of parents in Lakeview, in which they were asked to name the most important issues that should be immediately addressed regarding school improvement, a clearly different experience was articulated by Black and white parents. Thirty-six percent of the African American parents said that racial and cultural issues must be addressed, compared to only 7 percent of the white parents.[2] Obviously, the perceptions about the significance of racial and cultural concerns were vastly different between the white parents and the African American parents in Lakeview.

Because of this liberal denial or ignorance—ignoring of—the significance of race and racism by the dominant white majority, it is not surprising that the Lakeview School District has not systematically incorporated race-relations education on the agenda for school reform and improvement. However, not all whites have been in such sedimented denial about the significance of racism. Some teachers have indicated a desire for the district to provide opportunities for staff development on race relations and multicultural education. They felt unprepared to effectively teach Lakeview's increasingly diverse student population and unable to deal with the increasing racial tensions in their schools. Nevertheless, despite this interest shown by many teachers, by the mid-1990s opportunities for such professional development were eroding. Under the guise of "total quality improvement," the administration eventually abolished the Department of Human Relations and reduced offerings for staff development on multicultural and race-relations education, focusing more staff development efforts on various models of "total quality improvement." This was not unique to Lakeview, but reflected a larger trend in the 1990s, as many districts nationwide dismantled their human relations departments and focused more on the customer market model of service for "quality control."

The Lakeview School District's myopic vision on race relations reflects the perceptions of the dominant white society. Their vision—or lack of it—must be seen in this broader context. The dismal outcomes for students of color in Lakeview schools were certainly affected by the pressing societal problems, such as increased unemployment or underemployment, the dismantling of welfare, increasing poverty and homelessness, all of which placed terrible stresses on families. Such factors also affect educational attainment. But there was also the problem of how students of color were perceived and treated by the teachers, over 90 percent of whom were whites who did not otherwise have much contact with communities of color.

LAKEVIEW TEACHERS' PERCEPTIONS OF RACISM IN THEIR SCHOOLS

While approaching the issue of racism in education is a much broader issue than the roles of teachers alone, still, because they play a pivotal role being the professional group that has the most ongoing contact with our children, we must consider how teachers perceive the problem of racism in their classrooms and schools, especially since this will influence how they interpret and respond to racial issues. Yet there has been relatively little focus in the literature about how teachers understand this complex problem. Most of the literature that has emerged periodically since the 1930s has examined the racial attitudes and perceptions of children. Indeed, as Banks (1995) observes, "few [studies] examine the teacher in any detail or treat the teacher as the variable." And as Sleeter (1992) notes, most of the literature on multicultural education focuses on pre-service teachers, with little attention to in-service teachers. In this section, I examine the teacher as the variable and discuss the contradictory ways in which white teachers perceive the issue of racism in their schools, in this liberal but unequal, peaceful while simmering school district in Lakeview, "one of the most attractive places to live" in America.

As I discussed at the beginning of this book, from my personal experiences with my children, as well as observations of teachers' work in schools, I had become increasingly concerned about the misconceptions that many whites have regarding racial matters. If we are going to introduce teachers to an antiracist or a critical multicultural pedagogy, we must first discern perceptions and understandings about racism, especially considering the process through which many white teachers have often been taught certain racist constructions in the first place. For in addition to having been socialized in segregated white communities, for many teachers, the experience of teaching in multiracial schools in which white and Black children are effectively segregated may actually lead to a sharpening or reinforcement of racial stereotypes among white teachers rather than a lessening of them. For example, for the white teacher (as well as the white student), the phenomenon whereby the detention room or the special education classes may be filled with mostly students of color may be interpreted as a mark of inferiority itself, rather than as a sign of different or inferior treatment.

I knew that asking people about their attitudes or feelings about other races, or how they felt about prejudice and discrimination, would not necessarily capture the deep, "hard-wired" attitudes about race and racism. When I'd given teachers questionnaires designed to elicit responses about how they felt about racism or about their tolerance toward diverse "others," they rarely stated that they did not like a particular group, or that they believed that all members of a group have a certain deficiency. This is not surprising, for as Banks (1995) and Jones (1981) remind us, scores on racial-attitude measures are often influenced by the participants' prior knowledge of the socially acceptable responses, making it difficult to assess real attitudes and beliefs accurately. Many whites would not say they identify with the dictionary definition of a racist, one who adheres to "the belief that race is the primary determinant of human traits and capacities and that racial differences produce an inherent superiority of a particular race."[3] This definition absolves most white people from any responsibility or recognition of racism, since, except overtly white supremacists, most whites would not say that they believe there is an inborn superiority of one group over another.

Because most whites cannot recognize themselves in such a definition of racism, it appears to be something that exists somewhere else outside of themselves, someone else's problem. Thus, in order to begin to assess teachers' interpretative frameworks regarding racism in their schools, the first thing I ask teachers to do is to address the issue of racism as they perceive it in their own schools.

We shall now turn to the data I collected in the Lakeview School District from questionnaires that inquired about teachers' perceptions of racism. These questionnaires were given to teachers[4] in several mandatory, all-school in-services.[5] I asked teachers to answer anonymously on a questionnaire the following question: "Write down any examples or incidents that you think indicate racism or racial insensitivity (whether or not you believe such incidents were intentional or unintentional) that you have witnessed, heard about, or experienced in your work in school(s). Don't feel pressured to write anything if you don't feel that you have such examples." A follow-up question asked if they could recall how they felt about the particular incident or if they said or did anything about it.

At a strategic point in the workshop, I read and discussed their examples aloud to the entire group. My goal in this process of putting racism "on the table" is to enable teachers to see where they are as a group, as many are so isolated that they may question their own sensitivity—perhaps they think they are being ultrasensitive if they sense that something is wrong, or possibly they totally deny that there are any race-related problems in their school. Hearing many other perceptions coming from one's own peers is a valuable method of beginning to unfold and define the problem as being systemic.

These questionnaires did not ask for any demographic data, such as gender or race, since there were only one or two teachers of color in each school and sometimes only a handful of men, and I did not want to compromise their anonymity. Such open-ended questions can be particularly useful tools for revealing participants' points of view without predetermining them through prior selection of questionnaire categories, as may be done in a Likert-type scale. I asked teachers to fill out the questionnaire before I told them anything about my background or perspective in order to minimize my influence on how they might respond. I wanted to get at their more spontaneous reactions, perceptions, or feelings and avoid attempts for some to be "teacher pleasers," trying to accommodate me with their responses.

THE SAMPLE

Data for this study were collected from teachers who attended mandatory, all-school in-services. These included the entire staffs of an elementary school, a middle school, and a high school. Because these were mandatory workshops, this data provided me with special insight, as it represented the thinking of teachers in general, and not just those who voluntarily signed up for my longer classes. To aid in interpretation of this data, I also examined selections from taped interviews and field notes from my longer staff development courses, in which I had the opportunity to engage participants in further dialogue and debate. This juxtaposition helped me better understand the reasoning behind some of the responses given to the questionnaire. A total of 222 teachers attended these mandatory in-services.[6] Of these, 189 responded to the questionnaire; 33 people (11.7 percent) did not respond. Respondents provided a total of 281 examples of perceived racism in their schools. The teachers' responses were analyzed and coded according to major themes, which were then condensed into three major categories: attribution of racial problems to Blacks; attribution of racial problems to whites; attribution of racial problems to institutional/cultural factors.

HOW WHITE TEACHERS PERCEIVE RACISM: WHAT DO THEY SEE? WHAT DO THEY NOT SEE?

An analysis of this data reveals that when referring to examples or incidents of racism, nearly all of the respondents answered the question or posed the problem in Black and white terms. Only one or two people from each school cited racism against or by Native Americans, Asians, or Latinos as a problem in their school. In all other cases, racism, regardless of how they interpreted its causes or manifestations, was seen essentially as a Black and white phenomenon. Table 6.1 illustrates the major categories of causality that the teachers cited.

TABLE 6.1
TEACHERS' PERCEPTIONS OF RACISM IN THEIR SCHOOLS: MAJOR THEMES

Major Theme 1: Attribution of Racial Problems to Blacks	*Frequency*
1. Black students get away with stuff/preferential treatment	26
2. Teacher called racist by Blacks, "That's reverse discrimination"	22
3. Black students have bad home environment	20
4. Black staff are to blame for our problems of racism	16
5. Black students are heard making racist remarks	15
6. Black students act intimidating	12
7. Black parents act racist	9
8. Hallway control problems due to Blacks	8
Subtotal of frequencies for the theme	*(45.5%)* 128

Major Theme 2: Attribution of Racial Problems to Whites	*Frequency*
1. White teachers are heard making racist remarks	46
2. White students are heard making racist remarks	32
3. White staff treats Black students worse	27
4. White parents act racist	7
5. White teachers and students are intolerant of cultural diversity	3
6. White students wearing racist clothing (e.g., racist logos)	2
Subtotal of frequencies for the theme	*(41.6%)* 117

Major Theme 3: Attribution of Racial Problems to Institutional/Cultural Factors	*Frequency*
1. It's "natural" for students to segregate themselves	20
2. Students of color are not represented in school cultural activities	10
3. Racism in curricular materials	4
4. Racist graffiti in school	1
5. Special education discriminates against Black students	1
Subtotal of frequencies for the theme	*(12.8%)* 36
TOTAL	**99.9%**

Total number of examples cited: 281
Total number of respondents: 189

Major Theme 1:
Attribution of Racial Problems to Blacks

As table 6.1 indicates, in their examples of racial problems in their school, nearly half of the respondents assigned causality to Blacks. This section examines in more detail some examples of the typical responses they gave.

"Black students come from bad home environments and do not value education"

> When you are dealing with Black students and you bring the parents in, as a professional you must interpret that the parent may not know how to reinforce positive behavior at home. We need to describe what is expected of the student at school and what should be consistent at home. Teachers sometimes get tired of hearing "It's a cultural thing" or "They just don't know." (high school teacher)

> It's hard to teach children who come from a culture where they don't value education and their home life is so chaotic. Then we get blamed as teachers when they don't reinforce learning at home. (elementary school teacher)

> On conference days, we rarely have any Black parents who show up. We send notices home, we have refreshments and we are there for them, but they are not interested. Our staff is very hard-working and dedicated, but some of these parents obviously are not. This makes it very hard for the kids to get an education if it is not reinforced at home. (elementary school teacher)

The time-worn myth that it really doesn't matter what teachers do because "these people do not value education" is deeply ingrained in the thinking of many white Americans regarding African Americans. Most white Americans are ignorant of the reality of education as a tool of struggle historically in the African American community (Perry, 1993). While there is some truth to the noninvolvement of many African American parents, as Irvine[7] reminds us, citing Siddle Walker, we ought to ask when African Americans stopped becoming involved in their children's education, rather than why they aren't involved. For one of the unintended effects of the 1954 *Brown v. Board of Education* decision was that due to entrenched white racism, many African American teachers were fired in the South in the newly desegregated schools and were unwelcome in the North. As Irvine argues, if indeed African American parents did stop becoming involved, it was only after African American children were treated like other people's children.[8]

If, in fact, many African American parents do not participate in school events or parent–teacher conferences, the teacher may assume, "That is how those people are" or "Education is not important to them," rather than asking why the conferences or social activities, the latter often organized by the white, middle-class-dominated PTA, are not drawing all parents into the school. They may conclude that it is because "They do not care," rather than that it may be due to the alienating climate and the superficial nature of these (usually fifteen-minute) conferences. Additionally, because only one school in Lakeview was located in a nonwhite neighborhood, there may also have been problems of transportation. On the other hand, I was also aware of many cases where parents had tried to become involved but were shunned or ignored by teachers.

In lengthy discussions in my staff development classes, I found that teachers rarely examined the ways in which school events were organized, who organized them, or who was included or centered in these activities. On several occasions when I visited some of these events, I saw how African American students were marginalized at the same time that African American culture was being appropriated. For example, at one cultural event, the school jazz band was the featured performance. The band did not have a single African American student. I saw only one African American family attending this event. At another event, at a school in which African American children constituted 50 percent of the student population, the annual parent–teacher cultural event was organized around the theme of country-western music and line dancing, a favorite of many of the teachers, but not a cultural form that was embraced by or inclusive of many of the African American families in the school.

"Black students are 'intimidating'"

Three or four Black fellows were in the hallway talking loudly. I went up to them and asked them to move on; in so asking, I put a finger on one young man's arm. His response was "Don't you touch me, whitey." I was really taken aback, because I was just "hearing" and "seeing" students in an area in which they weren't to be, and they were disturbing us. (high school teacher)

When in the halls and confronting the students in the halls without a pass or authorization, most students respond positively. However, I am either verbally abused, completely ignored, or put on the defensive most frequently by Black students, especially the Black females. Usually there is a complete lack of cooperation and refusal to do what is asked of them. Why? I don't get this kind of intimidating treatment from any of the other minority students. (high school teacher)

I feel there is a growing perception that some Black students' misbehavior is being ignored because of fear of making waves, and that nothing will be done. I've talked about this with other teachers—most agree. (high school teacher)

This theme of Black students being threatening and "getting away with stuff" was one that came up frequently in my longer staff-development classes, especially from middle and high school teachers, who often complained about

hall behavior. The hallways were often the only place where some white teachers had contact with Black students, since, particularly in the "gifted" programs
or math or science classes, these students may have been tracked out of such
classes long ago. Hence it was the hallway encounter that seemed to reinforce
the stereotypes. In our discussions about this problem, it was sometimes revealed
that many white high school teachers feared the Black students and avoided
speaking to them, even avoiding eye contact. Often teachers would admit that
they did not even bother to try to get to know the Black students' names unless
they were going to "write them up."

In a discussion in one of my classes, for example, one teacher who had been
very resentful of the Black students ignoring him in the hallway was urged by
another teacher to try to know them as individuals. "Have you ever thought of
going up to the kid and just talking to him by name? Not for any other reason
but to know who he is as a human being, not to write him up?" In the process
of unraveling the racial stereotypes that led to his fear of the Black students, this
teacher eventually came to recognize his own prejudices. After several weeks, he
reported to the class that he had begun to take the time to find out the Black students' names and make small talk and said, "I began to see them as kids like my
own. These guys are starting to be friendly with me now." When he realized that
his taking the role of hall cop, in which he projected a cold, defensive demeanor,
was itself the obstacle to forming any positive relationships, he was able to try to
build some rapport with the students who had previously given him a "hard
time." This kind of incident illustrates a serious alienation and fear of relating to
the "other," whom this teacher had characterized and objectified as the dangerous Black male or the threatening Black female. The ultimate problem for this
white teacher was not only to get to know the Black student, but to get to know
himself and become conscious of the stereotypes and assumptions that he carried
around in his head. It is important to note that this humble self-reflection did
not come without a great deal of effort. It was only after this teacher had been in
my class for five weeks and had been exposed to some historical and sociological
background to the social construction of race, and particularly of "whiteness,"
that he was willing to step back and examine his assumptions.

While doing similar research with white high school students, it became
clear that often they were more aware than the white teachers of this disparate
treatment of Black students. When I asked them about perceived problems of
racism in their schools, 25 percent wrote that they frequently witnessed their
own white privilege as they would be walking down the halls with no pass while
they witnessed the hall duty teacher immediately going to the Black students for
hall pass checks. The following are two examples of white students' consciousness of their own preferential treatment.

As a female with fair skin, I know I can walk through the halls of ———— High School and not be stopped, so long as I act like I know where I am going. However, I have often seen Black students stopped who are doing nothing more serious than I.

I walk, without a pass, to the foreign language office almost every day. I have never been stopped or questioned, but I have seen many Black/African American kids stopped and questioned (they did have passes).

"Black students are favored or not being held accountable for their actions or behavior" (what some refer to as "reverse discrimination")

I think it is racist (maybe reverse discrimination) to make excuses for minorities, consequently not helping them own up to their own responsibilities. It catches up to them at some point—usually, too late. I would like to see the schools put more emphasis on helping African American children adjust socially in the real world that they will enter as adults. (middle school teacher)

We need to work to eliminate race as an issue in school. Eliminate or change the focus of groups and funds whose membership or allocation is determined by race. Mixed messages are sent when we say all races are important and should be treated equally, but then create organizations to favor students based on race. (middle school teacher)

The feeling that black students were enjoying special privileges and that there was too much focus on multicultural issues often came up in class discussions. In such cases, people were unaware of the relative "privileged" positioning that whites already had in a Eurocentric, white Amerocentric school culture and curriculum.

"I was accused of being racist!"

Often when Black students reacted to racially insensitive behavior or accused the white teacher or hall monitor of being racist, the white teacher turned the situation on its head and felt that she or he, and white teachers in general, were the real victims of racism.

A student called me "whitey" and said that he knew that I and all white people hated Black people and that's why I picked on him. He further stated that he hated white people, too. I felt sad that he may believe this, wondering what he was hearing and from whom he was learning these ideas. (elementary school teacher)

I've heard children and/or some parents of color blaming individual children's poor behavior and lack of academic behavior on racism of white teachers. Isn't this racism? Assuming if someone is not a person of color, they are racist? I feel angry and intimidated. Things seem to be getting worse. Aren't we singling out differences too much? Singling out certain groups for special classes/opportunities, full scholarships based on color, etc. Is this fair? (middle school teacher)

During searches on minority students, they complain that they were searched just because they were Black. Many times when I discipline students, they say I'm being racist. Some Black students really have a grudge against society as a whole and take it out on white teachers. We also had an employee who felt everyone was out to get her because she was Black. She was very bitter and hard to supervise. I expressed acceptance at all times, but she gets away with everything. (middle school teacher)

In my 22 years at ——— High School, I cannot remember ever witnessing an incident of racism. On the other hand, I as a faculty member have been accused of being racist several times. (high school teacher)

"It's the Black parents who are racist"

Black parents were often cited as problematic or were faulted if they complained that the school or the teacher was racist.

Parents complain that teachers singled out the "Black students' classes" and "poor classes" for our "head check" when we were having our lice problem. I have found that the parents of color tend to be a little more paranoid that teachers are "picking on them." It's almost a reverse discrimination that they think we're "out to get them." I feel bad that they think this way—it's a matter of mass education. I have found that we can talk until we're blue in the face to explain why we do [certain things] and it doesn't help—we're still "out to get them," as they put it. (elementary school teacher)

As the above example illustrates, the teacher often feels defensive about the accusation and perhaps may indeed feel that he or she was being "fair." Yet sometimes there is a great social distance between the Black parent and the white teacher, as well as a historic mistrust that the white teacher often does not have the knowledge to contextualize. Rather than trying to engage the Black parent or student, the teacher will more likely shut down and focus his or her anger at the parent or student for making him or her feel uncomfortable. On the other hand, often the Black parent or student has indeed experienced discriminatory treatment from white staff members. Since many white people do not understand or recognize the covert aspects of racism or their own white privilege, they often feel that unless they have used a racial epithet, they cannot be accused of any racist behavior.

"Our Black staff are uncooperative and unsupportive of the white teachers"

In schools with "blame the victim" thinking, it is often the one or two Black staff members in the school who are held responsible for the lack of racial harmony.

> Last year we hired two Black teachers (one was a parent liaison), but it didn't solve any problems. It was more trouble than it was worth. They tended to stick together, always ate lunch together, and made no effort to include any white teachers. They actually made things worse by polarizing some of the Black parents against the [white] teachers.

Such an example is emblematic of the kinds of problems that I had often heard expressed in conversations with Black teachers—they found themselves tokenized and felt "used" to do what all teachers should have been doing. For example, rather than deal with a discipline problem with a Black child and try to relate to the child themselves, white teachers often sent the child immediately to the Black teacher. African American teachers were also very conscious of being observed and interpreted by their white colleagues. Attempts to eat lunch together or share common experiences were often perceived as exclusionary and resented by their white colleagues. The perception that the staff was "integrated" usually varied greatly between Blacks and whites. Many white teachers believed that they were already integrated if they could visibly see a person of color.

"Naming names"

Despite my request for anonymity in these questionnaires, several respondents from the high school and middle school actually named the Black staff in their school who they believed were "the problem." Occasionally in my discussions with teachers, I would hear such remarks as "We want Black teachers, but what kind of a Black teacher?" I came to call this sentiment "Get us the 'right' kind, or get 'em outa' here!"

> I'd find a minority leader who could and would do his job. Mr. ———— is truly an adversary. Now Mrs. ———— is doing a good job, but [she] is demonstrating that she herself has a problem. She is not the kind we need. I feel that the rest of the staff is really trying.

> This school should appoint a new minority coordinator who is willing to heal the wounds and work with everyone. Mrs. ———— needs to stop encouraging children to view themselves as "victims." If our few Black "teachers" would be a positive model, we could start working in the right direction.

Black staff were sometimes perceived by white teachers as being "racist" if they ostensibly did not cooperate with or defend the white teachers when the latter were being charged with racism by Black students or parents. One teacher wrote of being called a "racist" by a student, and that "when Mr. ———— [a Black administrator] got involved, he did not adequately defend me. I guess I should have just dictated to [him] how to do his job."

While several people named names of Blacks in a questionnaire in which I had asked for anonymity and confidentiality, in no case did anyone ever mention the name of a white teacher. This is especially significant, since 16 percent of the responses were in reference to hearing their white colleagues make racist or racially insensitive remarks.[9] Yet their identity was never revealed, and the problem was more often couched in terms of a generalized problem of insensitivity, but never as intolerable behavior for the job. In discussions with teachers about such issues as the racist behavior of a white colleague, I often heard comments like "Oh, he's just like that," "He's mean to everyone," or "She must have just been having a bad day," when trying to understand the behavior of some racist white teachers or staff toward Blacks. Since this was an open-ended, gestalt-like question, the spontaneous responses of the teachers were very revealing of a "white racial ethic" among many of the teachers—a double standard being applied for Blacks and whites. Whites were likely being protected, whereas Blacks were "public property" when it came to exposing perceived racism.

Major Theme 2:
Attribution of Racial Problems to Whites

While nearly half (46 percent) of all teachers surveyed tended to perceive racism as being caused by Blacks in one way or another, it is very important to stress here that 40 percent did not do so. This major category of responses focused on the ways in which whites were seen as contributing to racial tensions in the school, perceiving that in various ways, it was sometimes their white colleagues, parents, or students who were contributing to the problem of racism in their schools. This section examines the ways in which these teachers perceived and acknowledged racism coming from their white colleagues.

Coded language and behavior of white racism

In our efforts to probe more deeply into the problem of racism in education, we often look for the less obvious or covert expressions (such as in the omissions or distortions of people of color in the curricula, in the teaching staff, or the institutional arrangements that guarantee racist outcomes), under the assumption that the more blatant forms of racism are an aberration, especially with "professional," "educated" people. Overt expressions of racism are more frequently expected from the "redneck" or "Archie Bunker" stereotype.[10] However, according to what many teachers said they saw and heard, we should not assume that the overt expressions of racism are somehow now submerged. In fact, over one-fourth of the teachers[11] reported hearing fellow white teachers make racially insensitive or hostile remarks about Blacks. While no overt racial epithets were reported, the language was clearly contemptuous, though it was couched in the coded language of racism used often to refer to Blacks or other people of color, such as the "other," "those people," "those people from [the big city]," or even "those people from the apartments." The following examples are typical of the kinds of coded language or behaviors that some teachers reported witnessing from some of their white colleagues.

> I was in a conversation with other teachers and an educational assistant, and we were talking about a Black student, and one person said, "Well, you know, those people always . . ." (elementary school teacher)

> I observed a teacher listing all the Black students who had "bombed out" of a class to a student who was asking about joining that class. I also observed the teacher making personal comments to a student about their facial bone structure and joking about "Polynesian background on your mother's side." The student seemed confused by the tone of voice and teasing but was not as aware as I was that this was a racial negative at their expense. (high school teacher)

> I hear teachers comment that an individual is probably guilty of wrongdoing, simply because of his racial orientation: It's probably a Black kid. (elementary school teacher)

> When calling roll, this teacher says [to a student of color], "White? How'd YOU get a name like WHITE?" I heard another teacher comment, "This was a manageable class until they put those Black kids in here!" It would seem that these attitudes are so ingrained that most of us aren't aware of them. How do we reach those who don't want to be reached? (high school teacher)

> I've heard these remarks from teachers: "A big Black kid came into my room" . . . a "tall skinny one" (one what?) . . . when told a [Black] student was talented in dancing—answer, "Aren't they all?" . . . saying the parents [of Black students] are concerned—as if it's rare . . . hearing racial jokes. I felt sick about these comments from the teachers. I commented to my friends—got up and left the lunch table. Told people I didn't like the joke. I could've taken a risk and said how the comments sounded to me and had a discussion about it, but it would've been a risk to say something to colleagues who don't know they are so ignorant. (high school teacher)

> Lots of kids are identified as Black kids, where white students are not identified as white kids—mostly it's the teachers and secretaries who do this. I thought—this is the beginning of extreme generalization. I suppose I could've pointed out to

them their "error" in logical thinking, but it seems so futile, I guess. (high school teacher)

At the middle school, many of the examples given were also blatant.

A teaching partner of mine made some pretty negative remarks about "Black names"—the names some African American parents give their children, saying that she'd be embarrassed if she had such a name and maybe that affects their self-esteem.

When issues are discussed (e.g., perhaps an incoming student who is reported to be a discipline problem), the question is asked, "Is he Black?" I've also heard teachers commenting on Black students doing well on a particular skill assignment with an obvious tone of "surprise" in their voice. I felt uncomfortable but said nothing. Then I felt uncomfortable and phony for saying nothing. I probably could have made a simple statement, such as: "Why does it surprise you that Sam does well in math? What does the student's color have to do with anything? Will that determine how we will handle discipline issues with him?"

After I complimented a teacher on the weekly music program she put together—more specifically, a dance routine that some boys had put together—she countered with, "That's about all they can do!" (The dance group was made up of African Americans.) I didn't know what to say.

Occasionally a teacher cited an incident in which a professional outside the school behaved in a racist or discriminatory manner, such as these two examples from high school teachers.

When referring a Black student for immediate dental care, I was asked by the dentist we usually call for referrals (over the phone) if the student was Black. He then told me that poor Black adolescents should have their teeth pulled out rather than having expensive reconstructive work done like root canals or expensive crowns.

When I send my [Black] business students out on job training, sometimes I notice that they are watched more carefully and treated differently than my white students.

Witnessing the unfair treatment of Black students

It is not only teacher talk that many reported hearing—many teachers reported observing white teachers treating Black students worse than white students. Nineteen percent of the middle school staff and 11 percent of the high school staff reported seeing such behavior. This included such behaviors as singling out Black students for discipline; asking Black students but not white students for hall passes; singling out Black students for detention for being late;

searching Black students for weapons or drugs. And there were other examples as well.

> Working with various classes in the LMC [library media center], we are constantly observing teachers' relationships with students. During a unit that lasted for two weeks, I became aware that the teacher was consistently ignoring Black students if they raised their hands. When a Black student actually asked a question, the answer was very abrupt. This went on the entire two weeks! As a result, I ended up helping the minority students in that class, but I felt uncomfortable about saying anything to the teacher.

> I have noticed that some of the teachers in my school cannot seem to accept a strong, assertive, independent-thinking African American young woman student, but can accept those African American students who they perceive "need" them. Those who are confident are seen as "threatening," whereas confident white girls are seen as "promising." Those who are "confident" are often treated like they are troublemakers, and I have noticed that they are watched closely.

> I've noticed that ESL [English as a second language] students (mostly Asian) are not welcomed in the Phys Ed classes at ———— School. The Phys Ed teachers complain about them.

While some teachers claimed to recognize racist attitudes or behaviors perpetrated by their white colleagues, they did not take any responsibility for counteracting it, and some expressed the view that not only was it not their responsibility to fight racism, but it was the responsibility of the few Black staff members to improve race relations in the school.

> Mrs. ———— gets angry with me whenever I send Black students who are in trouble to her room. This is something I and many of the other white teachers don't understand. How can she expect the white teachers to help them if she doesn't?

> We had an African American male teacher last year who really had a chip on his shoulder. He expected us to cooperate with him, but he wouldn't help out when we had our newspaper incident (when the African American students were upset over the article about their low grade point averages). He told one of the counselors, "That's your problem. You started it. You deal with it!" and expected us to just take care of it for him.

Silence: The persistence of racism

Although one out of four teachers reported witnessing racism or racial insensitivity from their white colleagues, in response to the question asking whether they did or said anything about it, they rarely reported that they challenged or refuted such remarks or behaviors. While many reported that they felt badly about racial slurs or insensitivity, they often expressed feeling powerless, embarrassed, afraid to rock the boat, or a sense of futility, so they behaved dangerously—they did nothing. Hence, we see another dimension of the persistence of racism: silence. If the students of color had sympathy from a white teacher, such teachers were often too silent to behave as allies—leaving these students in actuality with no one to defend them. And when Black students complained about being picked on it was difficult for many teachers to understand that there may be an objective reality in what the students were saying.

If one out of four teachers reported having heard racially insensitive remarks from their colleagues, one must assume that those who were the targets of such remarks heard or at least "felt" them as well. It would not be surprising to learn that many of the students of color had likely experienced discriminatory behavior or heard cruel remarks from some of the adults put in their charge. This is one of the reasons why it is valuable to read these responses aloud to the teachers, so that they may begin to see some of these behaviors as more systematic than they realize or may care to acknowledge—something the experiences of the students of color and their parents may have already taught them. Sometimes when I read such responses aloud, I also juxtaposed them with the reported or perceived "paranoia" of the Black parents or students. This illuminates the issue of witnessing. Historically, whites have always witnessed the degradation of people of color, from the first encounters with the Indigenous Peoples through slavery and colonization to the present. Rarely are people willing to face the contradictions between the so-called American creed of equality and the American reality of inequality and relative white privilege and power.

SOME CONCLUSIONS

While Lakeview was a school district known for "excellence" and tolerance, the academic outcomes for students of color were as problematic as for their counterparts in more economically depressed urban areas. Still, this "liberal" district proudly touted the rhetoric of "success for all" and other slogans of the "rainbow," without asking for whom there was such success. This "liberal" racism, while distinct from more overt racism, is nevertheless very dangerous. Yet it is a form of racism that persists, and we seem to have made little progress in recognizing this disguised form of racist self-interest. Writing over thirty years ago, educator Charles Wilson (1970) warned about the subtle manifestations of such racism:

> The racism which pervades the public school system is at one and the same time subtle, unintentional, unthinking, as well as brutal and deliberatively offensive. And more important, this middle-class racism is disguised in a clever rhetoric.

Sometimes the talk is liberal, affirming goodwill and genuine social concern and at other times speaking in a subtle racial code: "neighborhood schools," "jungle," "due process," "professional rights," "cultural deprivation," and oh yes—love for the children. But generally, behind the words exists an entire reality which protects the professional educators' self esteem at the expense of the children; protects the educators' status at the expense of the community's interests; protects whites at the expense of the Blacks; protects the middle class from competition with those who they feel aren't ready, or don't deserve the good things of this glutted society. (p. 307)

Most teachers seemed to show little awareness or understanding of the structural nature or roots of racism, or its institutional manifestations in education. Very few (5.6 percent) cited bias in the curriculum, and few cited other aspects of the school culture, such as bias in extracurricular activities, tracking, overrepresentation of children of color in special education, or the fact that their school had only one or two Black teachers, if any, as "evidence" of racism. And many took the immediately apprehended reality of problems that they may actually have experienced, such as Black students not following their orders, or Black parents' anger, as being the essence of that reality—as in, "That's how those people are." Invisible and unacknowledged white privilege clouded and distorted the lens, such that most of the Lakeview teachers were "disabled" from seeing their own portraits.

This problem of a lack of empathy and the tendency to "blame the victim" may actually escalate as teachers are becoming increasingly alienated from their labor. They may be more prone to scapegoat their students as the teaching profession comes under pressure to compete in the education "market." In such a "market," characterized by the defunding of public education and increased privatization in a global capitalist corporate economy, successful teaching and learning are measured by standardized tests. Such tests have the effect of replacing or negating teacher creativity. Indeed, Fine (1986) found that as teachers became more focused on routinized testing, there was a high correlation with derogatory attitudes toward the students. When the student does not respond "properly"—i.e., does not perform well on tests—this could reflect negatively on both the student and the teacher, who may be judged ineffective in her or his practice. This can contribute to resentment of those who are not "learning." Hence, when it comes to encountering people who have differences of any kind that do not "fit" within the very limited universe of discourse, the increasingly restrictive conditions of teaching and the pressures to "teach to the test" make it more difficult for the teacher to recognize the gifts and abilities that different people possess. It then becomes easier to blame the victim and reinforce all of the old stereotypes such as "those people don't value learning, anyway."

One of the critical aspects of most of the white Lakeview teachers' responses was how they framed their perceptions of racism, almost entirely positioning African Americans as the "other." In only two cases of nearly two hundred were Latinos or Asians cited as targets of racism, and never as the cause. Blacks were the only group targeted as problematic as a group. This does not mean that Blacks were perceived only as the cause, for a significant number of teachers did report witnessing or hearing whites victimizing or discriminating against Blacks more than any other group. In any case, other groups that were also having some similar problems in school, such as the Hmong or Latinos, whose educational success in Lakeview as elsewhere in the United States, was also problematic, were rarely cited in the examples given by teachers.

This should be put in the particular context of the demographics of the Lakeview School District, in which African American students were the largest racial minority. Hence, they were perceived by many whites as the critical mass "other," problematic in large numbers. However, it is not mere numbers that accounts for this reaction against African Americans. The posing of Blacks as the "ultimate other" has been observed and documented over the years by such scholars as Baldwin (1963), Du Bois (1964), Bowser and Hunt (1981), and by more recent scholars (Roediger, 1991; Frankenberg, 1993) as well. For example, in Frankenberg's (1993) research on the social construction of whiteness among white women, she similarly found that among the women in her study, "racist discourse frequently accords a hypervisibility to African Americans and a relative invisibility to Asian Americans and Native Americans; Latinos are also relatively less visible than African Americans in discursive terms" (p. 12).

Given that nearly all (94 percent) of the Lakeview teachers were white and grew up in a racially segregated society, most of them came out of a milieu that was likely to be increasingly far removed from the majority of their students of color. Many of these teachers found their relevance and effectiveness challenged as a result of the changing demographics as more students of color entered the Lakeview district. The situation was further compounded by an increasingly segregated job and housing market. Because teachers' perspectives are shaped by the same social forces that mold us in the society at large, it was not surprising to see that the cognitive categories they employed to understand their world reflected the stereotypes held by the dominant group of which they were members (Allport, 1979).

White teachers in Lakeview, as elsewhere in America, continue to live in a symbolic universe that is "white." In their own education, like that of the general public, they have been "victimized" by the lack of a serious education of the history of our country. Hence, many of their alleged characteristics of people of color were based on historic and culturally perpetuated stereotypes, which had become part of their stock of "knowledge" that they brought into the practice of teaching. Their perceptions of racism in their schools often reflected the dominant stereotypes and projections of Blacks, which perceived them as threatening, as intruders. Such historical stereotypes continue to be reinforced in the corporate capitalist popular news media regarding affirmative action and welfare bashing, and the use of Willie Horton–type stereotypes to demonize Black males and thus justify their increased incarceration.

There is little doubt that teachers have limited power when it comes to determining the social conditions of the larger society, which also contribute to the problems they experience in schools. However, it is important to realize that within the schools, they are members of a group that does have some power and ability to impose their own assumptions and categories on a subordinate group. In a society in which we have racial domination, racist assumptions, and categories that are left unchallenged will be reproduced in institutional practices. This is what Stuart Hall calls everyday or common-sense racism. These relations of racial domination may become uncritically accepted as "just the way things are" and come to be so normalized and institutionalized that they acquire a social inertia that seemingly does not require conscious reflection or intent.

In Lakeview, this uncritical habit of mind allowed many teachers to accept the status quo, not necessarily because they were passive or by nature uncritical, but because this is the dominant discourse in American education and culture. Alternative ways and means are not often seen as being within one's reach. Because of the subtleties of white privilege and relative entitlement, many white teachers revealed a confused or contradictory consciousness about racism and its manifestations, regardless of their intent. This is why it is important to understand and to measure racism not only by its intent, but also by its effects.

—◁◈▷—

In the last two chapters, I narrate my experience actualizing an antiracist professional development program for teachers similar to the framework I developed in chapter 5. First, I discuss my experiences with teachers as we unraveled and decoded our racist constructions and influences at the individual level. Then, in the final chapter, I move from our personal narratives to our collective narratives—facing history *in* ourselves. By this I mean something rather different from the concept of facing history *and* ourselves, to suggest that we must consider how history lives in us and through us.

CHAPTER SEVEN

Teaching Antiracist Education in Lakeview

unraveling the individual dimensions of racism

A S I DISCUSSED IN THE PREVIOUS CHAPTER, Lakeview teachers' perceptions reflected the dominant discourse among whites regarding race. Given the often distorted and superficial level of analysis expressed by many teachers, the challenge is to unravel the chain of causality of the racial inequities and the tensions that teachers may actually be experiencing in their work. This means we must reveal how we all have been educated to "not see." The one-time, "hit-and-run" multicultural workshop approach that most districts take may actually be dangerous for creating the illusion that issues are being addressed. A longer antiracism course that confronts the individual and the institutional dimensions of racism is essential to give the breadth and depth of analysis that the problem requires. In this and the following chapter, I discuss how I went about teaching such a course for teachers and how they responded to this antiracist pedagogy.

Examining teachers' perceptions of racism helped me clarify some of the obstacles that contributed to their failure to successfully teach all students. Most did not see themselves personally as being racist and were not conscious of the more subtle dimensions of racism or of the concept of white privilege. If whites "made it" it was because they worked harder. While these teachers may have rejected the notion that there was a genetically superior race, many believed that there was something in the culture of certain groups that caused their own failure. They often blamed the students for not fitting into the schools, rather than questioning why the schools were not serving the students.[1] Because so many "blamed the victim," it was important to help them understand the historical background to the conditions that contributed to the disparate outcomes and apparent alienation of many of their students of color. It was necessary to examine how the school culture, curriculum, activities, standards, and such are not "objective," but are affected by race, class, and gender biases reflecting a narrow Eurocentric and Amerocentric perspective.

It was evident that many of the Lakeview teachers subscribed to the myth of the "American Dream," even though they couldn't always buy into that dream themselves. Many of them knew they were sitting on the edge of a crisis in their professions, as they were under more stress now than when they had started out teaching. Because their own working conditions had become more constrained, with larger class sizes, more disengaged students, and increasing social problems such as unemployment, poverty, and homelessness affecting their classrooms, their power and effectiveness as teachers were challenged, and they were more likely to scapegoat the Black students. They were hampered in their knowing because of a distorted picture of history that they were taught in schools or through the popular culture.

Despite my philosophical differences with many of these teachers, I felt a solidarity with them as workers who were objectively in a very vulnerable position in their profession. They were at times under attack by the school board and the community for demanding better pay and improved working conditions. From the perspective of many parents, they were seen as abusing the job of teachers when they participated in teacher work slowdowns during contract negotiations. Some teachers were feeling on the defensive about some of the Black parents who charged the schools with being racist when they felt their children were being unfairly treated. And for those few teachers who were actually trying to introduce a multicultural curriculum, they often found themselves under attack by some of the white parents who felt that racial minorities were getting too much preferential treatment, or who believed that "too many" Blacks in their child's classroom were pulling down the "quality" of education. Because of these tensions, many of the Lakeview teachers chose to take my staff development class on antiracist education, which was offered as one of the possible continuing education classes in the district.

In the remainder of this chapter, I focus on some of the methods and curricula I used to help teachers examine the individual dimensions of racism and the social construction of "whiteness." In this process of unraveling the individual aspects of racism, it was apparent that many white teachers had a contradictory consciousness as they began to examine the impact of "whiteness" on their own socialization. I juxtapose this "white" consciousness with the racial frames of reference of teachers of color who perceived and experienced the problems of racism differently. How this antiracist pedagogy was received and negotiated by teachers is illustrated through their own voices, from their journals and class discussions. The examples I discuss here are representative of the issues raised and curricula addressed in my various classes and reflect the typical range of responses of the teachers.

WHO THE PARTICIPANTS WERE AND WHY THEY CAME

Sixteen percent of the certificated staff in the Lakeview school district took my classes during the mid 1990s. Of these, 80 percent were women and 20 percent were men, and 89 percent were white and 11 percent (thirty-eight people) were people of color.[2] This demographic profile tells little about the actual identities or individual backgrounds of these teachers; this is addressed in more detail later as I discuss the unfolding of the curriculum in my classes.

Why White Teachers Took the Class

While there were a number of circumstances that brought teachers to my class, in all cases teachers volunteered to attend. No one had been mandated to take it as a disciplinary or corrective measure. While most participants needed to take a staff-development course to maintain their teaching credential, there were numerous other courses they could choose. One may wonder, if teachers represent mainly a "white" reality, which has largely closed them off from the reality of people of color, why would they take a class on racism? In race-relations work, people often indicate that something besides idle curiosity or interest in the subject compels them to take such a class. While a few said that they personally had "no problems with racism" and were just taking the class for credit, the majority of participants expressed that they were motivated by a growing perception that something was wrong in the schools. Many were seriously disturbed by the conflict and tension in their schools or classrooms, which they thought was somehow related to the unfamiliar "new diversity" of the student population.

Glenda, a high school psychologist, wrote: "I work with many minority students, but I don't really know that much about them. I am looking for ways to help them better, relate better and understand their issues."

Megan, a hearing interpreter at a middle school, explained why she was taking the class: "I want to learn more about why there are such tensions between races or cultures. I am seeing it more and more, but I do not understand it."

Patricia, an elementary (ESL) and reading recovery teacher, wrote: "I work almost 100 percent with minority students. I am taking this class to develop a more acute awareness and sensitivity to racism/minority issues—particularly as they pertain to the classroom. Most of our materials don't represent the kids I teach."

According to Elaine, a middle school special education teacher: "I am here because I am concerned that all but one of the children in my [special education] classes are Black. I would like to figure out how that has happened. Are we doing something wrong?"

Except for Elaine, the majority of the teachers stated that their goal was to figure *them* [people of color] out, rather than asking why the schools or the teaching forces were so unrepresentative. Some people reported being concerned about "reverse racism," perceiving themselves as the victims because a Black parent or student had accused a teacher or the school of being racist. Some feared possible lawsuits, such as Barbara, a middle school teacher, who told the class: "I am concerned about reverse racism. One of our teachers is now being sued by a Black parent, and I think it's unfair. Many of our teachers are walking on eggshells. I want to learn strategies to build more effective communication so these things don't happen."

Janet, a high school learning disabilities (LD) teacher, wrote: "I am taking this class because I need the credit, but I am also concerned that too many of our kids hide behind race. You look at them the wrong way, and they call you a racist. They think they can get away with *anything*."

Others stated more benign reasons, such as a generation gap, as motivation for choosing the class. A high school math teacher said: "I am taking the class because as I age and as our student population changes, I need to take another close look at my teaching and interactions with students. I do not always understand this generation." The response of an elementary school teacher was, "It is a topic that has interested me since the sixties, when things seemed more hopeful. But lately I sense more tension and I am at a loss as to what to do about it."

Some admitted that they were taking the class because they were aware of feeling more prejudiced and intolerant of African American students, such as this high school science teacher who put in a nutshell the sentiments of many teachers:

I'm here for a variety of reasons:
1. My wife said I was being too closed-minded about the racism issues and should take the course to open my mind.
2. I get nothing but grief from Black students when I have hall encounters with them.
3. I'm tired of seeing our Black students wandering the halls and avoiding class attendance.
4. I have no Blacks in my chemistry classes, which is a shame that many are not challenging themselves and becoming contributing society members.
5. I am becoming increasingly biased as I observe our school atmosphere deteriorating somewhat.
6. Hopefully, I can learn to deal with my feelings and perhaps develop a more positive attitude. I feel that some of our Black students are genuinely great kids.

Similarly, Judith, a social worker in the Lakeview juvenile detention center, took the class because she found herself feeling hostility toward the incarcerated youth, who were primarily Black. She told the class:

> Where I work, it's always at least 70 percent Black. I mean . . . some of these kids are really bad, you know, selling crack and that sort of thing. I am beginning to find myself thinking that all Blacks are like that. I am coming here to see if there is any hope for these kids or if they are all just going to be criminals. I can actually feel myself becoming racist. That's all I see. I know I shouldn't feel that way, but I've been realizing that that's what I've been feeling. So I am here to see if there is anything I can do about it.

Rarely were people so candid as John or Judith about admitting their ill feelings toward their Black students. Many, however, did state that they were in the class because they feared they had unconscious biases or prejudices that were affecting their teaching, such as Emma, who worked in an elementary school where there was only one person of color on the staff. She wrote about the internal emotional conflicts she was feeling now that a small number of Black children were being bused to the school:

> I have always prided myself on being a nonprejudiced person. I have never thought of any particular group as being better or worse than any other group. I have had many Black friends. But lately, since these special-needs kids have been bused in, I am having some negative feelings, and I am not comfortable with that. This is mainly because I feel that I and the other white teachers are being used. We are expected to bend over backwards because some people have been victims. I feel myself getting angry because people are not helping themselves.

Why Teachers of Color Took the Class

Of the teachers of color who attended my classes, unlike some of the white teachers, no one ever said he or she was taking it only to fulfill credit requirements. They stated more direct concerns about the personal impact of racism on the job as a motivation for taking the class.

According to Janet, an African American high school educational disabilities (ED) teacher: "I wanted to take this class because racism is such an ugly issue that needs to be addressed. It affects me every day. I believe that by talking about this issue, I am able to gain valuable insight into other ethnic groups, beliefs, etc."

Rosalinda, a Latina woman who worked as a drug counselor, wrote:

> I work with the community with youth/parents and teachers, educating them around issues of DA [drugs and alcohol]. Often these children are obviously victims of racism. I'd like to get hints on how to counteract what's been inflicted on

them. Also, I am in contact with teachers who have asked me how they should deal with these students. At a personal level, I want to put words on what has happened to me—how to put what I've experienced into positive action.

Jerry, an African American fifth-grade teacher, explained:

I am here to learn new techniques for dealing with and facing issues of racism in our schools and outside of the schools. I also want ideas about how to deal with it from fellow staff. I would like to know more about how racism is as strong today and how it is still able or allowed to exist. I'm interested in learning how it is that people hate, dislike, stereotype, etc., when one doesn't have control of his/her color.

Wrote Annette, an African American middle school teacher:

A colleague approached me and said she was having difficulty relating to the Black kids in her class. She said they were all disrespectful, unwilling to learn, etc. I felt uncomfortable having to speak for thousands of African American people. I hope this class will help me understand what racism is and how to counteract such things from other teachers. I also want to become more sensitive to recognize racism in instructional materials.

Most teachers of color had experienced racism regularly, and unlike many of the white teachers, they did not need to be convinced of its existence. They were looking for tools to counteract it.

EXAMINING RACISM AND WHAT TEACHERS CAN DO ABOUT IT

In my classes, we proceeded along a route that began with an examination of the characteristics and definitions of race and racism and related terminology, then moved to becoming aware of how our own personal socializations have been affected by racism, particularly by the social construction of whiteness. We then related this personal experience to the institutional or systemic and historical features of racism, as manifested in political economy, ideology, and cultural and social institutions. Finally, we examined the possibilities—and the responsibility—teachers have to become agents of antiracist change. While one may be working toward change, in the case of race relations, these changes are often subtle and incremental and may not be measurable. Progress may mean helping a teacher to *recognize and stop* doing things that are damaging to good race relations.[3] My goal was to provide teachers with new perspectives from which to forge, each in his or her own way, antiracist education in their schools.

Because teachers (like everyone else in this society) have been negatively affected by racism, we must recognize the problems inherent whenever one is attempting to teach against the status quo, in particular to the very people who have been charged with maintaining it. The challenge is to go against the grain and question this authority in ways that don't backfire and alienate. If indeed it is true, as some suggest, that those in the teaching profession often tend to have been socialized and educated to be conventional and conformist, how do we introduce controversial issues to them?

LAYING THE GROUND RULES

Because we are dealing with controversial issues, it is useful to establish ground rules for discussion and interaction. If participants are fearful of speaking what is on their minds, a critical honest discussion cannot occur. Yet honesty can also be abusive if one has racist thoughts or intimidates others who do not agree. In order to put racism "on the table," it is important to have class participants construct their own ground rules rather than simply handing them a set of directives, as I had often seen others do in race-relations workshops. Usually the kinds of ground rules people developed included things like respecting different opinions, or at least one's right to have them; not making self-righteous judgments about others; having permission to make "mistakes," and giving others permission as well; listening thoughtfully; not dominating or "imperializing" space— that is, being conscious of not being so forceful that others cannot find space to speak; respecting others' silences and not projecting our own interpretations about what a silence may mean; not using racially derogatory language—specifically, not saying the "n" word in the class, even when we are referring to such language; being able to disagree with a person's ideas without putting the person down; and maintaining confidentiality.

  Although sometimes there is initial resistance to the notion that adults need ground rules, as we develop them and discuss the whys of them, there is usually a consensus that they will be useful. Often people reflect on the building of these guidelines in their journals. As one African American middle school teacher wrote in her journal, ground rules, provided they are not defined by the dominant group alone, can sometimes provide a safety net:

> We started the morning by discussing the ground rules for our class. At first I was worried, but then I appreciated being able to give input on the rules. It was important for my comfort level to request that everyone be sensitive. I was concerned at the beginning that the class would turn into a gripe session on how difficult it is to work with Black students. The topic of racism is a difficult subject to discuss and much more difficult for me since I am the only Woman of Color in the class. It's difficult for me to sit and share at this point. I might come off looking hostile. We need the ground rules.

Similarly, a white elementary teacher expressed in her journal some security in knowing that there were rules for participation, because she was concerned about what her own hidden biases and assumptions might reveal:

The ground rules for discussion made me feel secure in the fact that we as a class and as individuals want to recognize and counteract racism without fear of being attacked by others. . . . We need to be able to talk about it honestly without fear. It has to do with individual feelings and attitudes. We don't always know where or how we got our attitudes and feelings, but we need the safe space to talk about it.

Regarding the ground rule of confidentiality, I urge people to talk about our class discussions with others. To some, this seems a contradiction to the notion of confidentiality, which many initially interpret as a "vow of silence" once they leave the class, as in "What goes on in this room stays in this room." But I make the distinction between gossiping about others versus discussing the *ideas and debates* that came to life in the class, without attributing an idea or statement to a specific individual. In this way we can be instrumental in problematizing the issue of racism among our peers, rather than maintaining the silence that racism requires. I urge teachers to talk about the issues from the class, as well as to speak out and not to keep the "secret" if they suspect racist abuse is occurring in their school.

After this discussion about ground rules and the need to put the issue of racism on the table, a white middle school counselor reflected in his journal on the need to "break the silence":

Why don't we feel free to discuss openly the concept of race and our reactions to racial changes in our district's clientele? Lots of quiet conversations in huddles around the school. Lots of furtive looks. Lots of "stuffed" emotions churning inside and not brought out to look at and manage. Lots of myths and misunderstandings left unexpressed and therefore unchallenged and unchanged. The big elephant in the living room that no one openly talks about. How can we come to grips with the real issue if we won't voice the real issue?

While the actual developing of the ground rules takes only a short part of the class time, I have elaborated on this discussion because participants frequently reflected on them in their journals. When we are teaching about controversial issues, we cannot assume that just presenting the "facts" will suffice, for the emotions and biographies through which people mediate and negotiate that new information must be acknowledged, particularly when they are faced with a disjunction between what they've previously learned and what they hear in my class. It is important that people do not become defensive and shut down. In the process of discussing marginality, whites often feel defensive or marginalized themselves and repress their thoughts, leading to negative reactions that may surface later. It is far better to have a space where people may reveal what they are really thinking, even if it is unpleasant. People will more likely engage in a sincere discussion about controversy if they are able to feel some level of safety or fairness (not necessarily comfort) while doing so.

PROBLEMATIZING THE PERSONAL:
DOING RACE AND RACISM AWARENESS WORK WITH TEACHERS

As I discussed in chapter 1, one of the first things that I encountered when conducting workshops for teachers on the historical roots of racism was the need to set the stage for them to position themselves, in order to avoid the imposition of lecturing at them about something that they could not personally relate to. I could present all the "facts," but people were not necessarily able to contextualize them.

In my early classes with teachers, I had not focused on the individual awareness of racism in a systematic fashion, but attempted to work it into our discussions about the historical roots of racism. This soon proved to be inadequate, when I saw many people wanting to understand racism as a phenomenon that happened outside of themselves—something they could watch with disgust from afar while viewing *Eyes on the Prize* or other documentaries, or almost humorously via the "Archie Bunkers," whom they viewed as foolish bigots. But among many teachers who may have been repulsed by this shameful history, in the here and now they felt detached and sometimes even a stated hostility for many of the Black students or other students of color. There was a decided lack of empathy among some white teachers, who attributed the stressful conditions of their work to the presence of "too many" Black students in their school. ("It was fine until *they* came here.") These teachers viewed "them" as problems that needed fixing.

Others claimed the classic defense of "color blindness" and were in steadfast denial that they even noticed difference. A few of the white teachers sought out difference consciously and actually did have some experience with people of color, but sometimes the reasons were suspect. There was, for example, a white teacher who was married to Mexican man. She told the class that because she had a very light complexion and could not tan, she was attracted to marry a brown-skinned person so her children would have an attractive tan. (She made it clear that it shouldn't be too tan, however.) She frequently expressed resentment that our class should even be talking about racism, arguing, "I'm here to talk about multicultural education. If you go looking for racism, you are inviting it." She was angry that her Mexican husband complained about experiencing discrimination, because, as she told the class, "I have never seen it happen to him, and he cannot prove it." Unfortunately, her interracial and intercultural marriage hardly inoculated her from racist attitudes.

Before I could educate teachers about racism in society, and schools in particular, we would have to address the issue of the racial and racist constructions of reality in our own lives. It is important for white teachers to become conscious of the meaning of their own "whiteness" if they are to be able to recognize any racial bias in their own behavior and thinking. Before whites can develop empathy for those outside of their own experience, they have to become conscious of their own experience as whites. They have to examine the idea of "whiteness" as a socially, historically, and politically constructed "norm" that really is not so "normal" after all.

Yet I did not want to conduct the typical "race awareness training" workshop, which argues simplistically that all whites are racist. Such approaches leave participants stewing in guilt, cynicism, and complacency (for why struggle to change the inevitable?). As Sivanandan (1985) argues, race-awareness workshops often depoliticize racism, ignoring the influence of capitalism and slavery and negating the issue of resistance. While it is too simplistic to argue that all whites are racist, at the same time we need to come to terms with the fact that all white people are affected by racism and have a relative privilege—white privilege.

My approach would more accurately be termed *racism* awareness, in which we interrogate the impact of systemic or structural racism on the individual as well as on our social and cultural institutions. This is distinct from the dominant approaches to diversity, which focus on making people aware of their own ethnic and racial heritage so that people could realize that "we are all human beings in this great melting pot," or as popular posters in Lakeview proclaimed, "Celebrate our Diversity!" We must question why diversity or difference is an issue in the first place? Diverse from what? Different from what? Diversity and race are cultural and social constructions that are not fixed but are political and fluid, tied to relations of domination and power. Popular slogans like "Celebrate diversity!" tend to obscure the reality of these power relations and marginalize the experience of oppression and exploitation. My goal was to illuminate the fact that the most different thing about us is the way we are treated, and to question the reasons for this differential treatment.

THE RACIAL AND CULTURAL AUTOBIOGRAPHY: UNVEILING THE SUBJECTIVE DIMENSIONS OF RACE

What does it mean to grow up Black or brown or white in America? How do racial identities get constructed? And how do they become visible or invisible? How do factors like race, culture, and ethnicity shape people's lives? How does all of this affect the ways of being a teacher or a student? In order to unveil the subjective dimensions of race, early in my classes I asked people to position themselves as raced, classed, and gendered actors. I asked teachers to write a "racial/cultural autobiography," in which they are to describe their background or identity and any features that they thought were particularly influential in their own development, experience, and outlook on life. This might be race, class, gender, disability, nationality, ethnicity, sexual orientation, religion, language, geographic location, political or ideological perspective, or any factor that they think has had some impact upon who they think they are or how they think they think. I make it clear that no one is forced to disclose anything. For various reasons, we may choose not to share certain personal information, such as sexual orientation or disability, as it is possible that this information could be used against us. But all of these factors are important in how we see and are seen and are important parts of the discussion for those who want to bring them up.

In addition to the written autobiography, we also formed into small groups to discuss our early experiences. The collaborative character of this framing, done in small groups as well as with the group as a whole, is important so that people can reflect upon their commonalities and differences. As Brandt (1986) argues, group-centered collaborative learning is an important pedagogic device for antiracist teaching, "whereby members of the group can learn from each other not only the subject matter but of the 'real life' knowledge of themselves and their counterparts as they apply to the lesson in hand. This learning approach also encourages interaction between pupils both in the classroom and outside which opens the door to a cultural education that is done through the lived experiences" (p. 145).

I found that teachers often expressed appreciation when getting to know each other in more personal ways, for many of them had learned to maintain a professional social distance from their colleagues other than close friends. Because of the stresses and demands of managing the classroom, although the teacher is constantly surrounded by people, she or he may at the same time be lonely, with rarely the opportunity to have a connecting conversation with another adult or peer. Teachers often referred to the therapeutic effect that these discussions had and talked about how they were looking forward to the class each week. "We have been working together for all of these years and we never really talked about *this* with each other!" was the kind of remark often made at these sessions.

The Ethnic and Racial Identities of White Teachers

Nearly 90 percent of the teachers who took my classes were white, the majority coming from Northern European–American ancestry. Most grew up in small or medium-size Midwestern cities, though a few came came from rural areas or from large urban areas like Chicago or New York. Like the majority of teachers in America, they grew up in working-class or lower-middle-class families. While they shared certain class, race, and gender characteristics, one should not essentialize them, for they often had very different experiences growing up and coming into the teaching profession.

For example, there was Melissa, who grew up in a "stable" two-parent home. As she described it, "My mother was home making supper each day when I came home from school. It was kinda like the Cleaver family." Then there was Janice, who ran away from a father who raped her, forcing her to live on the streets panhandling, before she eventually found help and returned to high school. She then went on to college to become a teacher. Jennifer grew up being the only sighted person in her family and witnessed much discrimination against her blind parents. Maureen, a lesbian, grew up in poverty and dealt with issues of marginalization, abuse, and harassment since she was a child. Linda was divorced and, like several teachers who took my class, was working at another job on weekends to make ends meet. On the other hand, Phyllis lived in one of the posh areas of town with her highly paid doctor husband. As she recalled, "The most serious problem of my childhood was finding the proper match of socks for my skirts. I mean, I was really lucky and protected." Angela told the class that her father anglicized his Italian name so his kids could get into college. Liz grew up in a privileged community, where her father was a highly regarded sports coach who frequently took the family on trips to different countries. Paula's father was afflicted with polio when she was in second grade and, as she told the class, "from then on we never went anywhere because there was no such thing as wheelchair access back then."

Such disparate circumstances can certainly have profound effects on people's views and socializations. Nevertheless, no matter how diverse their backgrounds and upbringings, or how great the social distance between some of them, the underlying but invisible thread that tied most of them together was the happenstance that they were socialized as whites in a society that privileges "whiteness," and they were not aware of it. Nor was ethnicity of immediate concern. As Omi and Winant (1986), Roediger (1991), McCarthy and Crichlow (1993), and others argue, the issue of ethnicity in the United States is an unstable one. What may have been considered fixed and secure ethnic identities for whites a half century ago have faded and become more obscure, such that most whites no longer find it necessary to define themselves by their ethnic heritage, which has become progressively farther removed from the "old country" as language, culture, and traditions become irrelevant or are forgotten, denied, or "melt" away. Indeed, in their constructions of their cultural and racial autobiographies, ethnicity was rarely identified as a salient feature by the white teachers in Lakeview, the majority reporting that they had given little thought to their ethnicity, which was usually multiethnic, such as German-Swedish or Norwegian-English-Polish. Nor was language identified as an issue. With few exceptions, the teachers spoke no language but English.

The major awareness of "difference" that most reported experiencing in childhood was religious, and even this was within the Christian sects, mainly between Lutherans or Protestants and Catholics. "Now *that* was a mixed marriage where I came from!" was a not uncommon remark, heard particularly from those who grew up in small towns or rural areas. While many said they heard anti-Semitic references while growing up, most had never actually met a Jewish person until college. In fact, a story I heard several times from teachers concerned an experience in their college dorms, in which they described checking out the Jewish women or Black women in the showers "to see if they had tails or horns"!

When describing their racial or ethnic identity, "whiteness" was rarely explicitly stated. Most people expressed the view that they were "just Americans" and described themselves usually as a combination of European ethnicities, of which they were often not completely sure, though some professed to be interested in learning more about their backgrounds someday. Some claimed to feel no identity, others a loss of identity or ethnic roots. Some felt envious or romanticized racially oppressed groups like Latinos or Native Americans, whom they felt had a "culture," which "we whites do not have." While most did not discuss being white as an identity, some reported being conscious of being white when they felt their privileges or rights being threatened. They expressed apprehension that racial minorities were getting too much attention because of their ethnicity, while whites were being ignored. In such cases, they felt marginalized and believed that people of color were now having all the advantages "just because they are not white." Such concerns not only were revealed in the small group discussions where I asked the participants to focus on identity, but also were reflected in their journals. The following section looks at the major themes that emerged in our discussions about identity.

Loss of Identity

Regarding the issue of their own racial or ethnic identity, many white teachers professed to feeling culturally "blah"—to feeling they had no culture except that white-bread, "golden arches" culture that has invaded everywhere. "I don't feel anything, really. I mean, I'm not ethnic. I'm just ordinary American, and that's it," said one teacher. "What I know about my culture is lutefisk and meatballs," remarked another of Swedish descent. While a few may have expressed interest or pride in their European ancestry, typically there was no consciousness or recognition of the depths and distinctions of the historic cultures of their forebears, for they had little knowledge of those roots. Some claimed the classic "color blind" perspective, asserting they had never even noticed race: "When I see people, I see people, not color."

Bootstrap Ethnicity and the Melting Pot Myth

While most teachers said they were not that concerned about their ethnicity, sometimes it was seized upon opportunistically, a backlash reaction or fear that (racially oppressed) ethnics got "special" advantages. The assumption was that America was a melting pot where everyone could be included if they tried. It was the bootstrap mentality: "Why do the Blacks always get these special privileges?" wrote one teacher. "I'm half Polish and half Irish, and nobody ever did that for us. We got no affirmative action. We pulled ourselves up by our bootstraps." Typically, there was an uncritical acceptance of the assimilationist myth, as expressed in the following exchange between Librada, a Chicana, and Josephine, a white woman of Italian descent. Librada was recommending the movie *Stand and Deliver* to the class. She explained how in the film, "at-risk" students of color were tutored and inspired by their teacher so successfully that they all excelled on their standardized tests, but this was not the end of their problems.

"Do you know what happened to them?" Librada asked the class. "The authorities didn't believe them. They accused them of cheating, and they were forced to take the test again! *Our* kids have to work twice as hard!"

Josephine responded: "Look, that didn't just happen to you because you're Black or Hispanic! It happened to the Italians too. When I went to college, they had me take the entrance exams again because they didn't believe an Italian could have such a high I.Q. That stuff doesn't only happen to Blacks or Chicanos!"

"Do you think it's fair that these kids always have to do more, to try harder?" Librada asked.

"We did!" Josephine said. "I always tell my Black kids, 'You *have* to do more. You can't make excuses! You *have* to work harder.'"

Librada continued: "Do you think we should accept a system that tells some people, 'Oh, it's okay to sit on your ass,' and tell others, 'You have to work harder to prove yourself to those people who are sitting on their asses'? Do you think we women need to put in more time for less pay than our male coworkers? Or our principals who get paid a helluva lot more than we do, so that *they* can be convinced of our capability?"

"I'm not saying it's fair—but we did it," said Josephine. "We survived because we did it. We can't be victims. The Italians went through it too."

This argument exemplified the fallacies of the assimilationist paradigm for people of color. It is true that historically Italians and other Southern Europeans, Jewish, or Irish people have experienced racial or ethnic discrimination and have even been considered "not white" at various historical periods. And while ethnic prejudices and stereotypes may still persist, white ethnics have been able to "melt" their ethnicity and have assimilated to a greater degree, particularly if they affiliated with other whites or segregated themselves or acted "white." Most of us are still being taught the assimilationist myth that "we are a nation of immigrants." This negates the qualitatively different historical experiences and treatment of people of color, who were either invaded or forced here in chains or more recently often came as a result of America's military presence in their lands. While European ethnics were forced to shed their ethnic attachments in order to be accepted, for people of color, race has continued to form the basis for their subordination.

While there were some like Josephine who felt entitled because of her past ethnic minority status, there were also some whites who felt that their whiteness was leaving them out of the fold of "opportunity." They expressed resentment that nonwhite ethnics should have any "privileges" in America, especially when they were struggling "just to get by." For example, Karen, a high school teacher, worked an extra job on weekends at a grocery store to make ends meet, even though both she and her husband had full-time jobs. The store was located near an area where many international university students of color lived. On the first day of class, she said:

> I work on weekends at the X supermarket. Sometimes these people come into the store and they are on WIC [supplemental food program for Women, Infants and Children] and use coupons to pay for their food, and this really makes me angry. I'm thinking, like okay, so why should you get all this help, all this free food, and you're not even a citizen? My dad is just a working-class guy, and he would never take anything that he didn't earn. When we were growing up, we were working-class people, lived in a small house, and we never got help. And now I have to wait on these people who are not even from this country and they are using this WIC money. It is the part of my job that I hate.

The following week, when we were discussing the "English Only" movement, Karen told the class that while working at the grocery store, these same patrons really bothered her.

> They don't even seem to have tried to learn English when they come here. They want me to explain to them how to use the automatic teller machine, and I feel myself resenting taking the time to help them. Meanwhile, there is this long line of people that I have to wait on, and they think I should give them special English lessons. It really bothers me!

Karen certainly deserved to be angry that she had to have two jobs to make ends meet, but her anger was displaced at the foreigner rather than her underpaid and undervalued status in the teaching profession. Similarly, Joan, an elementary teacher who worked at a women's clothing store on weekends, told the class that she understood Karen's point.

> I don't like it when I've been working all day and I'm really tired, like especially this last Christmas, we were really busy, and these women from other countries, I don't know if they are from Japan or where, but they just talk among themselves. Maybe this doesn't sound right, but sometimes I feel like they're talking about me. It's not that I don't like them or anything like that. But I just feel if you are going to come to this country you should learn the language.

Remarks such as both of the above women made indicate the need to help people interrogate their taken-for-granted assumptions about who belongs here and why anybody is here in the first place. In this particular case, I related to the class the story told to Robert Moore (cited in Brandt, 1986) about a Sri Lankan in London, who, upon being asked by an Englishman, "Why are you people over here, anyway?" responded, "We are over here because you are over there." I then asked people to reflect upon who it is that is here—how did they get here and why did they come? Generally, our history and social studies texts have not critically examined our own colonial experience as colonizer, nor our government's true history of military interventions historically as well as in the present (Loewen, 1995; Parenti, 1995). We must consider our government's policies to maintain American hegemony that have affected many countries throughout the world, such as in Southeast Asia, Central America, Africa, the Middle East, the Caribbean, and elsewhere. American military and foreign policies have contributed to the destabilization of governments and economies, such that people are often forced to flee their own countries, often to the United States, to make a living. There is also the movement of capital by the elites from country to country, which often causes mass migrations of working-class people in search of jobs. As James Loewen (1995) demonstrates in *Lies My Teacher Told Me*, our educational system teaches us to not question, but to accept the myth of our "manifest destiny"—the American entitlement to dominate the world. He argues that those who have more formal education actually tend to have a stronger, unquestioning allegiance to the status quo, and that education is the primary method of this socialization.

The "Culture Vultures": Romanticizing and Appropriating the "Other"

While whites usually do not have to question their "whiteness" or their ethnicity—indeed, it is so "normal" and taken for granted that they may actually forget about it or "lose" it. Occasionally, a teacher reported giving much thought to others' ethnicity, romanticizing nonwhite cultures as being more "down to earth" or, as one teacher put it, "not constipated like white culture seems to be." It was not unusual for some to attribute perceived simplicity, collectivity, and community only to nonwhite peoples. They were not conscious of the fact that as white people, they too are descended from tribal or communal peoples. Nor were they aware of how, historically, the qualities of collectivity were subverted by the demands of a capitalist economy and culture. Some expressed a sentimental longing for a way of life that was distinguished from late-twentieth-century commercial and materialistic American culture. Dineen, for example, talked about going to Native American sweat lodges and wanting to "get into" Indian culture. Or as Sarah, a middle school Spanish teacher, told the class in her introduction to her background:

> Well I'm part English and Welsh mainly, but, you know? I really don't *feel* English, or Welsh, or even American, really. [laughs] I mean, I really *feel* Spanish. I think I was supposed to be born Spanish. [laughs] I don't know, sometimes I think about reincarnation, and I think that I musta been Spanish in my other life! [laughs] You know? I have always wanted to be Spanish. I just love everything about the culture. I love the food. I love the clothes. I love the people, the music. Ahh, I mean—I went to Spain and to Mexico, and I loved it! I just felt like I belonged there. That's really part of the reason why I decided to teach Spanish. Our [white] culture has nothing like that.

Sarah was all for "multicultural education," but her desire to be "multicultural" bordered on cultural appropriation. She seemed to have no sense of what her remark about even *feeling* Spanish or her frequent vacations to Spanish-speaking countries meant to the two Latina women in the class who could not afford to go home to visit their families. Sarah often took it upon herself to explain their culture to them. She was the consummate liberal, proud of her "tolerance," yet she was appropriating other cultures for her entertainment. If there was an international dinner going on in town, she would announce it to the class and talk about how "neat" she thought it would be, and how she was going to wear her Mexican clothes there. She would often greet Francisca, one of the Chicana teachers in the class, in Spanish, and Francisca would purposely answer her in English. Francisca often questioned many of the issues that Sarah would bring up as solutions. "How do you think that by your going to this international dinner, you are making a contribution? What are you going to do beyond the international food fest?"

Sarah assumed that she was already sufficiently sensitized by virtue of her love affair with "Spanishness." In the beginning of the class, she occupied much "space," talking authoritatively and confidently. She was used to being the cultural conduit for the other white teachers in the school. But as the course progressed, the tension between her appropriation of other cultures and the close proximity with which she found herself and her authority challenged by someone who was the "real thing"—Francisca—began to force her to reexamine her "authority."

For example, one week, Francisca brought up the issue of approaches to bilingual education. She related a conversation she had the week before that had been disturbing her, regarding an ESL teacher who made a rule that after the first week or two of class, the students could no longer speak in their native languages in his classroom, even when they were working in small groups with each other. He told Francisca that he wanted the Mexican girls in his class to stop speaking to each other in Spanish when they were working in small groups, because he "knew" they were just gossiping, and besides, they would never learn English. Francisca was concerned that if these girls could not feel comfortable with who they were and were prevented from having relaxed, affirming conversations with each other in their own language, they would eventually come to scorn their language and culture. They would more likely feel alienated at school and begin to form negative associations with it.

Sarah disagreed. "But if you want to learn another language, you *have* to immerse yourself. I mean, when I was in Mexico, I *couldn't* speak English. I had to speak Spanish if I was going to learn Spanish. We were just told we could not speak English!"

"Well, it's not just like that for us," Francisca told her. "I see Mexican girls in this school who are now embarrassed to speak Spanish with each other in the hall because it's not cool, and even when they don't have to, if they are in school, they speak English with each other. . . . I think it's because they are becoming ashamed of speaking Spanish now. I see it in their faces."

"Well, I don't agree!" Sarah said. "I have kids in my class who would love to hear them speak Spanish! . . . I mean, kids are really interested, they are fascinated with other languages. They are always going up to the foreign kids and asking them to say something in their language."

Francisca responded with a sense of desperation in her voice, as she was trying to get Sarah to understand:

> But that's not the same as respect! That's just making *objects* of them. Those white kids aren't asking them because they are really sincerely trying to learn that language or the culture! That's not the same thing. They are not asking them to participate in activities or invite them to their houses to play, or that sort of thing, you know? They just want them to perform for them!
>
> *You* don't know what it is like to be ashamed of your language. When you were in Mexico, you were a Gringo—you went there to learn a language. You were an American! You did not have to give up your identity and leave your country

behind to do that. How can *you* tell people, when they are here in this white Anglo culture and everything is constructed around that culture, and the whole school and all of the teachers and everything, that they cannot speak their language—that's what the colonizers have always done! Don't you see that people should just be able to feel comfortable with their own language? They have to feel comfortable with their language even when they are learning a new one, or they will come to reject their own language and culture! They will reject themselves!

I see girls in the hallway who *avoid* me because they know I will greet them in Spanish, and they are trying to blend in and pretend they are not Chicanas. That's what racism has done! Because they are here for different reasons than you going down to Mexico to study Spanish. Their parents were forced to come here, where everything is so cold, for work! Not like you going on a vacation! They are here to pick your vegetables! They *have* to learn English. They are forced to learn English. You did not *have* to learn Spanish, you see?!

"Well, I guess I never thought of it in that way," said Sarah. "I mean, I see what you're saying. But you know, I'm just concerned that they learn English. . . ."

For Sarah as well as others, these class discussions were often their first opportunity to have their "good intentions" examined more critically. Sarah later wrote in her journal, "I think I am beginning to see what you are talking about when you asked us to examine the difference between appreciation and appropriation."

The Invisible Presence of People of Color in the White Racial Autobiography

As described above, to further interrogate the meaning of their whiteness, I asked teachers to write a racial and cultural autobiography in which they reflected upon their histories in five-year segments, considering such aspects as their awareness of race and racial prejudices; the racial and ethnic composition of their schools, neighborhoods, and families; and influential experiences, educational materials, or moments that affected their views about race. Whether from an urban or rural background, according to what people wrote in their racial autobiographies or reported to the class, the vast majority of white teachers had had no personal relationship with any people of color in their childhood. People of color, if they were present at all, usually formed an invisible backdrop, such as this teacher remarked in one of the small-group discussions:

Now that I think of it, there *were* people of color. I think they were Mexican or Hispanic. They could have been Black. I just don't know! You know? I can't believe it, but I don't even know *what* they were! [laughs] But they didn't live there. I never met any of them. They came to work in the fields or the cannery. I remember everyone would lock their doors when these people came to town. We never locked our doors otherwise; that's why I remember it.

Or as John, a high school teacher, put it, he had an "awareness around the edges of consciousness" that "they" were "there." As he recalled in his racial autobiography:

> [Up to age fourteen], these were basically white, Anglo-Saxon, Protestant years during which I lived in Texas. Those were the people my family knew and interacted with, the people who surrounded me. When I started school [in the early fifties], all the first-graders were put into classrooms full of white children. There were some Hispanic children, as I recall, but they went to a separate room—something about language. They are now but a small memory of my early school days, a recollection that they were in the school; but we and they never interacted.
>
> Visiting my relatives in Albuquerque, I heard of "Mexicans" and of "Old Mexico"; but "Mexicans" were some vague group of "them" with whom my relatives and I never interacted personally. If "Mexicans" existed in reality for me, they were yard workers or maids. Because the people I saw and interacted with regularly were like me, I had only an awareness around the edges of consciousness of other types of people who existed as rather undefined "they," usually poorer, less motivated and less skilled than "we."
>
> From ages fifteen to twenty-one we moved to an area where a large number of "minority" people lived, specifically African Americans; however, they lived in the north part of town and had separate schools and shopping areas from the rest of us. Again, my experience of people unlike my family and the people I most closely came in contact with was that "they" were poorer, less motivated, and less skilled than "we" were. Even in college, the minorities I saw were maids, janitors, or yard workers for the most part. There were Hispanic students in the Spanish Department, sons and daughters of educated families, or students from Spanish-speaking countries. I became acquainted with Hispanics who were like me in many ways, and who were part of my "we" group. My horizons changed.
>
> From ages twenty-two to thirty-five I moved to Lakeview from Texas. One of my first surprises was seeing white women working as maids at the university. I recall thinking how strange it was that the maids weren't African American.

While virtually "invisible" in real life, the *idea* of people of color—of the "other"—also contributed to the popular mythology and the racist folklore or nursery rhymes introduced from early childhood that most recalled learning as part of the collective white experience, while at the same time having little knowledge of any of the folk tales of their own European ancestors. Another white elementary school teacher related one of her early memories to the small group:

> I remember we were told to be careful in the summer, because my dad always said the gypsies would kidnap us if we were not careful. And I really believed it! But I never saw any. But I could *picture* them. They were not white, but I don't know what. . . . [laughs] I don't think there are even gypsies in Minnesota! Are there? Were they Mexicans?

White Avoidance and White Flight

Another theme that came up frequently concerned memories of white flight. For those who may have lived near an area where there were people of color, whites usually saw them episodically, as in driving past (not through) their run-down neighborhoods. Many teachers reported wondering as children why "they" lived in such poor conditions. Many of those who came from large cities like Chicago or New York, where people of color were numerically near or in the majority, nevertheless also related growing up in segregated white environments, traveling the "white route" to get from place to place. "White flight" and racial tensions often characterized certain memorable "passages" of their childhood. Clara, a white middle school teacher, wrote in her racial autobiography:

> I was totally unaware of any racial differences from one to five years old. My family lived on the South Side of Chicago in a neighborhood changing from all white to Black. My kindergarten class was integrated, but I was unaware of any differences in my class or of the racial tension that existed at that time in my neighborhood.
>
> My family moved when I was in second grade. My neighborhood shortly thereafter began to change from white to Black. My first awareness of racial differences occurred during this time and was related to the racial tensions in my neighborhood. As the neighborhood became more integrated, tensions grew and members of my family were victimized. I remember being very frightened when my sixth-grade brother came home all beat up from the movie theater, where he was surrounded by Black youths. I remember my father's anger and the racial slurs that he made. . . . I remember my parents discussing other neighbors moving and how close "they" were getting.

More often than actually being beat up, people reported living with the fear that it might happen, naturalizing such behavior. These portrayals seemed to normalize such bullyish behavior among Blacks, as though it never occurred among and between white children. Although many of the teachers had been of the generation to experience school integration, this was not often recalled as a positive encounter, and usually their lives remained relatively segregated. They rarely reported that they went into Black or Latino communities or had a cross-racial friendship. Their parents often prevented such friendships from happening. Mary wrote about her early negative associations:

> I grew up in Boston. My sister and I went to a Catholic girls school but we lived near a public school, and when they integrated it, my parents no longer let us walk by the school on the way home. We had to go two blocks out of our way to get home because we were afraid we would be beat up by the Black kids. It never happened, but we were afraid, 'cause they would say things to us when we walked by

the school. Perhaps we were afraid for nothing. When they began moving near our neighborhood, our parents moved to the 'burbs.

Others reported that they were taught *not* to have cross-racial relationships by the the time they were preteens. Linda, an elementary teacher, related in her autobiography:

> It was during these years [ages five to ten] that my friends and I began telling racial jokes, although I didn't think I thought of them as racial, since I had friends of color at the time. It probably wasn't until a few years later that I realized these comments may hurt someone's feelings. It was also during these years that our neighborhood began going from mostly white people to mostly people of color. I began hearing my dad making racial comments and also my brother. Although I always felt uncomfortable about such comments, as I look back now, I realize the impact they had on me. I began to think of Black people as poor, bad, dirty, and lazy. Although I had several friends of color, they were different from "those other people." As more Black families moved into our neighborhood, I tried to make friends with them. However, they did not want to be friends with me. On several occasions, they tried to beat me up and were always teasing me. The comments they made to me always made mention of the fact that I was white. I soon became afraid of most Black people, and my family moved to another neighborhood—an all-white neighborhood.
>
> During the years that I was in junior high, my circle of friends changed, and I (for whatever reason) no longer had friends of color. It was also during this time that I began entering accelerated classes. I also knew which classes were in the lower track, and I began to realize that the majority of students in those classes were of color. I equated this with the idea that they didn't care about school and didn't try. Looking back now, I see that as junior high ended and I entered high school, my world as I knew it became more and more "white." When I came to college, I became more aware of more subtle forms of racism. At the university, there were a lot of complaints against fraternities about racial slurs. But when these incidents occurred, I saw nothing wrong with most of them until I heard others talking about it and it made me start to think. I think I have a hard time seeing racism because I have a hard time believing that people can be so cruel and insensitive.

Occasionally someone reported actively upholding segregation, such as Lena, a white elementary teacher who grew up in Mississippi. With much embarrassment, she told the class:

> I happen to remember segregation very well. Too well! In fact, you're lookin' at the one who kept the Black people out of the public library. [Hiding her face in her hands.] Do you know what my first job was? I was sixteen years old, and I was the one who had the job of making sure no Blacks got in that library. And I just did what those awful white folks told me to do. I didn't ask questions or say, "This is wrong." I just did it, like a damned fool. And I'm not proud of that, either!

Many teachers related early experiences of being exposed to overtly racist talk by a parent or other family member, such as hearing racial slurs at home, being admonished not to associate with Blacks, or as one teacher put it, "hearing people of color jokes just for fun—they would *never* have said it if a member of that group was around." These were not only childhood memories, however. Often someone in the class would talk about the problems they were having now in their own home, especially with a family member who had very racist views or used overtly racist language. While many reported hearing a family member use derogatory language or stereotypes toward Chinese or Native American people, the most common racial slurs were directed at Blacks. The word n—— was heard by many, sometimes from the very people they loved the most, such as a family member or relative, and it was applied not only to people, but to objects of all kinds, like black rocks ("n—— heads"), Brazil nuts ("n—— toes"), checker pieces, licorice candies ("n—— babies"), and church pagan dolls ("n—— baby dolls"), to name just a few of the more common examples.

Yet even though everyday racism formed such a common cultural backdrop, most of the white teachers said they never consciously thought about race and racism until they were well into their teens. Then the issue of race emerged when their parents forbade them to date Blacks or to bring Black friends into their homes. Many teachers reported that they had not personally met a Black person until they went to college. For white men, it was often a military experience that brought them into daily contact with people of color, where, as one high school teacher said, "We all got along just fine in the military. We were all the same. And we were all treated the same. Those were the rules, and in the military you don't argue with the rules. So we got along fine with the Black guys." I should note here that I often heard quite the opposite response from African Americans who had been in the military. More frequently, their interpretation of that encounter was, as one Black teacher related, "You ain't seen racism till you been in the military!"

Often a painful or embarrassing recollection was shared about a parent whose rhetoric was a model of equality and tolerance, but whose behavior was otherwise when it came to their own daughter or son marrying or even befriending "one." Such was the case with Sharon, who shared with the class: "I *never* heard my parents say anything bad about anyone, [they] never used the 'n' word, [but they] absolutely freaked out when I brought a Black guy from college home for Thanksgiving one year. It was awful. They told me to never ever do that again. And I never did."

Occasionally, a teacher revealed how growing up in a family where one or both parents were disabled gave her a taste of what it feels like to be "othered" and marginalized, or the object of someone else's curious or frightened gaze. But the status of being marginalized did not necessarily bring with it an added empathy when it came to race, as Betty, a middle school teacher, revealed. In her introduction to her background and early awareness about race matters, Betty told the class that as a child, she was the only sighted person in her family. She wrote in her journal:

> Both my mother and my father were born blind. People sometimes acted like we were strange, and I remember how that felt. I know how that feels. But I think the experience helped me to grow up thinking about what people have to go through. I was always very concerned about others, and so were my parents. They taught me to love everyone.

Yet despite the fact that her blind mother taught her much about love and empathy for others, especially those who had problems or disabilities, Betty told the group:

> The only kind of intolerance I saw from my mother was, I remember, she used to tell me [when I was in high school] that Blacks were bad and not to hang out with them. Even though she couldn't see them, she hated them just like other people did! I could never understand that. Now what really bothers me is that my younger sister is being told the same thing by my mother. She is telling her not to play with Black kids and not to bring them home. Whenever I go home, I am really trying to talk to my sister so she will not grow up prejudiced.

Others related growing up in an atmosphere of "liberalism," where their parents took in children of color as foster children or brought home a nonwhite business associate for dinner, only to later discover that their parents harbored real prejudices and fears if they thought that their daughter might get personally or intimately involved with "one." Others carefully avoided interactions with the Black community.

Nonracist or Antiracist Influences

Occasionally, a white teacher related what she described as an antiracist or a nonracist upbringing. Cindy, a hearing interpreter who was the only hearing child in a deaf family, was brought up in a racially integrated environment until she was seven, when the family moved to a small town. She recalled in her journal a story her mother told her about Cindy's early childhood:

> Although I have no recollection of this particular incident, my mother told me years ago of my first reaction when I saw a Black person for the first time. I was three years old. I went on a city bus with my mother, when I saw a Black man board the bus and I shouted, "Mom, Mom—look, that man is made of chocolate!" She calmly explained to me that he wasn't made of chocolate, but that people have many different colors of skin. She said nothing more than that. Today I think about that and think she handled my comment well and responded to it without scolding me or telling me to be quiet.

Cindy saw in her parents' daily activities and interactions that they respected people of color. African American friends came for dinner, and they went on picnics together and hung out at each other's houses. Having grown up in a deaf family, Cindy recalled that when she was a child, "I did not like hearing [white] people because I could feel their prejudice and superior attitude about deaf people." She said that she did not experience the same level of intolerance from African Americans. Of her high school years, she wrote:

> I became very good friends with people of color. Many times I was the only "white" person around. It never bothered me, and I always felt comfortable being in situations where I was the minority. I suppose that the fact that I grew up in a "deaf world" in a hearing society affected me in that I would feel comfortable wherever I go. In fact, sometimes I felt more safe and valuable around my Black friends. We accepted each other, and they are friends that I can really trust.

Despite Cindy's relatively "enlightened" consciousness and the fact that she was now married to an African American man with whom she had a son, there were some things that she said she had not really critically analyzed until she took my class, such as the racism inherent even in sign language. She reflected upon this in her journal:

> One influence I just thought of was language. My native language is American Sign Language, and it is extremely prejudiced. People of color are depicted through visual/physical features in sign language. For example: African in sign language is the letter "A" on the nose (signifying the physical feature of a broad nose). The sign for Jew is also the same sign for selfish or stingy. It's made by scrubbing your chin. (It also shows that all Jews have beards.) Chinese, Japanese, Korean, etc., are signs by the eyes to indicate the different slants of the eyes. Many of these signs are changing to be more culturally aware. I find it very interesting that even American Sign Language followed stereotypes and racial prejudice.

Of those untypical examples where a teacher reported hearing an "antiracist" attitude expressed by a family member, it was often a seed of contention in the family. Carol, a high school LD teacher, grew up in an Italian American family, where she recalls receiving very contradictory messages regarding race from her parents, as well as from from her peers, who taunted her about her "dark" skin. She wrote in her racial autobiography:

> I was born in Chicago, but grew up in a rural area. As a young child, I think I received two very different messages from my parents regarding Blacks and other people of color. My father would frequently make racist comments but would talk very fondly about a Black coworker and invite him over to our house. My mother never went along with my dad's racist comments and frequently got in arguments

with him about his comments. When my mother lived in Chicago, she had close friends who were African Americans. I remember her once showing me a picture of her bowling team, and it stuck out in my mind that there were black women on the team. When I started school at a Catholic elementary school, I remember being teased about being dark and having curly hair. Most all of the other kids had a very fair complexion and more money than we had. I felt like no one liked us or wanted us here at this school.

My mother worked at a factory when we were kids. I can remember her telling me how hot it was, how you could hardly breathe and could not stop working for any reason. I was mad at the people who ran the factory; they were hurting my mom and they were white. I knew they took advantage of the people who worked for them, especially the people my mom spoke of who came up from the South looking for work. Later, my mother worked hard to get a union into that china factory, and I recall how it was sort of secretive and fearful. What's important about the china factory is I saw my mother stand up and risk for her rights and the rights of those less able to protect themselves. Fairness and human dignity were important to her. This was in conflict with the racist comments my dad would make.

As I grew older and moved away from my family and the white environment I grew up in, I had to question my own racism. . . . When I think of my own race, I think of being Italian, not white. I think of my grandparents, who spoke Italian, and how I was told they came over here on "the boat." I think that I and my brothers looked dark and different from the kids we went to school with. I wonder how things would have been different if my parents had stayed in Chicago and let us grow up in the neighborhood around other Italians. My parents moved out of Chicago to give us something better. . . . I don't know what is better. When I was growing up, I didn't want to be Italian, I just wanted to fit in, to be white, real white.

I believe that I am "less of a racist" now because of my mother's views, the experiences I have had with people of different races and the feelings of being left out and "not as good as" when I was a child.

Yet Carol speculated, if she had she not been raised in such a WASP environment where she experienced being othered, whether she too would have become more racist:

I wonder if I had been brought up in a Chicago Italian neighborhood like my father, who, although he is very conscious of the negative Italian stereotypes, is still racist against Blacks, whether I would not have learned more quickly how to have racist attitudes against Blacks, like he did. My mother was the exception, and thank god for her influence.

Carol's and Cindy's early reflections on race and class were not typical of white teachers. The vast majority said that until taking my class, they had never thought about and had never been asked to reflect upon their early socializations and experiences from the perspective of race. They saw themselves as racially undefined or "normal." If they thought about race, it was about "them" but not about "us."

Most had never examined "whiteness" as a marker of privilege. If they did think about "whiteness," it was usually in the context of losing something because they were not people of color or believing that nonwhites were getting special privileges at their expense. Similar observations have been discussed by others (Tatum, 1992; Fine et al., 1997; Hurtado and Stewart, 1997). As Hurtado and Stewart (1997) note: "Whiteness becomes much more definable when the privilege it accords its owners is lost." For example, Fine and her colleagues (1997) document white working-class men's frustrations as they see their jobs "being taken over by people of color. It is in the loss of their way of life, which includes their job, that they begin to articulate what it means to be white" (p. 299).

The point of this examination and collaborative sharing of teachers' racial identities and experiences was not to indict white teachers as simply being racists, but rather to reveal how individual identities and experiences become racialized in the United States, and why this has remained so invisible to most whites. This invisible "whiteness of being" shapes white peoples' assumptions about "other" people as well as about themselves.

Most of the teachers related being fascinated with our discussions as they began to think about looking at themselves from the outside in and the inside out. However, while people appreciated these self-reflective autobiographical exercises, I was concerned that merely talking about our backgrounds without contextualizing them historically was something that people often voyeuristically "enjoy" while reinforcing the empty rhetoric of "celebrating diversity." But that is not the point of talking autobiographically. We also need to focus on the problem of the differential treatment that people have been subjected to and the *reasons* for racial and economic inequality. It is important that we examine the historical and structural context of how and when and why this "whiteness" was invented and naturalized. (I elaborate upon this in the following chapter.)

THE RACIAL EXPERIENCES OF TEACHERS OF COLOR

While approximately 16 percent of the white Lakeview teachers took my classes, nearly half of the Black teachers did so, as did a smaller number of other teachers of color. For teachers and other staff of color, their knowledge and experiences were quite different from those of their white colleagues. While most of the white teachers said that they had never had to think about themselves from a racial standpoint before, the teachers of color often reported that they could rarely *not* think of their racial positioning. Most wrote and spoke of having a highly developed awareness from their early years about the race privilege that whites have. However, in terms of recognizing the nature and causes of institutionalized racism, they did not necessarily come into my class with much further formal education or knowledge of the historical or structural aspects of racism.[4]

The Oppressive Presence of Whiteness in the Autobiography of Teachers of Color

Like their white counterparts, the teachers of color also had a range of experiences and backgrounds. For example, William described himself as the son of sharecroppers from Mississippi; Salina, the daughter of Mexican migrant farm workers; Emily, a child of the newly emerging "Black bourgeoisie," brought up in an upper-class white village in New England; and Sandra, an African American who had worked in the schools in Lakeview as a custodian before becoming a teacher. Maria, a "biracial" Mexican American whose father was white and mother was Mexican, lived until she was ten in a totally white, middle-class environment where there was no affirmation or acknowledgment of her Mexican identity. She considered herself white until her parents got divorced and she found herself suddenly poor and on welfare, shopping with food stamps instead of cash, perceived and treated no longer as white, but now often called a "wetback." Rosa, from Mexico, told the class that in Mexico, she had always considered herself a middle-class white, until moving to the States. After living in Lakeview for several years, she realized that she would never be considered white in the United States, and now, she told the class, "I would never want to be considered white again after what I have experienced here." Despite the diversity in their class backgrounds, the teachers of color often shared similar experiences by virtue of their membership in racially oppressed groups.

Early Loss of Innocence about Race

In distinct contrast to the white teachers, most teachers of color reported that their consciousness of race was often a negative experience that they had at an early age, usually before they were five years old. Many of their memories were traumatic, such as William, who recalled pouring a bottle of bleach into the bathtub when he was very young, to "whiten" himself, severely damaging his skin and causing his mother great heartache. Or Carolyn, who remembered how she felt when the teacher read *Little Black Sambo* aloud to her whole first-grade class and hearing the white kids on the playground taunt her, calling her "Sambo." For others, the experience was not quite as dramatic, such as Emily, who grew up in a working-class Black segregated neighborhood in Chicago in the late fifties. She wrote in her racial autobiography:

At the age of five, I discovered I was Black. My kindergarten teacher had us draw a self-portrait. I colored my picture pink. My cousins laughed and teased me. Probably my confusion about skin color was because I never saw people of my race represented in the media. Needless to say, after all of the teasing, I colored the people in my later pictures brown.

Emily attended college, where she was among a very small minority of Black students. She associated mainly with the Black students and joined a Black sorority. After graduating, she taught school in Chicago in the inner city for ten years.

Encountering "Liberal" Racism in Lakeview

Unlike most white teachers, who reported that they rarely thought about race or being white, for most of the teachers of color who took my classes, race was described as the most salient feature of their identity, especially after they moved to Lakeview, where, despite its liberal reputation, they were confronted with racism. As William told the class:

When I was growing up in Mississippi, I didn't have to think about being Black. We were all Black. The teacher, the dentist, the undertaker. We knew who we were, and we knew who you white folks were, too! We stayed away from you down there! [laughs] When I moved up here, there wasn't a single day these people weren't gonna remind me, let me know that I am Black and that they gave me a job here. And that I was one of the first Black teachers in Lakeview.

Coming to "liberal" Lakeview was often cited by many of the teachers of color as their introduction to a "new," more subtle kind of racism. In their journals and class discussions, they often focused on their more recent experiences in Lakeview. For example, Emily, an African American, mentioned above, left Chicago and moved with her husband to Lakeview, where she had been offered a teaching job. They looked forward to moving away from the big city to comfortable Lakeview, where they could begin to raise a family. But it was there that she found herself encountering racism on a very personal level, both as a teacher and a parent. Emily wrote in her journal:

In the liberal town of [Lakeview] at the age of thirty-two, I had my first experience with racial prejudice. I was a teacher at ——— Middle School, and I worked with a team of four female teachers who had worked together for many years. They gave me and a wonderful Jewish teacher a very hard time. I think we both felt but never voiced the thought to each other that racism was the underlying reason for the mistreatment. The Jewish teacher died of cancer at the age of thirty-two. I often wondered if the overwhelming stress we dealt with might have contributed to her getting cancer. Her death was devastating to me. I liked her a lot. I received a call about her death on my birthday.

In one of our class discussions and in her journal, she related the story of her son in kindergarten, who was accused of pushing another child. The teacher telephoned to tell her that her son had "attacked" another child. She wrote:

> My son is a very gentle, quiet child. I thought maybe he was just trying to get used to school because it was his first time in a school situation. Not only did the teacher call, but she wrote a long letter home explaining that this was inappropriate behavior in our schools, implying that this child must have a high tolerance for violence in his family. I showed the letter to the principal, and he agreed that it was inappropriate and spoke to the teacher.

As Emily related this story to the class, she found herself fighting tears until eventually she went into the bathroom to cry. Many of the white teachers also became emotional and, crying, followed Emily to the bathroom. Several of the class members admitted that they had seen fellow white teachers treating black parents as rudely as Emily had been treated. As I discussed in the previous chapter, many white teachers reported witnessing Black children being treated badly or talked about in derogatory ways by other white teachers. Most said they felt uncomfortable but did not intervene. Now these teachers were seeing the results of their own indifference or refusal to take a stand. They could not imagine how to intervene because they really did not have to. Furthermore, in a racist context, to problematize such matters, whites run the risk of giving up the "comfort" of their white privilege, or of becoming marginalized by the powers that be, when perceived as a "race traitor." For white people, challenging racism means challenging a status quo of which they may be immediate beneficiaries. Emily's story was a very common one for Black parents. There was no "privilege" that Emily could count on to protect herself. Her college degree and the fact of her being a fellow teacher did not warrant any protection from racism for her own children. They were still treated as "Black" children. Emily wrote in her journal that night:

> The women in our class felt overwhelmed with the knowledge they have now about how pervasive racism is in our society. I, too, become overwhelmed and depressed about this subject. What is especially scary is that I'm raising a son, and the media in [Lakeview] has perpetuated a very negative image of Black males. I will do my best to let him know that what others think should in no way define him. He also has a loving, caring father who is an excellent role model.

The case of Emily also illustrates one of the tensions in doing race-relations work. Asking people to relate their personal experiences, particularly those who have been victimized, is a sensitive and invasive issue, especially when you have to continue living with such experiences. It is one thing to talk about discrimination and prejudice when you have been an observer or scholar or bystander from the dominant group. Looking upon the situation from afar, for some people there may even be the cathartic cleansing of the confessional—that you got it out of your system or you lived through someone else's pain and experience and you are still okay. You may even believe you are a "better" person for it. Hearing someone else's pain or misfortune can have the effect of reassuring people how "lucky" their own circumstance really is. This distance from the problem is one of the privileges of the dominant group. One might analogize this to the difference between a woman testifying to a group of women about being raped or sexually abused, compared to relating the same experience in a context where she is the only woman in a group of men to whom she must prove the seriousness of the case.

While it is necessary to put the "stuff on the table" in order that it be faced and dealt with, it is also important to understand the effects of that "stuff" on our different lived realities. I recall a conversation I had with an acquaintance who was doing a race-awareness workshop with health professionals. She had consulted with me about doing an exercise on stereotypes in which the group would "brainstorm" all of the stereotypes about different ethnic groups, purportedly in an effort to challenge them. I told her that I did not think such an exercise could be effectively managed, especially when there was not enough time to negate or challenge the stereotypes, because I feared that such attempts could end up actually reinforcing them. But she decided to do the exercise anyway. Later, she told me that it was an extremely painful experience. She was able to participate and maintain her professional "scholarly objectivity" in the naming of the foolish or cruel stereotypes of all the ethnic groups, until they got to Jews. But as a Jewish woman, she found herself suddenly having a different set of reactions, many of them physiological as well as psychological:

> We were going along, you know, I had the group really involved in naming the stereotypes, and they were all coming up with these stupid, ridiculous stereotypes about Blacks, Latinos, Indians, etc. And when these people started identifying the stereotypes of Jews, and I was going along just jotting all the stuff on the board as fast as I could, before I knew it I found myself consumed with anger and fear. I was looking into their eyes and seeing the way they were seeing *me*! I heard things said about Jews that I never heard before. I knew this was just an exercise that I had asked them to do. And the fact that they really got into it really made me suspicious. I felt my blood pressure rise, my face got red. They were talking about *me*! My people! My history! My tongue became as dry as wood. I thought the top of my head would blow off. I didn't give a damn about putting up a professional front. When I looked at them, I imagined I was looking at Nazis and began to wonder what their parents did in the war . . . how many of them had maybe been offered protection here by the U.S. government after the war. When I got back to

my hotel room, I had the chills and went straight to bed. And I was thinking—why didn't I have the same reaction when we were naming the stereotypes of the others?

The experience of revealing one's pain to those who may have contributed to it was also related by Rosetta, an African American woman, who wrote:

> In most classes like this that I have taken, I have refused to share what really happens to us. I get tired of seeing those white women cry. Or you look at them and they have tears in their eyes, and you know they are just feeling guilty. The men are quiet. Then they go home and feel like they have done a good thing. It has been difficult for me to be in this class. I have found myself dealing with things that I haven't thought about for years. Things I suppressed. I appreciate the historical knowledge you give us each time because it helps for the white people in this class to see how things are. It helps me too. That African American people are not just "oversensitive" individuals. I also appreciate that white people have to look at how their own racism has distorted them.

Racism obviously mattered for the daily quality of life on and off the job for the teachers of color in Lakeview, and they frequently brought these realities into our class discussions. William and Henry, both African Americans, related incidents that had "ruined the weekend," when they would go out fishing only to be followed out onto the lake by a warden or state official, who would demand to see their fishing license or boat owner's license. On one occasion, William was over an hour late to my class. He had been stopped and detained by the police on his way to class, with his two sons in the car, under suspicion for a robbery that had just been committed. Other African American teachers related stories of being followed while shopping, or being stopped for questioning by the police.

I also shared examples of my own children's mistreatment. In a recent incident, my son's (African American) friend, on his way to visit my son, was detained and handcuffed in front of my house, while the street was blockaded with seven police cars from midnight till 4:00 A.M.—in a raging July thunderstorm. My son's friend was being held under "suspicion" of a robbery. The police would not allow me to give them any information, nor would they give me any information. The following day, when I did my own investigation and interviewed the store owner, I found that the suspect in no way resembled my son's friend except that he was supposedly a Black male. For the white teachers, hearing about these realities from people they were beginning to know personally made a profound impact, as most said they had never believed that such things could happen in Lakeview. Robert, a white middle school teacher, wrote in his journal:

One thing that has impacted on me this week has been the revelations about police brutality. I have read about it before, and the Rodney King case was important, but I never thought of it as a problem here in Lakeview. I have heard some of the African American boys in [the middle school] talk about police, but I thought they were exaggerating. Hearing William's stories and some of the other things that the African American teachers in this class have shared this week has made a deep impression on me. Before, I guess I considered this a problem only in the abstract, as something that happened in L.A. I will definitely listen to the African American kids' experiences with more credibility after taking this class.

Being Marginalized as a Professional and as a Parent

Teachers of color reported daily racial struggles in and out of the classroom. Brenda, an African American woman who worked as an educational assistant, related several stories of her encounters not only as a worker in the schools, but also as a Black woman, as a parent, and as a member of the teacher's union. She took my class, she said, because she felt that she had undergone so much stress and harassment that she hoped the class would help her find a way to share and deal with the stress. Brenda was also going to the university part-time to earn a B.A. degree in psychology. She had not always worked as an educational assistant. At one time, she had worked in the physical therapy department at a high school. She was forced to leave that job, however. "My supervisor constantly spied on me and checked up on *me specifically*," she explained. She felt that the supervising teacher resented her because she was Black. She told me: "I knew the school principal would do nothing about my complaints. The stress was so bad, I didn't feel it was even worth the money. Other Black teachers left, too, because of the harassment and stress. One of them is even driving out of town every day, just to work—he works in a suburban school."

Brenda then found a position at a middle school as an educational assistant, with a significant cut in pay, from $11.67 to $6.50 per hour. Even after four years as an educational assistant, she was getting $7.00 per hour. But here again she ran into problems that were race related. Not just problems with her personally, but with the way Black students were being treated. She related the story of how her protests about the poor treatment of Black students led to her being treated rudely and being marginalized by the assistant principal:

One day, I walked into the assistant principal's office, and there was a group of Black boys waiting in there to see him. I left and went back to my room, and a little while later these boys came into my room. They were very upset, and they told me that when Mr. B [the assistant principal] came into the office, he frisked them and made them empty their pockets, and told them he suspected that they had been smoking (like drugs). He found nothing and he let them go. They came straight to my room. I told them to call their parents immediately and let them know what had just happened. They did. Well, Mr. B was *really* mad at me and told me I had no right to get involved, that it was none of my business. I told him that anytime I saw any kid being mistreated, it *was* my business. After that he constantly bothered me and harassed me. He could not tolerate an outspoken Black woman. Eventually I had to leave because I saw it was not going to get better. And it was making me sick. I had serious health problems from the stress.

Aside from working conditions where harassment or marginalization was a daily part of the scene, either for the Black students or for herself, the union did little to defend her as an educational assistant. Brenda felt that because many of the educational assistants were people of color, the union had done little to address their interests and only used them as a "bargaining chip" when it came time for union negotiations. The role that African American educational assistants played was often central to the survival of African American children in a school. They often found themselves the only people in the school who had the cultural knowledge, empathy or understanding to work with the African American children, and they were heavily relied upon by white teachers, many of whom feared or avoided interacting with the Black students or their parents. At the middle schools and high schools, the assistants were sometimes crucial to preventing racial fights. Yet their positions, while often central, were extremely tenuous, with no job protection or benefits. They not only were peacekeepers, but often did the instructional work of teachers as well, engaging in tutoring and teaching the African American students or making home visits to their parents when white teachers refused to go into the Black community.

When Brenda came to take my class again the following year, she told me that her struggle continued, although she had a somewhat better job paywise. Now she worked with attendance records in a middle school, making $11.67 per hour. "Can you believe that?" Brenda said. "If you work with paper, you get almost twice as much as when you are working with ED [educationally disabled] kids! Shows you who's important to them, doesn't it?"

As a mother, Brenda still fought other battles constantly on behalf of her own children. She frequently had to go to school to intervene on behalf of her daughter, who she felt was being discriminated against both because she was Black and because she, like her mother, articulates her rights. She related another recent incident:

My daughter and her friend were cleaning out their lockers at the end of the school year, and the janitor comes over to them and acts like they are sneaking into the school, and he asks them what right they have to be there. Lots of other white kids were doing the same thing, and he didn't question any of them. My daughter replied in kind, asking him what right he has to be there, since he was being so rude to them. Then the janitor calls the police on my daughter and her friend, who also happened to be the daughter of the only Black person on the school board. Well, the police take them into the office, and my daughter calls me, and I say, "Don't move, I am on my way. I am leaving right this minute." When I get there, do you know what? The police would not even speak to or ask questions of either myself or the other girl's father [who the police did not know is a school-board member]. The principal told me, "Oh, he's [the janitor's] just like that."

Maybe the kids shouldn't have talked back to the janitor, but then again, maybe the janitor shouldn't have singled them out among all of the other kids cleaning out their lockers as not belonging to their school. But they were the only Black kids. And the only ones he questioned and suspected as not belonging there. Meanwhile, as we were standing there talking to the cops, all kinds of kids came into the school, and no one asked *them* anything, even though the school was closed by now. I asked him [the janitor], "Why don't you ask *those* kids what they are doing in the school?" And to think that they actually bring in the police because a Black kid *says something*! That's what they want more police for!

Brenda emphasized that even in the process of trying to be an involved active parent, she felt invisible:

It's everywhere. Like when I went to the principal's office to deal with another problem, when they tried to give my daughter an F in Spanish, even though she was doing well in Spanish—even her tutor who I had come over twice a week from the university said she really didn't even need a tutor 'cause she was doing so well—and while I was waiting for the principal, the secretary would not even offer me a chair. Can you believe that? I had to stand up for about half an hour waiting to see the principal; she would not even have eye contact with me! Then I get into the meeting and they have called in all these people—a union rep, a lawyer, and some other authorities to have this meeting with me, and all I've brought in with me is another Black teacher who is also a parent rep. Now *I* am an educated Black woman, and I know how to stick up for myself, but can you imagine how it feels, how hard it is for a poor woman who may be shy to come into such a place to defend her interests? And then they say, well, Black parents won't come to the meetings! Well, how do they treat them when they do come?!

Whether one was working as an educational assistant or a highly placed administrator, the problem of being ignored or mistreated applied. One African American Ph.D. in the district said that despite having been in the district a number of years, he always felt like an outsider. Another wrote of being recognized or consulted only when he was needed to serve on a committee to ensure racial representation:

Reflecting over the last five years, I realize now that any level of bending over backwards to work with a number of my fellow educators is perceived by them as just not being enough. Whatever I may or may not do will not change the color of my skin. How I am seen and received by many white educators will not be enough to bridge the gap of color prejudice. Skin color, I have come to see, is the defining ingredient which determines the degree of fully working together in an environment that is predominantly white. Under circumstances where a person of color occupies a position of responsibility, and some white workers cannot avoid him, or perhaps need him to accomplish a task, then the person of color at that time (and only at that time) becomes a tangible person. Once the need to work together on some chore has passed, the person of color is once again relegated to invisible status. Even the pleasantry of a morning greeting is lost.

The majority of African Americans have probably always known about being invisible in a predominantly white workplace. It is a relatively new experience for me. I had not known what alienation was like and it caught me by surprise. . . . My white colleagues will never embrace me fully, because they don't need to. Being white in America is enough. And the advantages in that reality are enough, or so it seems.

Because most of the teachers of color who took my class were African American, the above examples concerned their experiences; however, other teachers of color were also similarly affected. For example, in several cases, Latina teachers talked about their experiences of marginalization and frequently reported feeling ignored or patronized by other teachers and disrespected by the white students in ways that they thought were racially prejudiced. For the teachers of color, even among those who had been able to achieve a higher socioeconomic status, they often found that social class did not buy them out of the experience of racial discrimination. Clearly, the struggle against racism was one that could not be deferred by teachers of color.

EXAMINING HOW WHITE SUPREMACY OBJECTIFIES THE "OTHER" AND NORMALIZES "WHITENESS"

As I said earlier, most of the white teachers were not aware of their own whiteness and had never had to think about what it means to be white. The fact that teachers of color and white teachers grew up and in many respects remained in two separate worlds was well known to most of the teachers of color but was rarely discussed by the white teachers, who often expressed surprise to hear about these different realities. Not only was it important that they become aware of this difference in treatment and opportunity, but they also needed to unravel how we got to such a place. Why did these two separate and unequal worlds not disturb the consciousness of white society?

We needed to examine the broader historical context to understand how white supremacy has affected our culture. This white chauvinism was usually not overt, nor was it recognizable to whites. In a place like "liberal" Lakeview, people prided themselves on their "multicultural" tolerance and "celebration of diversity," yet many people were more tolerant of diversity if it was "exotic," such as the comments made by the teacher who said that her colleagues enjoyed having the students of color of international professors from Japan or India, but thought that having "too many" Black kids in their school was a problem.

In my classes, I wanted teachers to become aware of this romanticization or exotification, which leads not to real inclusion, but to objectification or paternalism toward people of color. It also tends to pit groups against each other when one is considered a more "model" minority. And we needed to challenge the persistent myths that people of color can simply assimilate if they choose to or just try harder, or that they necessarily want to assimilate into the dominant white culture. We needed to consider how we have all been socialized to believe in the "rightness of whiteness."

To open up discussion about some of the ways in which people of color are objectified and marginalized, I showed a video, "It Does Happen Here" (1989), produced by a group of students of color at the University of Wisconsin. In it, they were having a conversation among themselves focusing on "what I never want to hear again." The students talked about the day-to-day stereotypes, experiences, and incidents that they had all endured on the basis of being students of color in a mainly white environment, where all of the authority figures were white and where people of color were, by and large, left out of the curriculum and the general culture of the school. They also discussed how it feels to be exotified or objectified by whites and described seemingly complimentary but stereotypical remarks that white people had said to them, such as "Asian women are so cute and quiet" or that it must be really "neat" to be a Native American. Some of the African American students discussed their discomfort when professors focused on Black students in the classroom (presumably as "representatives" of their race) when issues of race were discussed, to ask them what they thought, when their opinions were never solicited at other times.

Some of the white teachers felt defensive when they heard people of color in the video express their discomfort with this objectification. For example, when a Chicano man from Texas said he was tired of white people always asking him, "What country are you from?"—assuming that because his skin was not white, he was not from the United States (even though his people were, in fact, the original inhabitants of this country)—it surprised some white teachers that anyone could be insulted by such an "innocent" question. Or when a Native American woman said, "What I never want to hear again when I tell people my ethnic heritage is 'That's neat!' It's not neat!" This remark often offended some whites, who felt she had an "attitude problem" and should not be so critical of others' "goodwill." Laura, a fourth-grade teacher, told the class:

> I can hear *myself* saying that. I can't understand why anyone would be offended by that. I would mean that kind of a statement as a compliment. I never mean anything bad. I *do* think it's great to be an Indian. We white people don't have anything like that. They have contributed so much, and they should be proud. I can't see why she would be so defensive! Besides, when you first meet a person, isn't that just a normal kind of a thing to say? To try to show them that you appreciate knowing them? That woman seemed too bitter. I think she has a chip on her shoulder.

This comment opened up much discussion about the assumptions made by many whites that lead to the objectification of those who are not members of the dominant group. Most whites go through life without understanding the "critical gaze" that white society imposes on others, nor do they see the gaze of the "other" upon the dominant white culture. When they do see it, they may take offense and "blame the victim" for being "oversensitive." This is part of the social construction of "whiteness"—the normative and unconscious formation of the white self. Many whites had never heard a conversation among people of color critiquing whites' behavior. They had never heard an analysis from people of color about the stress of everyday covert racism. Many had a difficult time understanding why certain behaviors were perceived as racially insensitive or paternalistic by a person of color, when it was not necessarily the conscious intent of the white person to do or say anything racist. Yet the question was, Why did it feel racist for those on the receiving end?

While many of the white teachers were wrestling with the notions of paternalism or the exotifying or mystifying of people of color, the subjects of this analysis did not have the same difficulty understanding this subtle racial objectification. "Is it *neat* to be forced to live on a reservation where there are no jobs, poor land, poverty, and where your culture and language have been robbed from you?" asked an African American woman in one of my classes during one such discussion. But for many of the white teachers, it would require more time and discussion before they could begin to see from a different perspective. After all, they never meant anything bad, so why should people of color be so defensive? "Why can't we all just get along?" said Christine, a first-grade teacher who, like many of her peers, had no historical background to understand the issue. As she reflected in her journal:

> I'm trying to sort out my reactions/ideas to the Native American woman who didn't want to hear that her heritage was "neat." I'm wondering if part of my inclination to say something along those lines isn't largely due to the way we are raised

to be female. Female children are raised in this culture to be "nice." Comments like the one suggested are culturally acceptable "nice" responses. We feel the need to verbally respond and come up with reinforced positive inane "neat" responses.

While Christine made a valid point about the superficial ways that people are taught to communicate in our culture, she dehistoricized the problem and minimized the Native American woman's experience. This sort of behavior was felt as racist or paternalistic, not only because of its superficiality, but also because of the underlying assumptions and stereotypes that contributed to the exotification of the Indigenous Peoples and the objectification of people of color. Those on the receiving end of the critical gaze were being treated as a curiosity, tolerable and even enjoyable as long as they stay in their place. This level of racial insensitivity, which involves cultural appropriation, was a topic that many whites struggled with.

Challenging "Color Blindness"

Another issue we discussed in the class was the issue of group pride in a hostile environment. As the students of color in the video were reflecting on what gave them pride and strength, many expressed that they were proud to be people of color because their people had survived despite the oppression they had to endure. But for some of the white teachers, this idea of group pride was seen as threatening. Jane, a white high school teacher, expressed the view that group identity was actually hindering her students' ability to be a part of the school. She told the class that at a recent school event, the Black students had refused to sing the National Anthem: "When the whole school stood up to sing, they just sat there. It was horrible. This Black pride can be dangerous and divisive. Besides, if people of color are told they should feel proud on the basis of race, shouldn't white people also be proud to be white? Is it okay for a Black person to be racist?"

As it happened, Jane was also a leader of the school's "multicultural" committee. In further discussion, it became clear that she felt that the multicultural committee had already done its part for the Black students in her school, and they were now so unappreciative and unpatriotic. She frequently talked about how she was color-blind but feared that some of the Black students were racist. While she put up pictures of Martin Luther King in her school, she preferred the sanitized version of this great leader. She could not recognize that these students were becoming critical thinkers in the tradition of Martin Luther King and other activists, who were taking a principled stand similar to Muhammad Ali's refusal to fight in Vietnam or the stance of the Black athletes at the Olympic games in Mexico when they showed the Black Power salute. This teacher's fear of the Black students' increasing political consciousness, or what Freire refers to as "conscientization," was an example of the missionary approach of "helping"—but on one's own terms. "When I see people, I see people, not color. When these students refuse to participate, it just makes it difficult for everyone," Jane complained to the class. Jane's perspective was typical of many who consider themselves nonprejudiced or "color-blind." As Thompson (1999) notes:

> Color-blind definitions of racism usually assume that racism does not have a material or institutional form; instead, racism is considered to be a matter of personal attitudes or perceptions. Thus, under the terms of colorblind racism, Chicana/os or African Americans who call a policy racist may themselves be identified as racist because they have used race as a perceptual filter. Using colorblind frameworks, it is as easy to call people of color racist as it is to call whites racist. If anything, it may be easier to call people of color racist, since people of color are more likely than whites to challenge the terms of colorblindness.

Many teachers had initial responses similar to Jane's and viewed the Black students' pride as racist. But as we put the issue into historical context, many came to understand that pride in a people's survival under adversity did not equate with racist supremacy. Maureen, a white elementary teacher, had an empathy for, perhaps even an identification with, the oppressed as she tried to help her colleagues see beyond their fears. She said her perspective was informed by her early experiences being ostracized as a poor child and in later life being harassed as a lesbian. She told the class and later wrote in her journal:

> When I watched the video of students who were asked, "What makes you proud to be a person of color?" my first reaction to their answers was dismay. I thought, "Uh-oh, they didn't understand the question" because they kept answering, "I'm proud to be a Latina woman" or "I'm proud to be Black." . . . Maybe it was a matter of editing; maybe that wasn't the original question. Two of the three people who finally tried to answer the question said they were proud that they were survivors. My dismay hung on. "Is that the best you guys could do?" Given the course of history, and the state of the world today, well, yeah, I suppose it was a pretty appropriate answer. Which made me feel even more dismal—for a minute. Then I realized that it was recognition of determination, perseverance, courage, and a collective refusal to give up.

Making a comparison with her recent experience playing a soccer game as the underdog, she said that though they lost the game, they were so outnumbered that they felt they had won:

> There is a trivial connection in my own recent experience that was pretty vivid for me. Our soccer team played a much, much better team yesterday; we had seven

players, they had twenty; I still hurt all over. . . . We weren't expected to win; the ref suggested we forfeit before the game even started; we were told the game would be called when the other team scored five goals. . . . Halfway through the first half, they had only scored two, and we realized we could hang on for a while, maybe. . . . We did; at half-time we were thrilled and proud that they hadn't beaten us yet. . . . The bad news is, they eventually kicked our butts, but the good news is, pride in perseverance (even without prevailing) has meaning for me now. And if a little soccer game, at the cost of mere bruises, stiff muscles, and a little bit of superficial blood, could make me feel proud, IMAGINE the pride associated with generation after generation of perseverance in the face of socially sanctioned malice (including slavery, rape, murder, personal and economic oppression, overt, covert, and institutionalized racism, often perpetrated by those sworn to protect and defend). . . . What I'm trying to say is, I'm impressed. I'd be proud, too.

CONFRONTING WHITENESS

Such discussions revealed the more subtle, covert aspects and consequences of white chauvinism, which affects not only the victims, but the perpetrators as well. It is important for teachers to interrogate the idea of "whiteness" and the presumption of the "rightness of whiteness" in a culture in which being not white means being the "other." We must question the effects of such distortions on those who—perhaps unconsciously—perpetuate them. In order to understand why "others" seem so "sensitive," we need to see how "whiteness" has become normalized, invisible, and undefined for whites and oppressive for people of color.

This is where a historical perspective was germane to the discussion. Most people had no knowledge of the concept of white supremacy. If they had heard the term before, it was usually in reference to racist groups like the Ku Klux Klan. How did this happen that whites are so unconscious of their own "whiteness"? What is "whiteness"? There is no white language or country. The construction of the white American self is part of the legacy of capitalism and slavery. As Europeans who had traditionally defined themselves by national, linguistic, or ethnic identities became "Americans," they were forced to shed their ethnic attachments and redefine themselves and their identities in opposition to, in not being, "them." Their identity depended on who they were *not*. This complex process is tied to the roots of slavery and colonialism and the racist ideologies that justified the extreme brutality of domination. The process whereby people, by virtue of their membership in an oppressed group, become marginalized may be difficult for those in the dominant group to comprehend, since they have been socialized to *not* see. "Whiteness" is unexamined in mainstream American culture. A common reaction from whites toward people of the racially oppressed group is that "they" are too defensive, and therefore it's "their problem because I did not mean to insult them."

EXAMINING HOW THE "OTHER" GETS CONSTRUCTED IN THE WHITE IMAGINATION

How the "other" gets constructed in the white imagination is something most white people are unconscious of. For the "other" is often simply a part of the "natural" landscape. In my classes, we addressed the obvious as well as the more subtle ways in which people of color have been made either invisible or hyper-visible, resulting in persistent stereotypes. These stereotypes are transmitted in elusive and often entertaining or even nurturing ways. Most white people have been introduced to these stereotypes at an early age in an "enjoyable" manner, through such nursery rhymes as "Ten Little Indians" or "Eenie Meenie Minie Mo," or through television cartoons, which are particularly powerful mechanisms for imprinting stereotyped images into our culture.

But there are also "respectable" routes through which the "other" becomes formed in the white imagination often found in the school culture. During one visit to a school, I saw a very offensive bulletin board display in a teacher's middle school classroom where I happened to be giving an in-service. The board was a collage of images from *National Geographic* magazine, of bare-breasted African women, or mostly unclothed Indigenous Australians or "natives" from anywhere, but all nonwhite and partially "undressed" or otherwise showing a lack of "modesty," which placed them "closer to nature." Most of the images also involved some sort of ritual practice, and interspersed along with the images of the people on this large wall mural were pictures of orangutans, baboons, and other monkeys. The visual impact was clearly one of primitivizing the people and equating them with the monkeys. When I pointed out to the teacher that this portrayal was reinforcing stereotypes, he became defensive. He felt it was very "multicultural" and said he chose those images particularly because "the *National Geographic* is a very highly regarded magazine, you know." The fact that it came from a well-regarded cultural journal legitimized it for this teacher.

This reminded me that I had observed many teachers using images from the *National Geographic* magazine to "multiculturalize" their classrooms. In their book *Reading National Geographic*, Collins and Lutz (1993) examined the role of the *National Geographic* in perpetuating exotified notions of people of color and, in particular, conflating Black women and sexuality. To problematize this issue, I gave teachers an excerpt from this book that discussed how particular images have contributed to the process of decontextualizing people from their culture, so that one knows only these "primitive" images about another country and absolutely nothing about the peoples, cultures, beliefs, economy, causes of poverty, or the relationship of all of this to colonialism and imperialism. Many of the older teachers reported that, in fact, the *National Geographic* magazine was their first introduction to people of color in any magazine.

Janice, a middle school teacher, wrote in her journal:

> The article on the *National Geographic* showing racism in the magazine . . . made me think about the perspectives of minorities in a white culture. It was interesting to have it put to words about how black cultures were portrayed. I can remember as a young girl looking at the pictures in those magazines and seeing the African cultures in what may have been traditional form. Often the women were scantily clothed. Looking back, I probably thought that it was like this that most black people lived. I also remember that the pictures were very colorful and eye catching.

Another elementary teacher wrote in her journal: "As I read the article about the *Geographic*, it made me think about the legitimacy with which my siblings and I were allowed to sit and stare at Black women's breasts in the comfort of our own living room. I cannot imagine us being able to look at pictures of white women's exposed breasts without getting in trouble."

Of course, the idea is not to blame *National Geographic* magazine for the racist stereotypes of the day, but to illustrate how the academy and respectable cultural creations may have influenced our racial consciousness. It also makes one realize just how rare and precious are positive everyday images of people of color in all forms of media. As one teacher wrote: "After reading the article on the *Geographic*, I had to ask myself why I had ever used it in the first place. It occurs to me that it is not easy to find images of people of color. It seems like all there is *Ebony* and the Janet Jackson type of glamour. Why are there no other places I can find positive images of regular people?"

CONCLUSIONS: FROM SELF-REFLECTION TO TAKING ACTION

Typically, white teachers reported that they had never examined the issue of the construction of a "white" identity or investigated how often, unconsciously, they had been taught to construct a particular image of the "other." The fact that the vast majority of white teachers reported that they had never before critically examined these issues illuminates the serious concerns that many people of color have about the effects of this ignorance on the assessments that white teachers often make about children of color in their schools. This was not lost on the teachers who took my class. In their discussions and evaluations, many people expressed that they had been shortchanged in their preparation to become teachers. Many were troubled that they had never been exposed to a discussion of these issues, such as this typical example from a white middle school teacher, who wrote in her journal:

> Taking this class has made me very angry at the education I have received. Or should I say have not received. I feel that I—*we*—have been cheated education-ally. How could I have received my certification without even talking about these issues before? This class has shown me that it is not only our students of color who are suffering. As a white person, a parent and a teacher, I can see now, after tak-ing this class, how we have all suffered from what you have called "historical amnesia."

While many of the white teachers reported that racist attitudes were ex-pressed in their families, they very rarely admitted to now holding such beliefs. Yet despite their stated concerns about the inequalities they were witnessing in their schools, which had brought many of them to take my class, frequently their interpretations of the causes of these social problems revealed an uncon-scious acceptance of racial stereotypes. The purpose of my class was to interrupt this discourse and introduce people to other ways of seeing from a critical, anti-racist perspective.

These discussions with teachers about the impact of racism and race con-sciousness or unconsciousness in their lives helped illustrate how people of color and white people in the United States often have different material realities and experiences, and hence distinctly different "racial frames of reference" (Figueroa, 1984). In discussing the concept of racial frames of reference, Figueroa argues that there are two main aspects to the construction of reality: one being that people act on the basis of their definition of a given situation—or, "if men [*sic*] define social situations as real, they are real in their consequences"—and the sec-ond being that the situation that one may find oneself in is not solely the result of one's own making, but is the result of the interaction with and among others. The assumptions, stereotypes, and myths that serve to define situations are what Figueroa terms the racial frames of reference, which provide

> definitions and boundaries along which power is distributed, and in terms of which relations and social interactions are patterned in terms of an inherent and basically inexplicit interpretive process. The racial frame of reference is rooted essentially at the level of the subsidiary awareness on the taken-for-granted, at the level of hidden structure or even of the social "deep structure." (p. 20)

I wanted teachers to recognize that the unconscious racism embedded in this deep structure contributes to the distortions and ordering of the world through such racial lenses or frames of reference. Antiracist pedagogy seeks to unveil this by constructing a critical framework for recognizing and counteracting our racist constructions of reality as they affect individuals as well as institutions.

Understanding our individual narratives is central to comprehending our collective narratives. Reflecting on the personal is important whenever we are talking about working for social change and building democratic movements in a racially divided society. We must ask ourselves, Who are we, and what is our relationship to the problem and to those most affected by the problem? To guard against the kind of unconscious arrogance or missionary zeal that may come with the territory, we must become self-reflective and conscious of our own historical positioning and our taken-for-granted assumptions.

The purpose of such self-reflection is to help us take more informed action. But in order for such reflections to be more than an egoistic or guilt-ridden exploration of the "self," as frequently happens with many approaches to "race-awareness training" or "whiteness" studies, we must place these contemplations in the historical and socioeconomic contexts in which our dramas unfold. We must face our history. We should not forget that we had slavery in the United States for a longer period than we have *not* had slavery. To not face that peculiar distinction of our past, to not examine how it has affected the social geography of race, means to not face ourselves. In the process of this unmasking, inevitably for some there may be grief or resentment, sorrow and guilt, anger or despair (Tatum, 1992). These difficult emotions can be intensified by our talking about it. How can we harvest these bitter seeds and plant them as seeds of resistance and renewal? How can we see ourselves and others as agents of change rather than only as victims of the past? In the final chapter, I discuss some of the ways in which we struggled with facing history *in* ourselves as we began to investigate the roots of racism from a structural and historical perspective.

CHAPTER EIGHT

From the Individual to the Collective Narrative

facing history __in__ ourselves

WHILE WE NEED TO BE AWARE OF OUR INDIVIDUAL positioning in society and the meaning of difference, neither should individual difference be mystified. The most different thing about us is the way we are treated as members of particular groups; hence, it is imperative that we examine power relations and the genesis of this differential treatment in the larger structural and historical context. This history is the backdrop for understanding how our racial constructions of reality affect the culture of our society and our schools.

The social construction of race and of "whiteness" come out of a particular historical and cultural context. In order to understand the genesis of the problem of racism, we must understand its relationship to the particular society in which we find ourselves—namely, a capitalist society formed out of slavery, characterized by increasing extremes of wealth and poverty and increasing corporate control. One cannot understand the failure to integrate our schools or to truly integrate people of color into American society in general without understanding American slavery and its aftermath.

EXAMINING THE SOCIAL GEOGRAPHY OF RACE: CENTRAL THEMES

I examined several themes with teachers in order to help map out what Frankenberg (1993) refers to as the social geography of race. These included the historic and symbolic significance of the Columbus "discovery" in framing our sense of our past; the relationships among slavery, colonialism, capitalism, and white supremacy, and how they have affected our views of the world; white privilege and its invisibility (to whites); the role of the corporate media and popular culture in creating and maintaining racist stereotypes; and an examination of the larger picture of globalism or globalization—namely, corporate transnational capitalism.

FACING HISTORY

Depending upon who is writing (or reading) it, history can be dangerous. Or it can be liberating. Much is at stake in preserving and disseminating one's story or record. Indeed, as historian Gerda Lerner (1979), one of the founders of women's history, shows, the record for over half the human race (females) was not even allowed to be written until very recently. Similarly, the history and voices of working-class people and people of color in general have also been silenced until relatively recently (Zinn, 1980). While we have made great strides in opening up fields like the histories of racial minority groups, labor history, or women's history, such histories have not been resurrected without a struggle. An example of this struggle concerns the conspiracy to keep African American history "in its place" to keep it separate from the "real" American history, to preserve it as a sanitized version that does not challenge the status quo. Those who seek to uncover the truth often encounter great resistance. A classic illustration of this is the treatment of historian Herbert Aptheker (Kailin, 1998), whose seminal work, *American Negro Slave Revolts* (1943), was a major challenge to the "magnolia school" of American history, which promoted the image of slavery as a benign, patriarchal institution. One of the major historians of this school, Walter Lynwood Fleming (1905), described the plantation as "a chapel of ease," characterizing slavery as fit for both the enslaved Africans and the slave masters. Indeed, until the second half of the twentieth century, the "official" story according to the prominent mainstream scholars of the day, such as Dunning (1897) and Phillips (1929), was that there was actually little resistance to slavery, since slaves were inherently "childlike" and "docile," accepting their condition.

These views were promulgated not only by the official "scholars" of the day, but also by the artists and writers who imprinted the "romantic" image of slavery into the popular imagination. Unfortunately, this view cannot be simply relegated to the past, for this myth of slavery as a benign institution persists, as Loewen (1995) points out, exemplified in the continuing popularity of the "classic" book and film *Gone with the Wind*. Loewen writes:

The superstructure of racism has long outlived the social structure of slavery that generated it. The following passage from Margaret Mitchell's *Gone with the Wind*, written in the 1930's shows racism alive and well in that decade. The narrator is interpreting reconstruction: "The former field hands found themselves suddenly elevated to the seats of the mighty. There they conducted themselves as creatures of small intelligence might naturally be expected to do. Like monkeys or small children turned loose among treasured objects whose value is beyond their comprehension, they ran wild—either from perverse pleasure in destruction or simply because of their ignorance." White supremacy permeates Mitchell's best-seller. (p. 144)

As Loewen notes, "although this book was written in the 1930s, it remains very popular, and in 1988, when the American Library Association asked library patrons to name the best book in the library, *Gone with the Wind* won an actual majority against all other books ever published" (p. 144). However, there has been a scholarship of resistance that countered such racist historiography and culture[1] but these views have, until recently, been ignored or suppressed in academia. Historian Herbert Aptheker (1943) was among the few who challenged the "official" story and documented the continual resistance to slavery by the African people held in bondage. Because Aptheker's work revealed the centrality of this struggle against racism throughout our history (and also because he had a Marxist perspective), he was until recently, marginalized and discredited by the mainstream of the American historical profession (Kailin, 1998). This was regardless of the enormous contributions of his works, which included many that are now considered pivotal, such as *American Negro Slave Revolts* (1943); *The Negro in the Civil War* (1938), or *A Documentary History of the Negro People in the United States* (1951–74); and scores of other works. Not only was Aptheker's work marginalized or ignored until relatively recently, but he was effectively banned from teaching at any American university from 1936 to the late 1970s.[2] This is serious not simply because of the injustice against an individual scholar whose work went against the grain, but also because of the damage to the general public, whose right to know our history and to challenge knowledge constructions has been affected. It is about an affront to the national polity, as an entire nation continues to be puzzled and confused about its own past and its identity and history. How different would the future be if we knew the truth about the past.

How can we face our history if we do not know it? Without a fair and open opportunity to study various historical and philosophical perspectives, we cannot have the background in order to subject knowledge to a critical interpretation. We are robbed of our right to know. Our view of history is part of our identity, part of our knowing who we are or can become. As James Baldwin

(1963/1988) wrote in the 1960s in his essay, "A Talk to Teachers," "If I am not what I have been told I am, then it means that *you're not what you thought you were either!*" Or, as Bob Marley sang it, "If you know your history then you would know where you coming from. Then you wouldn't have to ask me who the heck do I think I am."[3] If we are to employ an antiracist or a critical multicultural perspective, it is imperative that we examine our history so we can better understand individual racial attitudes and the manifestations of institutional racism in education. In my classes with teachers, I introduce alternative perspectives to the dominant discourse of American history that have often been suppressed, ignored, or marginalized in academia, calling upon the ideas of such scholars as Carter G. Woodson, Charles Wesley, W. E. B. Du Bois, and Herbert Aptheker,[4] as well as the more recent works of progressive scholars and activists such as Howard Zinn (1999), Manning Marable (1983, 1995), Jack Weatherford (1988), David Roediger (1991), and Michael Parenti (1995), among others. I also used some of the more recent popularly written and accessible publications from the publisher Rethinking Schools.[5]

OPENING PANDORA'S BOX OF HISTORY: COUNTERING/ENCOUNTERING COLUMBUS

When Pandora opened the box that contained all of society's ills, *she* was blamed for releasing the evils of human life. What happens when one becomes the bearer of "bad news"? Countering the lies of history is often profoundly disturbing. It is certainly disconcerting to discover that we have all been fed a diet of lies. Where does one begin to unravel the frazzled chain of causality? From a structuralist perspective, it is important to consider the centrality of chattel slavery and of colonialism to the development of the Americas. The myth of the Columbus "discovery" continues to be an important part of the elementary social-studies curriculum.

We examined the legacy of the Columbus encounter on the development of Native American and African American history, beginning our historical exploration of Cristobel Colon (Columbus) and colonization by listening to a taped lecture by scholar Manning Marable,[6] in which he discussed the impact of Columbus on African American history. Marable traced the legacy of Columbus as a symbolic figure who played a major role in the development of colonialism and slavery. He discussed such issues as the genocide against the Indigenous Peoples, the trans-Atlantic slave trade, and its connections to the development of mercantile capitalism. Marable also discussed the eventual development of the concept of "whiteness" and white supremacist ideologies used to justify the inhumanity of chattel slavery. He related this to the continuing and persistent problems of contemporary racism and increasing class divisions, concluding that we must build toward a multicultural democracy if we are to have a more just society. In the latter part of the lecture, Marable emphasized the importance of coalition building for this democratic vision and the necessity of including people of color, poor and working-class whites, gays and lesbians, and the disabled—if we are to have a "multicultural democracy."

As we began to explore the contradictions between the traditional teachings and such interpretations as Marable's, which have been excluded from the dominant discourse, it was apparent that most of the teachers were hearing a radically different version of the story for the first time. Most of the teachers said that though they celebrated Columbus Day, they had not given much thought to the meaning of the Columbus story. Many felt a profound sorrow and guilt upon hearing about Columbus's culpability. Others were angry that they had been cheated out of this knowledge. But some were angry at the message and the messenger. The following responses exemplify the range of teachers' responses when we examined this "unconventional" historical perspective. Janet, a high school teacher, told the class after listening to the lecture:

> I am very, very moved by this tape. I do not know much about this history, so much of it was very new to me. But I have watched things on TV and try to get information when I can because I think it's very interesting. I remember watching "Roots" and being impressed by that. But there was something that happened when I listened to this tape just now that I think only now I am just beginning to understand. I mean how it *really* was. When he talked about the way those African people were crammed into those slave ships, I really began to *see* it. For the first time, I think I really began to see them as people, as human beings, and how inhuman, how horrible it was. It is incredible that any people survived that. It just struck me how strong people can really be. I had really not thought of it like that before.

Not everyone was receptive to a critical reinterpretation of history, however. Some of the whites, albeit a minority, but a vocal one, felt that an attack on white supremacy was tantamount to an attack on white people. They took the position of what I came to call "the white man under siege." For example, Marable's call for coalition building and inclusion of all marginalized groups, which included gays and lesbians, evoked not only hostilities from some toward Native Americans, but also other deep-seated prejudices against gay people. Mike, a high school teacher, saw this perspective not only as an assault upon his history, but upon his very "manhood." He very angrily told the class:

> Well I'm gonna tell you what I think about this guy Marable. This whole thing is a crock of shit, if you'll excuse my language. Ya know, I am so sick of hearing about

those *poor little Indians* and all the terrible things the nasty white man did to them. They weren't sweet little angels, you know; what they were doing to each other was much worse than anything Columbus ever did! They were cannibals! Cannibals! Do you even know what Ojibwa means? It means cook until puckered! That's what it means! Because they were referring to how long they had to cook a guy before they ate him! And for another thing, let me tell you something, about what this Marable guy who's talking about all this gay stuff for democracy—you should see what these homosexual guys are doing to each other; do you know how they do it? Do you want them in your school teaching these kids?

Such a reaction is so outrageous that it is almost laughable, until one considers that someone with this mentality is teaching our students. According to Pfaff (1993), in actuality, Ojibwe means "roast until puckered" in reference to the distinctive style of puckered moccasins worn by the Ojibwe people. Mike's selective distortion of language and understanding recalls the persistent images from the old movies and cartoons of the forties and fifties (when he was growing up) that depicted "cannibal natives" around huge vats. Evidently he had never been forced to challenge these stereotypes. For him, both the Indians and the gays were the feared, dangerous "other." In another class, an African American woman was similarly disturbed by the reference to justice for gay people. "I really liked what he had to say until he started talking about the gays, and I just stopped listening after that," she told the class. These expressions of intolerance highlight the need for antiracism educators to be prepared to articulate not only the problems of racism, but also related issues of stereotyping and discrimination that affect multiple groups. While there is a real centrality to the race problem in America, ultimately, as Audre Lorde argues, there can be no "hierarchy of oppressions." This highlights the importance of Marable's call for linking these oppressions and the necessity for building coalitions among oppressed groups.

Another high school teacher, upon hearing such a perspective on the impact of Columbus, took the position that this was history with a "bad attitude" and complained to the class that his even having to listen to the tape was like having experienced a "drive-by shooting." Obviously, facing our history is not without tremendous resistance from some people. While such reactions were not typical, neither were they an aberration, and there were sometimes teachers in my classes who expressed such views, who felt threatened and did not hide the stereotypes ("drive-by shootings") lurking in their heads. I should note that such expressions of anger were heard much more frequently when the participants were all white people. Such racial comments were rarely expressed out loud if my class had any teachers of color.

Aside from this overt resistance from a few of the teachers to the larger political message, by and large people tried to process (rather than react to) this information, which was a disjunction with what they had been taught. Sometimes people expressed skepticism that they were being asked to judge seventeenth-century people by twentieth-century standards. This problem of "presentism" is indeed a valid point to consider, but it is also important to point out that even at the time of slavery, there were those who vigorously opposed slavery and genocide, not the least of whom were the African peoples and the Indigenous Peoples themselves. And although they were in the minority, there were also antiracist whites—many of whom remain unnamed and whom we shall probably never know because their stories were discredited or stifled, or because of the danger of holding such a position against the dominant ruling class (Aptheker, 1992; Loewen, 1995). Because of the way in which history has traditionally been taught, many people see history as "dead" or boring and irrelevant to their lives. It is compartmentalized as a separate discipline to be left to the historians. Hence, it is important to weave together the historical background with the personal and the institutional dimensions of racism.

Taking the Class Home

Many teachers related that they were taking our class discussions home to family or friends as they were beginning to rethink history. Sandy, a high school special education teacher, wrote in her journal after hearing the Marable tape:

Tonight I had a lesson in "displaced anger," and I'm trying to figure out if that concept plays any role in racism and prejudice. Some people argue that a people's history that happened long ago has no place in today's society. I guess that they would argue that the anger of today's people of color has no basis in the history of today. Their anger is misplaced and should be discounted. I guess there was a time—no, I know there was a time—when I did not understand what slavery had to do with anything today. But I chose to try to understand the argument rather than discount it. I did find much truth and cannot discount how different it has been for minority cultures that have come to the U.S. for acceptance and understanding or seeking refuge, as well as those who were brought here against their will. To be judged or to be stereotyped is now unacceptable to me.

Later, Sandy wrote that the class was influencing her personal relationships:

I had a discussion tonight with my fiancé, and he asked me about our class. I told him that I talked about him and mentioned that he was a racist. I spoke to him about vocabulary that he uses and things that he says. He says he's just prejudiced against people who expect handouts and cry about all of the injustices of long ago. I said, I know you're prejudiced. You judge people by the color of their skin. That's being racist. I suggested that he start reading some of the materials that I'm bringing home from this class. . . . I think I'm making a dent at home, and it really feels good. The best thing I can do is keep making him aware of his attitudes and set an example.

Susan, an elementary teacher who was in one of my weeklong summer classes, arrived exhausted to the class the morning after we listened to the Marable lecture. As we were discussing how we were thinking about the class thus far, Susan told the class:

> I just wanted to let you know that if I seem like a zombie this morning, it's because I called my best friend up in California last night at 1:00 A.M. because I couldn't stop thinking about the Marable tape. I tried to sleep and I began looking at the *Rethinking Columbus* book you gave us. It was such an unbelievably new view of Columbus. At my school, they put a lot of effort into Columbus Day. I think I can really understand certain issues more clearly now, especially about all of these stereotypes about Native Americans. I haven't talked to my friend in California for over a year, and we haven't had this kind of a talk about *ideas* in years, since we were in college! I read her stuff out of the book and told her about this class for three hours! Finally at 4:00 A.M., I told her, "I have to get up in two hours. I am exhausted!" I went to sleep thinking about what I could do for Columbus Day this year. I can't believe I am even thinking about a class. Usually I'm sitting in a class like this writing grocery lists and thinking about what I have to get done when I get home, where I have to stop off or shop, or, you know, whatever. I'm getting married in two months, and until last night, all I've been thinking about is the wedding. And now here I am thinking about Columbus and this class and who I am!

Whatever the reaction, one thing that was clear was that this examination of the origins of racism and this interpretation of history were usually "new" to the participants. Even many of those who had relatively more exposure to "alternative" viewpoints, such as Maureen, who had gone to a university on the West Coast, where she had taken classes in women's studies from a "radical" feminist professor, related that she had never critically examined race before. She wrote in her journal:

> I think the Manning Marable tape had the most impact for me, because I had never heard the connection before. It's the biggest new thing I've learned. In this class was the first time it occurred to me that the fact that Christopher Columbus enslaved people of a different color had a significant advantage for the Europeans, because it was such a visual marker of who ruled and who was ruled. So it wasn't until we were listening to Manning Marable that it dawned on me that Columbus played a big part in African slavery. Of course, he said it straight out; this isn't any major revolutionary breakthrough on my part. Once the Europeans (Spanish, in particular) had begun to exhaust their "supply" of [Indians], they logically pursued the trend to Africa. . . . The Columbus connection was a bombshell for me.

Resistance to Change

With all of the recent debates about "multicultural education," or the "canon wars," some assume that there have actually been substantive revisions or discussions of these issues. Yet I found, as have others doing similar work (King and Ladson-Billings, 1988; King, 1991; Loewen, 1995), that the majority of teachers who took my classes had rarely engaged with such arguments that challenged the dominant discourse. This was not simply a question of generational differences in knowing for young teachers, but it was a reality whether we were talking about younger preservice teachers or experienced teachers of the sixties generation who were in my classes.

Recent publications like *Rethinking Schools* or *Rethinking Columbus* were still unknown by the majority of the teachers.[7] This was not surprising, because the Lakeview school district did little to make such alternatives available. I found that it was not only the problem of a lack of resources, but sometimes a stifling of alternative resources. For example, when I examined the social studies collection of one of the high schools, I discovered that they were still using biased and distorted history texts. These were not old discards, but were newer texts. At that same school, I also came across a book that offered an alternative to the racist views or distortions of American history. Although this book had been distributed to all school libraries by the state's department of public instruction, most teachers told me they had never heard of it. I learned why when I accidentally discovered a dust-covered pile of the books stashed away in a corner of the social-studies resources room. They had never been opened! Change was resisted in this school by the all-white, nearly all-male (one female) social-studies staff. As an African American teacher in that school told me, when she had tried to get Black history added to the curriculum, they would allow it only if included in a course on "family studies." In addition to the suppressing or ignoring of the historical record, there is also the continuing problem of the domination of history teaching by white males. Lakeview had few female social-studies teachers and only one teacher of color who taught social studies in the district. With this sabotaging of history, it was not surprising to discover that the teaching and learning of history has changed little in our schools.

THE MAPPING OF WHITE SUPREMACY: COLONIALISM AND RACIST REPRESENTATIONS OF THE WORLD

Another illustration of how white supremacy affects the curriculum can be found in the mapping of the world. We examined the issue of our geographical representations of space and place in something as seemingly "objective" and "scientific" as maps, which often reinforce white supremacist representations of the world. We juxtaposed the Peters Projection map, produced by Arno Peters in 1967, with the still frequently used traditional Mercator Projection map, produced four hundred years ago, which distorts the world to the advantage of the European colonial powers. While many correctly argued that it is not unusual for a country to place itself center stage in its own map making, upon a critical examination of these maps, people came to discover that in the Mercator map, it just *happens* that all of the countries of people of color are portrayed much smaller than they actually are, relative to the European countries, which are portrayed much larger than they actually are.

I was not advocating an uncritical acceptance of the Peters map as *the* corrective, however, for that map as well is not without controversy. Although it is a more realistic representation of the comparative sizes of countries or continents, it still places Europe at the top of the world. Of course, top and bottom are purely relative, since it depends upon the point in the cosmos from which one is looking at the planet Earth. And there are always problems of representation with any effort to represent a global configuration on a flat surface. The point of this discussion was to get people to critically examine our taken-for-granted assumptions and biases. I wanted people to see that there could be other perspectives and interpretations of the curricula that we often use, and to become more conscious of how Eurocentrism and racist assumptions may continue to distort our picture of the world. I also wanted participants to see that all representations are controversial and potentially dangerous if taken uncritically at face value.

With regard to geographical representations we also examined our knowledge base of Africa, a continent actually larger than China, India, Europe, the United States of America, Argentina, and New Zealand *combined*. In addition to the size of Africa, which covers 22 percent of the world's land area and is the second largest landmass after Asia, we discussed the centrality of the location and the importance historically of the continent, not only in relation to the development of the Americas, but also because of its strategic position such that it has long been encountered by both the East and the West (Mazrui, 1986). Africa as a major cultural center of the world and, as anthropologists argue, the birthplace of humankind has never received the kind of attention in our educational system that Europe or even a single country like Germany or France received.

After our discussion about the maps, a middle school teacher told the class that, in fact, she was aware of a box of the Peters Projection maps that had been sitting for the last two years in one of the resource rooms in her school. They had been ordered by someone who was no longer on staff, and no one knew what they were for. She told the class that until we had examined the maps in my class: "I just figured they were maps and I already had a map in my room, but I didn't realize that they were showing a different perspective and the significance of that. I am going to make sure that everyone knows about this when I get back to school!"

Many teachers reported or wrote in their journals that they had never thought about this issue of representation before and were going to buy the Peters map and display it in juxtaposition with the more traditional map. Juanita, an African American teacher, wrote: "The big eye-opener was the presentation of the Peters map. I had never seen that map, and I find it incredible that a 'progressive' district like Lakeview is perpetuating racist inaccuracies."

This discussion helped people understand the significance of colonialism and the Eurocentric bias that has distorted our conceptions of knowledge and culture. It is not only the tendency to centralize one's perspective from where one stands or what one is familiar with, which many feel is only "human nature," after all. But it is also the appreciation of the relationships between knowledge and power. The dominant discourse has the power to create and preserve unscientific misrepresentations or distortions that perpetuate white supremacy.

These often unrecognized misrepresentations distort our knowledge not only about those who are marginalized, but also about whites' views of themselves and their historical roots. As Diop (1974), Bernal (1987), and others have shown, what we have come to regard as the classical Greek roots of our Western civilization were actually Afro-Asiatic as well. This process of mythifying the West and "whitening" Egypt began during the period of chattel slavery (Lumpkin, 1988). It continued as the rise of imperialism affected the writing of history so as to naturalize the "rightness of whiteness." Such perceptions are often introduced to children at an early age. Lumpkin (1988) found in her study of children's books that Egypt has often been portrayed as not really being a part of Africa, and it is often ignored as having contributed to the foundations of our Western civilization. Many pictorial illustrations suggest that the Egyptians were really Nordic-looking, blond-haired, blue-eyed Europeans. Through our discussions of these issues, I wanted people to appreciate that knowledge is neither neutral nor objective, and that there are class interests and power relations behind how knowledge gets framed and taught.

It is important to problematize the issue of human agency in constructing histories and therefore in deconstructing and reconstructing them. While it is not our fault that we have been taught distorted and biased views regarding race, class, and gender, it is our fault if we knowingly perpetuate these biases. Teachers need to know that there are alternative perspectives and resources available. We need to think about the connections between the historical lies, upon which the unspoken or unrecognized notions of white supremacy and our "manifest destiny" are based, and the lies of our times, those underlying assumptions we have today about the "at-risk" children in our schools.

With our discussions about history, some teachers expressed a new understanding of the sentiments they were hearing from some of the African American students when they were asking for "Afrocentric" teaching, as the following
participants reflected in their journals:

> After taking this class, I think now that I can see that there was actually some truth
> to it when some African American students charged our school with being racist.
> I want to get a copy of the map and use it as an example at our staff meeting. That
> is one of the examples that is really objective. (white middle school teacher)

> Often I (and my fellow teachers) have suspected Black students of playing the race
> card when they complain about the curriculum or charge our school or a teacher
> with being "racist." Many teachers automatically assume that they are just trying
> to get out of doing the work. I have also felt that way, and sometimes I think it is
> actually true. I am no longer so sure, however, that they always are using race as
> an excuse. One of the greatest lessons I have learned in this class from our discus-
> sions about the maps, the history, and becoming conscious of our own assump-
> tions, as well as our discussion in class today about the "race card," is that the
> Black students may be more aware of how white people have actually always been
> using the race card. By that I mean that they have always defined the world
> according to themselves. The Blacks can see us better than we can see ourselves.
> (white high school teacher)

In addition to being exposed to this historical background, I found that having teachers (both white teachers and teachers of color) first become conscious
of the racist constructions of reality in our personal lives helped them to understand the lack of objectivity in the standard curriculum. It is counterproductive
just to have workshops that introduce new materials to, or rather *at*, teachers. It
is probably even a waste of money to purchase new antiracist or multicultural
materials if the consciousness of those who are to use them is unexamined. One
cannot presume that teachers can have a commitment to antiracist education
without first giving them the opportunity to become informed in order to transform their perspectives.

A STRUCTURAL PERSPECTIVE: TALKING ABOUT CLASS, CAPITALISM, AND GLOBALIZATION

While we began our historical examination with Columbus, colonialism, and
slavery, it was important that we also relate this to the more recent developments
of global corporate capitalism. Such terms as "capitalism," "imperialism," or
"class" are rarely used in American society and indeed seem almost subversive.
Parenti (1998) observes that those who use such language are often dismissed as

"conspiracy theorists." The word "capitalism" is usually robbed of its intrinsic meaning, and the notion of the primacy of profit—before people—is not scrutinized. "Imperialism" is something we think of as in "the British empire," but one rarely hears the phrase "American empire." Yet the reality is that the American empire maintains the largest military in human history, with three hundred military bases around the world, and spends one-third of the world's military funds (Parenti, 1995). In just eight hours, the Pentagon spends more than the supplemental food program for Women, Infants and Children (WIC) spends in one year (Zepezauer and Naiman, 1996). As Parenti (1995) notes, imperialist development and the globalization of corporate capitalism leads to maldevelopment serving the wealthy, with the construction of luxury hotels instead of housing for the poor (who may actually be displaced in the building of those hotels), cash export crops for agribusiness instead of food for local markets, highways that are built to go from the mines to the ports instead of to serve the people living in the backcountry. The working conditions in the plants are also abominable. Nike, for example, has closed every plant in the United States, and in their Indonesian plants, workers earn 15 cents per hour working ten-hour days. Yet one may still pay a hundred dollars for a pair of Nike shoes in the United States (Parenti, 1995).

Since the fall of the socialist world and the now uncontested dominance of capitalism, we are in a period of even more intense globalization of capital, or what is referred to as "globalization." Karliner (1997) describes the impact of this globalization:

> Transnational corporations exert increasing influence over domestic and foreign policies of governments. At the same time, transnational corporations are moving to circumvent national governments. The borders and regulatory agencies of most governments are caving in to the New World Order of globalization, allowing corporations to assume an ever more stateless quality, leaving them less and less accountable to any government anywhere. These corporations, together with their host governments, are reorganizing world economic structures—and thus the balance of political power—through a series of intergovernmental trade and investment accords. These treaties serve as the frameworks within which globalization is evolving—allowing international corporate investment and trade to flourish across the Earth. They include: The Uruguay Round of the General Agreement on Tariffs and Trade (GATT), The World Trade Organization, which was created to enforce the GATT's rules, The proposed Multilateral Agreement on Investment, The North American Free Trade Agreement (NAFTA), The European Union (EU). These international trade and investment agreements allow corporations to circumvent the power and authority of national governments and local communities, thus endangering workers' rights, the environment and democratic political processes. (p. 53)

As industries leave the United States and relocate to places where labor costs are cheaper and where workers have few protections, racist ideology often resurfaces to obscure the causes of these developments. Many people are led to believe that "those people" have taken their jobs from them. This is why it is important to relate the important ideological role that racism has played historically in maintaining the hegemony of the ruling class. Racism is incredibly profitable and has been the source of maintaining the super exploitation of labor and super profits off the backs of peoples of color from throughout the world, as well as from white workers who are "extra exploited" in competition with the "super exploited" (Perlo and Welty, 1984). Ultimately, the capitalist class is no more patriotic to whites or to their own nation than they are to people of color, particularly considering that U.S. capitalism produces eight times more abroad than it does in the United States. The costs of empire are always borne by the working people both at home and abroad.

To cite current examples, when companies pull out of the United States to do business elsewhere because costs are cheaper (such as the example of General Motors in the documentary "Roger and Me"), this does not mean that the working classes reap those profits or get cheaper goods. Even where goods are indeed cheaper (such as the comparatively inexpensive prices for some consumer goods in the United States compared to many other countries), the economic and social destabilization that occurs when companies pull out of communities in favor of opening up "cost-effective" plants abroad is very costly to those who live in those abandoned communities—white people as well as people of color. The result of the globalization of capital or speculative money being moved anywhere it can find higher profit has tended to plantationize, rather than to develop, other economies and has resulted in the collapse of the economies of Russia, much of Asia, and now many countries in South America (Kagarlitsky, 1999).

Talking about global capitalism or globalization may seem too esoteric or not directly relevant to a group of schoolteachers. Yet it is very relevant to the material conditions of life for children in our schools, as well as for the working conditions of teachers. As public services including education become increasingly privatized, we see intensified pressures on school systems to "produce results." Less money for public education means the increased stress of larger class sizes for teachers (and for students), increasing pressures to "teach to the test" rather than to the needs of the children and numerous other challenges when there are not enough resources. For the children, there are also new pressures as a result of the new "efficient" economy. What happens to the child whose mother or father has just been "downsized" out of a job? How might that impact on the child in the classroom? Because of the fallout from the deindustrialization of America that has occurred rapidly since the 1980s, people are often confused about the causes of increased unemployment, job competition, and homelessness. Since our educational system and the media do not encourage us to examine the "big picture," people may focus instead upon the immediately apprehended reality without understanding the chain of causality, leading them to blame the victim. This is often expressed in fear of (Black) crime in the streets; hatred of government, which is seen as protecting the rights of (Black or brown) "welfare cheaters," or foreigners (people of color) taking over jobs at the expense of hard-working whites. Discussions of a structural perspective are certainly more immediate, as teachers, like others, are also affected by increasing privatization of so many of the functions of our economy and culture—such as public education, criminal justice, social welfare, transportation, and media—in the name of efficiency or to increase profits.

Such discussions are hardly esoteric, for teachers' work is profoundly affected as they increasingly find themselves expected to respond to such problems as hunger, homelessness, or anger and alienation that more of their students are bringing into their classrooms. Yet, as many of them told me, they had rarely analyzed these problems from a class or structural perspective. Some admitted that they found themselves frustrated, blaming the children with problems rather than the system that was creating problems for the children.

The new sanitized catchwords of the day, such as "contracting out," "outsourcing," "downsizing," or "total quality improvement," obscure the realities of meaner working conditions or the elimination of jobs, whether in the Lakeview schools or any other industry or occupation. In our discussions, we examined how this is operationalized locally, where plants are closing and where workers are now competing for jobs that may soon be contracted out to near-slave prison labor. This necessitates also talking about the increasing prisonization of society, or what Angela Davis (1998) refers to as the "prison industrial complex." Of course, we cannot talk about this "new" phenomenon of prisonization without also talking about institutionalized racism and profit and power. What does it mean when a young Black man is in prison for a nonviolent crime and is now working in a creamery for 17 cents per hour? Since the late 1990s, I have found less resistance to such discussions that offer a class analysis than I might have found ten years ago. Perhaps this is because many of the teachers in my classes knew or were related to people who had worked in those now closed-down factories—people who once embodied the "American Dream" once considered the "aristocracy of labor" in auto or other heavy industries. Barbara, a white middle school teacher, reflected in her journal after a very lengthy discussion we had about privatization:

> I have been thinking about our discussions yesterday about the traditions of community or collectivism that we have all had sometime in our past but which have been taken from us. I am thinking about how the dominant individualism and privatization are necessary parts of capitalism and imperialism.

As I was driving home tonight, I was listening to NPR [National Public Radio]. I couldn't believe what I was hearing. They were talking about legislation that would privatize certain roads so that people would have to pay higher tolls for public roads. There was a segment about the governor wanting to use prison labor for businesses. And I thought about what you told us about the company which makes library tables and the tables we were sitting at in our class, using low-paid prison labor to make office furniture. I have to tell you that I was skeptical when you began talking about how you thought prison labor would increasingly be used in our country. But after hearing that on the radio, I am no longer skeptical. This class has made me notice and listen differently. I am not sure if I would have paid attention to the radio in the same way before.

Similarly, Christine reflected in her journal:

Today I was struck by the power of profit or the profit motive. It is greed. It didn't seem as blatant until today that so much or all of the situation is due to profit motivation. But take away capitalism, and then we need to restructure everything. . . . As I drove home, I was thinking that we—I—live on way more than my share of the earth's land.

Some were less open to critiquing the system and maintained a "bootstrap" ideology, considering those who complained to be whiners. Jean told the class about her mother's struggles as a widow raising five children alone without help while working several minimum-wage jobs:

My mother never had it easy, a woman alone, raising five kids. But I never heard her whine about it. We didn't take welfare, and all of us kids made it. The newspapers are full of jobs. Sometimes you have to take things you don't want because you have to. Things may be getting worse, but I see nothing wrong with working at McDonald's. Some of these people just want the State to take care of them like children.

Jean's sentiments underscore the need to examine race in the context of a class system. What sort of society tells a widowed mother of five children that she must work several jobs just to survive? Interestingly, Jean was less vocal about the lack of support for her mother than she was about the possibility that "others" might receive some sort of affirmative support. But why should we believe that we can't spread justice around? I knew that just because many of the white people in my classes were willing to talk about the injustices of class inequality, this did not necessarily mean that they would have more empathy about racial inequities. And if history tells us anything, it is often at those moments in which there is scarcity, economic competition, and destabilization that racist ideologies and scapegoating become more prominent. This is why is instructive to look at the objective measures of how institutionalized racism impacts on people of color. In this instance, one can compare the statistics for whites and people of color on factors such as infant mortality; environmental racism; economic distributions of wealth and income; unemployment figures; rates of imprisonment and sentencing rates (including comparative death penalty sentences by race); apartheid in housing and employment; health care, bank loans, and home mortgage lending practices; and myriad other areas in which people of color fall significantly behind whites. In this sense, whites enjoy a relative privilege over people of color—a white privilege.

EXAMINING WHITE PRIVILEGE

In order to critically interrogate our experiences and assumptions, it is also imperative to examine the relative privilege that whiteness brings in the United States. The personal gains and achievements that whites often attribute to hard work and entitlement may also be influenced by skin color privilege. One of the more popular discussions of this is Peggy McIntosh's 1989 article, "White Privilege: Unpacking the Invisible Knapsack," in which she examines the relative privilege that even poor whites "enjoy," relating it to the relative privilege that men have over women, though men too may be oppressed. In the article, McIntosh lists some of the conditions that attach more privilege to skin color than to class, religion, ethnicity, gender, or other factors. Some of these skin-color privileges that whites can usually depend on but people of color cannot are listed by McIntosh as follows:

> I can turn on the television or open the front page of the paper and see people of my race widely represented; When I am told about our national heritage or about "civilization," I am shown that people of my color made it what it is; I can be sure that my children will be given curricular materials that testify to the existence of their race; I can swear or dress in second-hand clothes, or not answer letters, without having people attribute these choices to the bad morals, the poverty or the illiteracy of my race; I can be pretty sure that if I ask to talk to "the person in charge," I will be facing a person of my race; I can take a job with an affirmative action employer without having co-workers on the job suspect that I got it because of race; I am never asked to speak for all the people of my racial group; I can do well in a challenging situation without being called a credit to my race; If I should need to move, I can be pretty sure of renting or purchasing housing in an area which I can afford and in which I would want to live; I can be pretty sure that my neighbors in such a location will be neutral or pleasant to me; Whether I use checks, credit cards, or cash, I can count on my skin color not to work against the appearance of financial reliability. (p. 23)

After reading the "White Privilege" article, Maureen, an elementary teacher, related the issue of white privilege to her own feelings of dispossession, having grown up poor, to what she imagined people of color must experience:

> I really identified with the article by Peggy McIntosh about white privilege. One point she made really provoked a lot of thought for me. "I can be pretty sure that if I ask to talk to the 'person in charge,' I will be facing a person of my race." Yeah, I can. For me, that's a big deal, because of class issues. When I grew up, we sold a portion of our food stamps so that we could buy soap and we never, ever, absolutely never asked to talk to the "person in charge." I remember once at a restaurant, a waitress took my plate away before I was half-finished. My mom consoled me by giving me half of what she had left. We never returned faulty merchandise, and if something didn't fit when we got it home, well, that was a shame. I am only now learning to complain if service or goods are not acceptable, and I am consistently shocked to see that complaining gets results, and without fail, every time I find myself talking to the person in charge, I break out in icky, prickly sweat, my lips stick in weird places on my dry teeth, and I shake uncontrollably (and hope it's all invisible).
>
> So in my own prejudiced way, I am relieved if I find myself talking to someone who's not of my race, thinking that maybe this person hasn't always been an "in charge" kind of person, and maybe they'll sympathize with my discomfort. It's not that I talk any differently to them, I'm just more optimistic. I recognize that it's still a racist assumption. Guess it needs work, too.
>
> Anyway, where I was headed was that a white person can not only be pretty sure the manager will be of the same race, but absolutely positive that [he or she] will be of equal racial status with the manager. I don't know for sure what I'd be like if I'd grown up African-American, but I do know that if I woke up African American tomorrow, I would never ever ever ask to see "the person in charge"— nothing would ever be worth it.

Many whites are unaware or may not believe that people of color suffer from being harassed, excluded, marginalized, or discriminated against in so many daily aspects of life. Small daily affronts to people of color are rarely realized or reflected upon by white people, and those who complain are often dismissed as oversensitive whiners. When a Black teacher in the class talked about how she had problems cashing checks at the same store where her white colleague had never been asked for an ID, or when Black teachers described their experiences being stopped by police, most of the white teachers said they were unaware that such things happened in Lakeview. White privilege is usually invisible to those who have it.

We examined other ways in which the "rightness of whiteness" gets ingrained in the way certain consumer goods are named and categorized. For example, many women's pantyhose manufacturers still label their light-colored pantyhose "nude," despite the fact that all people do not have the same nude skin color, or that "flesh"-colored Band-Aids refer only to a particular color of "flesh." Even something as benign as "angel hair" spaghetti sends a powerful message about who is perceived as the sweet little angel—a blond-haired, blue-eyed representation. What would people think if they went to the grocery store and saw "Jew Pies" or "Polish Pies" in the ice cream section, where one can still find Eskimo Pies. We must consider how it would feel if we replaced the names of any oppressed ethnic group for the Native American logos and mascots that abound not only among white-owned sports teams, but also as logos for apartment complexes, names of automobiles, clothing manufacturers, and such.

While it is important for people to be conscious of the hidden meanings embedded in these "tribal" symbols, I am also concerned that we critically interrogate the very notion of privilege in the first place. In a democratic society, why should it be a "privilege" to be able to rent an apartment or to see one's peers represented in the workforce or in the media?

Reading McIntosh's "White Privilege" sometimes elicited a response that troubled me. Some people had a reaction of relief, as expressed by one white teacher: "Well, it sure made me feel like even though I think *I* may have problems, at least I am grateful that I am not a person of color." White privilege is a complicated notion, because for some it may be interpreted as an assumption that there are not enough democratic freedoms to be extended to all. Or even worse, it may make whites feel grateful for their whiteness. While the article is powerful for making white people become conscious of what people of color often endure in the daily quality of life, I am concerned that it could have the unintended effect of making people feel desperate to protect those "privileges" that they have, rather than seeing them as universal human rights that must be extended to all. By and large, however, the article was received as a revelation by most of the white teachers and, on the other hand, as an affirmation by teachers of color, who had long complained about the issues mentioned.

Kendra, an African American who worked as a teacher's aide in a high school, wrote in her journal: "I had never seen the list of things that white people have that we get used to not having. It is important that they read this so they will not see us as paranoid when we talk about the insults we have to put up with."

But another Black teacher was disturbed that her white colleagues seemed more receptive to the message when it came from a white person (McIntosh) than they were when it came from their Black colleagues. She told the class: "I've been telling my colleagues this for years! Why is it when some white lady tells them this, suddenly they all sit up and listen? When we tell them, they put us on the spot to prove it."

"Whiteness" as a social identity is invisible to whites, and the social and eco-

nomic benefits that have accrued to whites over the course of our history must
be understood in the context of white supremacy. While the issue of white privilege is essential for members of the dominant group to be aware of, at the same
time I am concerned with the simplistic way in which this notion is sometimes
understood. To reiterate a point made earlier by Marable (1995), we must go
"beyond a racialized description of how whites, as a monolithic category, benefit materially, psychologically, and politically from institutionalized racism to a
position which seeks allies to transform the political economy of capitalism
across the boundaries of race, gender and class" (p. 121). In order for whites to
be motivated to become allies, however, they must first understand the political
economy of racism. Many whites may not necessarily want to be allies if they do
not first have the opportunity to reflect upon how this relative white privilege
has been used to confuse, divide and prevent us from uniting against a common
oppressor. For even if whites have a relative privilege, in the long run whites also
stand to lose. If today they can take away rights or opportunities from people of
color, tomorrow they can more easily do the same to whites.

DEVELOPING MEDIA LITERACY

One of the reasons why whites have a difficult time believing that people of
color must contend with these daily racial insults is because of their lack of real
experience with people of color, due to neighborhood segregation and occupational apartheid. Though the vast majority of whites have grown up having little or no contact with people of color, at the same time, they did not grow in
our society without *any* consciousness of "others," but rather with particular
"tapes" in their minds. These tapes are racist representations and stereotypes of
people of color that percolate through the culture via television and popular culture. Most whites have been introduced to these stereotypes at an early age in an
"enjoyable" manner through nursery rhymes like "Ten Little Indians" or "Eenie
Meenie Minie Mo." They grew up watching "The Little Rascals," in which
Black children were wide-eyed, fearful, and superstitious, and seeing "wild"
Indians with tomahawks, and "Chinamen" who were identical by the thousands
in funny cartoons.

This has been the fare of fantasy in American culture, and it remains so to
this day. Cable television has brought back the old Bing Crosby and Shirley
Temple "blackface" movies and the most overtly racist of the old cartoons.
Hollywood has aggressively resurrected old stereotypes in the remaking of
movies like "The Little Rascals," whose Buckwheat character has now become a
doll one can order through popular women's magazines like *Woman's Day*.
Native American stereotypes are embraced by the "liberals" of the culture such
as actress Jane Fonda, who insisted on her right to do the "tomahawk chop" at

the Atlanta Braves games, despite the protestations of many Native Americans and others. Some school systems and sports teams around the country are defending their "right" to use Native Americans as mascots and logos, although importantly, there are increasing numbers of school districts that are consciously taking a stand against such practices. In the popular culture that is still being tailored for our children, Native American women may still be portrayed as property of white men or as "squaws" (the obscene racist term frequently used in Disney's movie *Pocahantas*).

Antiracist pedagogy involves asking teachers not only to examine such notions that they have been taught, but also to interrogate and analyze the mediums, mechanisms, and motivations for the continuation and revival of such racist discourse. While we may be conscious of the wrongness of racist imagery, we should also question the hidden logic behind its perpetuation. In discussions of the role of the corporate media in hegemonic discourse, we should examine the impact of television on our own, as well as our students', consciousness. One way of doing this is to do a content analysis of movies and television shows to become aware of who is really being represented and how; what kinds of roles are being played and by whom; how genders, races, classes, and languages are being represented; and who the commercial sponsors of these portrayals are. Television culture affects the way we see ourselves and others, and the way our students see and treat each other, as well. This racist culture distorts our ability to see the causes of the real problems in society.

Even when teachers may consciously reject stereotypes, they are not in control of the forces that affect the students and the culture of their schools. The impact of corporate-sponsored popular culture is felt in schools, where the subculture of the students is often negatively affected by the latest sitcoms, music videos, or popular movies. Children, particularly Black children, become commodified in this process, where the main option that is portrayed is of the gun-toting, drug-using, or drug-selling Black youth. Such stereotypes are so bombarded that the image of the "dangerous Black male" is often emulated by white boys as well. As we discussed these issues in my classes, teachers talked about the new role they saw emerging in the culture of white students in their classroom—the "wigger," a racist term used by white youth to describe the white boy trying to act tough or rude, or what was described as "acting black." One African American teacher told my class that at a small-town middle school where she had recently done her student teaching, they had a "Wigger Day," when the boys were all supposed to dress and act "Black." She was able to prevent it from happening—that time, anyway—by complaining to the principal, who claimed to be unaware of what "wigger" meant.

While it is relatively easy to recognize overtly offensive racist representations in the media, more subtle are the "liberal" approaches that offer us "Black" television entertainment, usually from the perspective of white corporate producers and their sponsors. Many people believe there is a representation of people of color simply by seeing that some television shows feature Blacks or Hispanics, though there is an almost total absence or marginalization of people of Asian or Native American descent. But we must still critically examine the kinds of roles and stereotypes that continue to be perpetuated. An effective documentary, *Color Adjustment*,[8] examines stereotypes of African Americans from the early years of television to the mid-1980s and analyzes the issue of corporate sponsorship and ideological control. The documentary demonstrates how some television sitcoms often continue the perpetuation of the buffoonish stereotypes of Blacks, while others lull the American public into believing that the civil-rights movement won the battle for inclusion. At the same time, some of the more politically progressive or critical shows on the air have been canceled after only one season, because corporate sponsors are not interested in their socially critical or antiracist content.

An examination of the media must go beyond identifying the perpetuation of stereotypes, to pose the larger question of the media's ultimate function. This must be placed in the context of who owns the media and who owns the press in America. As McChesney (1997) argues, the purpose of television is to sell products and make money. The media is now controlled by a handful of firms that dominate the world. This media apparatus "works to advance the cause of the global market and promote commercial values, while denigrating journalism and culture not conducive to the immediate bottom line or long-run corporate interests. It is a disaster for anything but the most superficial notion of democracy—a democracy where, to paraphrase John Jay's maxim, those who own the world ought to govern it" (p. 11).

The majority of teachers reported that they had never systematically critiqued television or other media before, even though many were conscious of the deleterious effects that television was having on children. Typical were these responses to our examination of the representations of people of color on television:

Watching the video *Color Adjustment* was just another cause for oppression among Black people. I was trying to think what it must be like to turn on the TV and rarely see your own race, and when they are seen on TV, they are depicted in such demeaning ways. It wasn't real life, and I was also concerned about how people of color were also glamorized when the fact was we were having real problems in our world. (white female, elementary school teacher)

The video [*Color Adjustment*] on the impact of television . . . brings to people the subtle ways we're conditioned to accept racism. It was fascinating to see how a medium used to install and reinforce classism and capitalism/consumerism was also used to install racism (as well as sexism, homophobia, ageism, etc.). The lack of African Americans, as well as other people of color, in television programming was startling, and the unrealistic portrayal of the few Blacks was revolting to watch. It was amazing to see the producers/directors justify this based on money (that it makes good business sense). (white female, middle school counselor)

As a young person I had very little contact with people of color, so the programming at that time seemed to represent my world (although my working-class family didn't act like Beaver's family). The real power of seeing [*Color Adjustment*] for me was how it demonstrated the power of the majority to influence large numbers of people. (white male, high school teacher)

Since taking this class, I have become more and more aware of the various forms of racism on TV. TV programming is consumed with racist imagery. This class has made me much more conscious of, for example, how the National Football League is racist. Out of the ninety-one quarterbacks, only eight are African Americans, with the largest percentage of players being African American. (African American female, elementary school teacher)

In addition to television and popular culture, we also examined newspapers, which are often thought to be more objective. We examined them for frequency and quality of representation of marginalized groups to become aware of how few diverse representations there are. It is not only racial balance that is lacking. There is also the issue of class. I asked the teachers to examine a collection of national, state, and local newspapers and to list all of the major sections of the typical daily newspaper in the United States. The typical list included world, national, and local news, sports, comics, business, neighborhoods, want ads, horoscopes, crossword puzzles, obituaries, advertising, stock-market report, women's section, real estate, and cooking. But what is missing? The list seemed complete. The missing topic is labor. In American newspapers, there is no labor section—no way to become aware of the treatment and responses of the labor movement and the working class on a regular basis. Those who actually do the work are virtually ignored by the press. That is a class issue that teachers should be aware of.

REFLECTING ON AND CRITIQUING OUR PRACTICE

Thus far I have discussed some of the central themes and typical responses to our examination of the institutional and individual aspects of racism. For the majority of teachers, this was a new discourse. I wanted to find out what they were going through intellectually and emotionally as they were processing this antiracist perspective and counterpoising it with what was happening around issues of race in their classrooms. How relevant was this analysis to their day-to-day experience in the classroom? I posed this question at the beginning of each class. These "check-ins" often revealed some of the most important internal struggles, revelations, and contradictions that people were experiencing in their schools, ranging from their individual roles as people who may have been contributing to racial problems, to those who were struggling to find methods for working effectively against racism. The following sentiments expressed by a white elementary teacher and a middle school teacher are typical of how people referred to these reflections on our practice:

> I thought "checking in" was a wonderful way for everyone to express how they are feeling. People were feeling uncomfortable, as I had suspected, and people, including myself, feel very disturbed about what we've been discussing. It's a lot easier to forget or push away things we don't want to deal with. But Julie will not let us do that. This class is great because I feel we are required to care, not just to study about stuff objectively. Julie always makes us think about the "so what?" or "what do you think that means?" and this helps us share how we are dealing with the uncomfortable problems we are examining.

> I appreciate being able to talk about how these issues are impacting me in the classroom. At all of the in-services I have had before, we are given information, but no one asks what we have to put up with or if we think this multicultural education can work. Many of us are tired of the district coming up with these "experts" who tell us what to do without even consulting us. The discussions at the beginning of each class help me compare what is happening at ———— School with other schools, and I find myself looking forward to them each week.

Talking about Discipline and Resistance

One issue that came up frequently during these "check-ins" was the problem, especially among many middle and high school teachers, of the discipline of Black students. Several teachers complained that there were often some Black kids "wandering the halls" when they should be in class. This was disruptive to the students who were in their classes, as well as counterproductive to those in the halls, who were building up a truancy record for themselves even though they were actually in the school while missing their classes. Bill, a high school math teacher, commented:

> One thing that really bothers me is that when we [white teachers] go up to these students and ask them why they are in the hallway or tell them to get to class, we are "blown off" by the Black students, who will say things like "I don't have to listen to no white teacher" or accusing us of picking on them 'cause they're Black, picking on them because we are racist, or they'll behave in ways that are seen as aggressive, rude, or disrespectful when we confront them in the hallways.

The "hallway problem" was reported by the white teachers and teachers of color alike. Often the Black and Latina teachers in my classes said that they approached the students, white or Black, and told them to get to class. They also said they tried to get to know their names, and most of the students knew their names because they were usually one of the few or perhaps the only teacher of color in the school. But the teachers of color also often reported their frustrations, for they perceived that they were the only adults interacting with the Black students, while the white teachers would be standing there in the hallway among themselves seeming to pretend that they didn't see what was going on. The Black students then knew that they didn't have to respond until they saw the teacher of color coming toward them. This created resentment among the white teachers, who felt their power diminishing as they watched the Black or Latina teacher manage the situation that they were avoiding or were unsuccessful at managing. On the other hand, another (though less frequent) response from some teachers of color was to do what some of their white peers were doing—ignore the students. As Al, an African American high school teacher, explained it to the white teachers in the class: "We get tired of doing your work for you. So sometimes I will just walk right by and not say a word, just like you do. You've got to be involved, too."

As we discussed this problem, people talked about why they did not know the Black students' names. Often it was because they didn't have them in their class, and so they never asked them. But also there was the problem of fear—some teachers admitted to being afraid of or defensive with the Black students, particularly if more than one student was involved. They did not engage them one on one and felt intimidated by Blacks in groups. The Black students often viewed the teachers doing hallway duty as cops without power and ignored them if there was no perceived relationship. Other Black students felt intimidated by the white teachers. As a result of our discussions, some teachers reported that they were now making an attempt to get to know the students, finding out their names, greeting them when they saw them, even when they didn't have them in classes. They often reported that the students seemed at first surprised, but then responded positively. One high school teacher wrote in her journal and shared with the class:

> I have found our discussion about Black students in the hallway to be helpful. It seems obvious that when you know a person by their name, they respond to you as a person! But isn't that true of us adults as well? When an administrator comes up to me and seems to walk right past me, I sure don't feel like being nice to him. I talked to this student at the beginning of the semester about roaming the halls, and he just talked back at me rudely, then just ignored me. I didn't want to start something big, so I just let it go. I thought about what some people in the class were suggesting the other week. When I was doing hall duty last week, I saw the same young man again hanging out. I found out his name from another student, and then, when he started up again, I walked over to him and said, "Hi Brandon, how's it going today?" He looked at me in a surprised way and then smiled. And

I asked him, "Shouldn't you be in class?" This time he didn't give me any back-talk! He went to class! Our discussions in the racism class gave me some ideas about what I or many of my peers may be doing unconsciously that makes the students feel that we do not like them. I think it is important to remember to treat people how we would like to be treated.

During one class session, we discussed the problem of the stereotypes that many white teachers entertained of Black students as being inherently undisciplined, or the view that their parents or communities did not value education. I asked the teachers how many of them had ever attended functions in the African American community. None of them had. One middle school teacher in particular perceived the Black children as being disrespectful and undisciplined. She frequently made references to the lack of respect for authority in their culture. I asked her how she could know so much about people she had so little experience with. Several weeks later, this teacher shared with the class that as a result of our discussion, she and another white teacher decided to attend a function at one of the Black churches. She wrote about the experience in her journal:

> Last week my teaching partner and I had the opportunity to go to ———— church for a program. The students from my school were really shocked to see us there, I could tell. They kept telling their friends, there's Miss ————! What I realized was that the students that are often the most disruptive at school were totally well behaved and respectful. I thought about what we talked about in class, about how people may feel when they are "dispossessed," about not wanting to relate to someone that they thought did not want to relate to them. I thought about the things in the "I Won't Learn" article, and it all became more obvious.

The fact that the teachers were strangers to the communities of their students underscores the serious effects of this segregation on their abilities to relate to the students or the students to relate to them. Their narrow experience in schools as "gatekeepers" reinforces their perspective that the reactive behavior they see, or may *think* they see, from some of the Black students is the essence of "how those people are," rather than perhaps being a reaction to how schools are, or how teachers are, or how they are being treated.

The problems of Black students "wandering" the hallways or disrespecting the white teacher are not unique to Black students and are not necessarily rectified by just getting to know a student's name or showing up at their church. Students may be skipping classes or not participating in them because they feel marginalized or turned off by the curriculum or resent the teachers' attitudes toward them. This is why it is important to teach politically and culturally relevant curricula that will engage all the students. Many teachers said that some of the African American students were so far behind in their classes, they may have been skipping class as a face-saving strategy. There was also the assumption made by some teachers that the students really were not capable of doing the work in the first place, hence they hid behind a tough facade to shield their inability to read or do the work. This is what is often behind the low expectations that some white teachers have for students of color. "Look, I'm happy if I can give one of these kids a C!" remarked one high school teacher in a discussion we had about student achievement.

Of course, there also are societal problems that teachers do not have direct control over, such as unemployment, gangs, drugs, or family instability, which may affect any student. These problems can impact on one's ability or willingness to learn or "do school" and certainly make teaching more difficult. The larger problem that must also be considered is the element of alienation and the possibility that such nonengagement with school may be either a conscious or unconscious response that educator Herb Kohl (1994b) refers to as "not-learning." Kohl defines this term:

> Learning to not-learn is an intellectual and social challenge; sometimes you have to work very hard at it. It consists of an active, often ingenious, willful rejection of even the most compassionate and well-designed teaching. Not-learning tends to take place when someone has to deal with unavoidable challenges to her or his personal and family loyalties, integrity, and identity. In such situations there are forced choices and no apparent middle ground. To agree to learn from a stranger who does not respect your integrity causes a major loss of self. The only alternative is to not-learn and reject their world. (p. 2)

If the curriculum and the culture of the school do not speak to particular students, and if their teachers are unfamiliar with their communities and their experiences and do not understand them, this contributes to a disassociation and rebellion. To help teachers reflect upon the notion of students refusing to become engaged, as a self-protective and intellectual (rather than "criminal") response, I gave them an excerpt from Kohl's 1994 book, *I Won't Learn from You and Other Thoughts on Creative Maladjustment*, which elaborates on this problem of student resistance. I asked teachers to reflect upon their own experience, asking them if there was any point in their lives when they felt that they were vulnerable to becoming invisibilized, and if they had ever reacted in such a way as simply refusing to become engaged, even though that may not have been in their own self-interest? Many teachers reported that there were times when they had been marginalized or treated differently, perhaps as females, or on issues of physical appearance, sexual orientation, physical abilities, or poverty. I asked them to consider how they responded. Did they accept the behavior? Did they resist it or fight it? Did they accommodate to others' perceptions or expectations? Did they internalize it and lower their own expectations? As they reflected on their own experiences of dealing with being treated differently, many realized that they had reacted to this resistant behavior from some of their students, without probing deeper into the causes.

While understanding the reasons for student resistance, it is important to be careful not to take the notion of resistance too far. For in our attempts to honor resistance, we must guard against sabotaging the interests of the student. This may happen when the white teacher tries to be too understanding of the student of color and demands or expects little because of feeling sorry for the student. This will not contribute to the student's success in any way. Often the "liberal" response to discipline or behavior issues comes not from neglect or hostility, but out of genuine confusion about how to react to another's oppression. Empathy alone is not sufficient; it may even exacerbate the student's self-destructive behavior and contribute to the child of color internalizing his or her own oppression. Such misplaced empathy is not an uncommon situation. Educators Sara Freedman and Marica Baynes (1984) write about how a white teacher and a Black teacher may respond to the alienation or rebelliousness of a Black student differently. Freedman, a "progressive" white educator, tells of her experiences with an angry Black child:

> When I was teaching in Newton, I had one kid in my class who was a Metco kid. The kid that I had in my class was very immature. There were times when he got very angry and I would have to think about what was the source of his anger. Was it that he was the only black kid in the class or is he just pissed off? His accent would change, he would become much more street black and his whole body language would change. I didn't quite know how to deal with it, whether or not to say to him, "That kind of behavior is appropriate, that isn't." I wasn't happy with all the anger he would express, but on the other hand do I say, "You have to express your anger, but you have to do it in a different way." I wanted to say, "I think you have a right to be angry. Perhaps this is not necessarily the best situation for you." (p. 14)

On the other hand, Baynes, a Black sixth-grade teacher who had also lived the Black child's experience, responded quite differently:

> I had the same experience as that little boy, I was always the only one and I found that either you are the rebel and you act out or you try desperately to assimilate or you're expected to be the perfect person. It's always because you are black that people react to you. For example, as a black teacher if the child had had temper tantrums in my room, I would have said, "You're having a temper tantrum and get your act together." But I would say the same thing to a white child. I wouldn't say, "Well I understand because you're a black kid and the only kid in the class, you have a right to act out." There's good behavior, there's appropriate behavior, and there's inappropriate behavior in all situations. "Now why is it that you are acting

that way? What's troubling you, let's talk about that. O.K. how can we get around that problem? That one problem." So the child does not internalize that it's all right for me to be disruptive and act up because I am black. Because then you cripple the kid and he goes along, "Oh, it's all right, I'm black, I'm bad." (p. 15)

Janice, an African American elementary teacher, reflected on our discussions about this issue in her journal:

Our class discussions have been stimulating and motivating. But maybe we could be less concerned about saving people of color and spend more time preparing these children to be tough enough to endure and have the skills to rebound or be resilient, to hang in there. We cannot shield our sons or daughters from the realities of racism. African American children need a school experience that will make them better prepared than their white peers. Anything teachers do less than helping arm African American children with the knowledge, skills, and attitude needed to struggle successfully against oppression is affording them the luxury of shielding themselves with a sugar-coated vision of the world. If African American students are to be equipped to battle against racism they will need excellent skills in reading, writing, math, understanding their history, critical thinking, problem solving, and decision making.

The problem of the friendly but unchallenging white teacher has negative consequences for preparing children to survive academically. Massey, Scott, and Dornbusch (1975), writing about the persistence of racism in newly desegregated schools in the mid-1970s, called it "racism without racists":

In the past many teachers expressed overt hostility toward minority students in their classrooms. Teachers are now expressing warmth toward Black students, but are not accompanying their friendliness with challenging academic standards. This lack of challenge and a distorted evaluation system are just as debilitating to students as the old overt hostility. The teachers, faced with students who lack basic skills and denied the resources to change the situation, become "the reluctant instrument of the establishment." Institutional racism thus persists without racist villains. It is a racism of the educational system that is unquestioned, self-perpetuating and powerful. (p. 10)

It is important for teachers to develop empathy, not pity, for the problems that some of their students are facing. Part of this process means becoming conscious of their own assumptions, which have often been framed from a deficit perspective. The teacher must ask, If this student is turned off to school, why is that, and what can we do to turn him or her on to school? What are we doing that is turning off learning? What are we doing that is inherently not inclusive? One does not lower expectations, but rather offers meaningful and relevant expectations. "High expectations for all" is a fine slogan, but we must have the resources (labor and time) to give all students the extra help that they may need and provide the tools to help students reach high.

STRUGGLING WITH CONTRADICTIONS

Unlearning racism is not a linear path, but as Tatum (1992) discusses regarding her experiences teaching courses on the psychology of racism, it is more like a spiral staircase—hence, there may not be clearly defined "stages" that people go through as they unlearn racism. In our discussions of the daily life of schools, one sees how people are struggling with the contradictions. Often these struggles were expressed in the safety of their journals. Ellen, a white middle school teacher, rarely spoke out loud but focused her reflections mainly in her journal. Many of her entries represented the kind of contradictory consciousness and the internal conflicts that come with the process of unlearning racism. As the following journal entry illustrates, she recognized the fallacy of the stereotype of the alleged lack of respect or family values but did not understand the alienation that may contribute to problems of resistance:

> I've noticed that actually in Black families, the children have more respect for their elders than the white children do. I know that if I really want to scare a kid, I don't threaten him with detention or the police. I threaten him with a phone call home. Sometimes I force a kid to call his mother right there on the spot and explain his misbehavior and why he did it. That usually cures the problem, at least in my class. But then I notice that the kid will be doing that same bad behavior somewhere else. I think it is important that we know that this kind of family discipline is often effective. But the problem I have is, Why is this behavior necessary from the Black kids in the first place? Are they trying to prove something to white people? Do they want to show you that they don't respect white people?

Ellen recognized the strengths of the Black family but didn't understand how institutional racism affected these same families. After our discussions of racial stereotypes in the media, Ellen wrote in her journal that she now had a new recognition of racism in the media and began to watch television more critically. Still, her new "sensitivity" did not yet extend to the school culture. She was protective of her white privilege and wrote in her journal that in her school there was "too much inclusion of people of color," that she feared they were "going towards reverse racism." While pictures of African American role models and heroes had recently been hung on the walls, along with white women, she thought that this was too much of a focus. She did not perceive the already predominantly Eurocentric curriculum and school culture as problematic, but was worried about efforts to celebrate African American culture, in particular,

Kwanza: "Why should Blacks be allowed to have a special holiday? It seems like they are just trying to throw it at us—as if to say, we have this and you cannot be a part of it because of the color of your skin. I wonder if this is not just as damaging—this reverse racism—as racism."

It was not until several weeks later that she was able to recognize how Eurocentrism was already embedded in the system. After a session where we viewed a segment of a videotape featuring Jane Elliot, the race-relations educator, Ellen felt "shock" at Elliot's statement that white people are racist and wrote:

> When she said "I am a racist," I was angry and shocked, but after thinking it over that evening, I understood what she was saying, especially after I read the articles in *Rethinking Columbus*. How can any of us be a part of this society and not be a racist? All of this is difficult for me to assemble just now. I am glad I signed up to take the part two class. Because I think I am only just beginning to understand what this is about.

Ellen's responses illustrate the complex issues that people must sort out in their attempts to unravel racism. While she saw things that many of her peers did not see, such as the strengths in most Black families, she did not yet see the racism or the sexism inherent in the structure that makes the fact of even having to think about putting up pictures of white women or of women and men of color, or having Black holidays (or such simple things as finding Black children on greeting cards) as problematic.

Coming to an antiracist consciousness is not a "politically correct" stance that one wakes up with one day. It is, rather, a perspective that comes about more typically through a process of examining and reexamining the personal and political dimensions of race and power relations, and the interrelationships between individual and institutionalized racism. In Ellen's case, she was developing a new consciousness about race incrementally as she began to ponder rather than react to the notion that the society is racist. And the fact that she came to the point of realizing that indeed there was a knowledge gap meant that she was ready to continue to learn, rather than have a process of self-protective reaction set in. This is more typical of the kind of incremental growth in knowledge and sensitivity that most people go through, rather than a single great revelatory moment. Antiracist education can help teachers have a different engagement with the world and their role in changing it.

FIGHTING CYNICISM AND DEFEATISM

For some teachers, the struggle was not over the acceptance of "new" ideas, as such. They were aware of the Eurocentric bias of the curriculum and had no arguments with the critical perspective of Columbus or a structural analysis of racism. In fact, some of them portrayed their own perspectives or upbringings as "Left," "activist," or otherwise progressive. For some of these teachers, the struggle was to fight a defeatist cynicism, for they were not sure that they even wanted to work with or try to "enlighten" their more biased peers. For example, in one class of high school teachers, there were several white males who were very bigoted and resistant. Jean, who was active in the teachers' union, was disgusted at their racist attitudes. But she was not vocal in class and didn't counter their arguments. One evening after class, she phoned to tell me that she thought I should cancel the class. "I can't stand to be in the same room with those creeps. You will never get anywhere with them, so why bother? This is just wasting all of our time. I think you should just cancel the class." I told her that she was welcome not to continue the class, though I was disappointed that she seemed willing to take a public stand for the union but not against the racist attitudes among some of her peers in the school. On the one hand, I agreed with her that this class would not likely change their bigoted attitudes, but on the other, I knew it was important that they heard that not everyone agreed or validated their attitudes. For these men, her silence was likely interpreted as consent. I reminded her that the students of color did not have the white privilege of removing themselves from such intolerance when they felt uncomfortable. I wanted people to be conscious of not falling back on their white privilege when they got "tired" of dealing with racism.

Unfortunately, one's union activism or "class consciousness" was not an indication of an antiracist consciousness. Some people had the cynical attitude that the system was so unfair and had already done so much damage that no change was possible, so why bother trying. Kathleen, a white teacher at a middle school where I taught a staff-development class, was another example of the contradictory consciousness exhibited by many people, including some who had been exposed to more "progressive" perspectives. Kathleen had described her parents as politically "Left" or radical. But like her more conventional peers in her middle school, she accepted the stereotypical associations of Blacks with dysfunctional families or lack of motivation or ambition. She was not far ahead of her less politically attuned peers when it came to recognizing racism. As an activist in the teachers' union, she also was single-minded when it came to defending the rights of teachers and took offense at any criticism of teachers. For example, after a newspaper article was published showing the Lakeview School District's failure to adequately educate the students of color, Kathleen was vocal in the class about defending the teachers from criticism:

> Well, there is some truth to the article, but it really angers me 'cause it's just a grain of truth and it doesn't tell the whole story. Our teachers are trying, it's the kids who are so disrespectful. The article says they need African American teachers?

What does that mean? When we had two last year, it didn't make any difference. In fact, they were problems and they really were not the kind, you know, they really were not good teachers. So what do we do?

Nancy, a white teacher at the middle school, added: "They are coming to us with low skills, and suddenly it's Lakeview's problem. Many kids come from a more competitive environment and they don't know how to get along in a place like Lakeview." Kathleen continued:

Many say they haven't learned the script, many of them never had that in their learning experience. You really see the differences in those who make a choice not to try. You know, we have high homework rules here, but that isn't part of their script; many white kids go home and continue to learn, but these people don't value learning. What do you want us to do, give them no homework so they can pass?

These sentiments were typical of many teachers who were resistant to examining their own or the school's role in perpetuating racial disparities. They saw the problem with the kid, not with the school. Viewing success narrowly as an outcome of good or bad choices, they believed that token efforts at integration were sufficient; it was up to the kids to take the opportunity to assimilate into the school. Often, when a problem was posed regarding racial discrimination, if they did not recognize it, their response was "Prove it." There were objectively real concerns with many of the poor Black children who were bused to the school, coming with less "cultural capital" and preparation than their more affluent white peers from that neighborhood, but the school's response was to accept them so long as they assimilated into the status quo as long as whites in the school did not have to move over.

In this middle school, we often spent much time discussing problems like the extremely disproportionate numbers of African American students who were always in detention after school. When I had originally visited this school (located in a desirable white, middle-class neighborhood to which a large number of Black students were bused), I came across a room of all Black students. Thinking it was perhaps a special cultural class for the Black students, I asked the teachers at the in-service what they were studying. "Oh, that's just the detention room," they told me. When I problematized this, many of the teachers became defensive. "Just because all of the kids in the detention room are Black does not mean that we are racist! Don't you think it's possible that they are doing something to put themselves there?" asked one of the teachers. After lengthy discussion, it was revealed that the reason why a large number of the Black kids were in detention that day (and many other days when I had observed this) was because their bus was late and they had been given detention by their individual teachers for coming in late.

I wanted teachers to begin to sort out causes and effects. For example, it was not uncommon for teachers to assume that because Black parents did not attend school events, this meant that they were disinterested in their children's education. "It's not in their script," Kathleen said. The injustice was that there was only one school in a Black neighborhood in Lakeview, yet the teachers did not see the absurdity of that. Moreover, there had been few attempts to involve parents of color in school events or in the planning of them. Hence, it was important for us to talk about how culture and power get distributed, expressed, and played out in school. The dominant paradigm of assimilation in education says, "You can join us, but you must be just like us." This means that if you are different from the dominant group, you cannot discover who you are. Assimilation involves a destruction of memory.

It always surprised (and frightened) me to find out how rarely teachers had been asked to examine the relations of domination and the "whiteness" of the culture in their schools. They may have been aware that there were few pictures of people of color on the walls of their school, for example, but went no further in examining other arrangements that automatically favored the dominant group.

Breakthroughs and Baby Steps

Gradually, as a result of our lengthy discussions about institutional racism, there were some small changes in perceptions and an increased willingness to admit and confront racism. In the case of the middle school discussed above, presenting the facts alone did not necessarily convince everyone about the reality of racism. Some people would need to really see it to believe it. The following example reveals the importance of connecting theory to praxis.

In my visits to the school, I had noticed that the school security guards, who were all white, more frequently questioned the Black students while often ignoring the white students. I asked if other teachers had ever observed this, and only the lone Latina teacher in the class said she had tried to raise this point with her colleagues before but was ignored or accused of being oversensitive. This led to a discussion of how African Americans experience the police and the increasing prisonization of Blacks. Many of the teachers expressed skepticism that race and racism could have anything to do with the fact that so many African Americans "happened" to be in prison.

In this class, it was a threatening experience for a student of color, in conjunction with our discussions of racism and prisons, that convinced the teachers of the reality of institutionalized racism. At one of the last sessions of the course, during our "check-in," Jill said that she needed to discuss a police incident that happened in the school the previous week. As she explained, there had been a basketball game the previous weekend at which one of the Black eighth-grade girls had a fight with another girl and was removed from the game. The girl angrily threatened another student, saying she was going to "kick her ass." When a teacher intervened, she verbally threatened her too. One of the teachers then called the police, but by the time the police arrived, the girl had left the gym. The policeman left. Then the Black girl came back, and again the police were called. The girl this time, when she realized that the police were coming, left the school grounds altogether. Shortly thereafter, a different policeman arrived. As he was walking into the gym, a Black student named Raymond happened to be coming toward him on his way out. Raymond was in a jovial mood and had been showing off to some girls. He was walking around in the gym with his arms in the air, making the victory sign, since his team had won the game. The policeman, upon seeing a young Black male coming toward him, immediately reacted aggressively. As Jill told the class:

> The cop crouched down on his knees. He had his arms outstretched like he was trying to capture or cage a wild animal or something! He grabbed Raymond, yelling, "Freeze!" and threw him against the wall and pinned him there with his hands behind his back and handcuffed him! And this kid was shocked—we all were shocked—and he [Raymond] was flailing his body and screaming things at the cop, like "You racist! You racist!" Meanwhile, the girls whom he had just been hanging out with were hysterical. I mean they were really hysterical. There was one girl who I was just so worried about, 'cause she was crying and shouting to the cop, "He didn't do anything, you racist motherfucker!" and like that, and I was afraid he was going to arrest her, too, so I did everything to try to get her away from the cop, and I was screaming at the cop, telling him, "Let him go. He's not the right one. He's not the one!" They were trying to pull at the cop and screaming, accusing him of being a racist.

Jill and Kathleen, who had been assigned to supervise the kids at the game, saw this whole incident. Jill said that she didn't know what to do, and all she could think to do was calm down one Black girl in particular who was crying and screaming hysterically. Both Jill and Kathleen said that they had to scream at the cop over and over, "You've got the wrong person!" The cop finally released Raymond, who was very upset. Kathleen said, "All I wanted to do was to get Raymond into a room where I could calm him down, so he didn't make matters worse. I mean, I know this kid. He's in special ed and he can be a real problem, but the funny thing is, this time he was so innocent, and then look what happens to him!" The policeman left, and afterward Kathleen and Jill were in different rooms trying to calm down these traumatized youngsters. That was the "end of the incident." Kathleen was upset but seemed resigned: "That's how the system is. There's nothing we can do about it." But for Jill in particular, it had a more profound impact, and she refused to let it go. She now identified this incident to the class as clearly a racist incident and told the class:

I have been thinking about this all week. And I can't help but think about those things that we've been talking about in this class, especially institutionalized racism. Before I took this class, I think I would have been confused about this, but now there's no doubt in my mind that the policeman was racist and that this was a racist incident. I felt so terrible for the girls, too, because they were so traumatized and I couldn't help them.

Kathleen added: "She's right. I mean, there's no other way to explain this. This really was a racist incident. There's no getting around it. I saw it. I was there. And I'm not terribly fond of Raymond. He can be a real—a real, you know, a real pain—but he really was victimized. It really was a racist thing that was happening."

I asked the teachers, "What did you tell the girls and Raymond?" Kathleen responded, "I just told them that they have every right to be upset, but they have to calm down or things will get worse."

I was concerned that their major response was only to "calm down" the students. If this was all they did, were they not glossing over and accommodating the cops? Of course, I wanted them to comfort the students, and I did not want the problem to escalate, but neither did I want it to stagnate. I then asked the teachers around the table, "Are there any opinions or suggestions about what could have been done?" The teachers pondered silently for a few minutes but could come up with no suggestions. They looked guilty; a few were clearly fighting tears and professed to feeling so helpless in the face of injustice.

I then asked them to problematize how we could make this incident into something that would not simply "victimize" us—how could we fight back? I asked them whether they had talked to Raymond's parents or the girls who had witnessed their friend's abuse. They said they had not. I asked them whether they had called the Police Department to report this abuse, and they said they had not. I asked them whether they would want to know if their own children had been handcuffed and thrown against the wall in school by police. They adamantly said, "Absolutely!" I asked them whether they felt the same value for the Black student in the school. They obviously felt very bad and realized that they had not done for another child what they would wish others might do for their own children.

I then asked them what other possibilities they might pursue so that they would not maintain their dangerous silence. Eventually someone suggested writing a letter of complaint, and another suggested calling the Police Department and expressing their concern. Several discussed the idea, but one teacher said, "Well, I don't know if the principal would want to sign it." I asked, "What does the principal have to do with this? Was he there? If he refused to sign such a letter, or to write one, would you keep a secret with him? Well, this is not my decision. I am just asking you to consider your point of power. This is something for you to decide."

The group discussed the issue among themselves at length. They began to question the appropriateness of the quick reaction of the teacher who had called the cops on an eighth-grade girl in the first place. This was hardly the first time there was a fight at school among middle school students. Why weren't other methods of intervention tried first? What else might have been done? At the end of their discussion, they voted unanimously to write a letter of complaint to the Police Department, as well as to forward a copy to the principal and the assistant principal, asking them to sign onto this letter. They also discussed putting the issue of when to call in the police on the agenda at the next staff meeting. One of them suggested that they should examine the school records to see if there were any patterns of calling in the police for discipline problems when it came to Black students. Another teacher reflected on my earlier question about the security guards and said that she, too, suspected one of them of selectively questioning the Black students in the hallway while ignoring the white students. This teacher later wrote in her journal that she was going to do some "action research" in the school and more systematically observe the security guards. Still another teacher wrote in her journal that she would call Raymond's parents and talk to them. In the course of this lengthy discussion, they came to agree that it was their responsibility to break the silence, and that if they did not, there was no reason why they should expect the Black students to trust them. While I cannot speak to the long-lasting impact of their decisions to take a stand, I think that what was accomplished at the least was a beginners' lesson in antiracist civic responsibility. And a brief moment of coming to terms with the possibility of our own human agency.

The necessity for being proactive is an integral ingredient of antiracism. Otherwise, one risks that such classes become nothing more than "whining sessions" in which people talk about how bad things are. While it is important to have a forum to talk about such problems, it is also critical to question, "What do you think you can do about it?" or "How do you think you can respond to it?" Often I had the class form small groups and brainstorm or do role plays in which they could practice or imagine themselves countering racism. It is one thing to have a heightened sensitivity or understanding about racism, but antiracist education can be realized only if we act on it. In doing this, we tap into another level of contradiction. We are not all born activists, after all. And we do not all resist in the same way. It is important for people to realize their own possibility to contribute, to identify their own points of power. In exposing ourselves to an activist perspective, we need to tap into our own educational programming and examine how our own impulse to activism has been suppressed or repressed. We need to understand how we can take a stand.

By becoming more conscious of the historical genesis of these problems, white teachers often began to more critically examine their own roles in relation to people of color. One such breakthrough occurred for Karen, the teacher referred to in the previous chapter who had expressed resentment about some people getting food stamps or coming to America and needing help with English. After she had been in my class for four weeks, she had one of those breakthroughs, one of those "aha!" moments. Karen came to see how institutionalized racism put people of color at a disadvantage and, by the same token, had worked to confer upon whites *relative* advantage. And she was able to see how racial arrogance and misplaced anger had affected her and separated her from a parent of color. In this case, she had found herself a member of an evaluation team in which she, along with three other white teachers, was charged with evaluating an African American student for special education. She told the class that as she sat in the meeting along with the student's mother, she knew something was wrong. The parent also felt uncomfortable in the meeting and got angry and "stormed out" of the meeting. She accused the team members of knowing nothing about her child. Karen told the class:

> Something happened to me then that could *never* have happened if I had not taken this class. I really mean that. Before this class, I probably would have reacted like the other women on the team did, you know, like "What's wrong with her?" or "See, she's really got a problem. No wonder her kid is having problems!" But this time, I was able to put myself in her shoes. I mean, my god, how would I feel if I was in her position? Here we were, these four white women, and we were telling *her* about *her* child, like we were some kind of authority or something. I felt awful. I really did not want to be in that position. I mean, how would you feel if you were that mother? Because of the discussions we have been having in this class, it helped me tremendously. I was able to understand that the parent was right. She told us we didn't know anything about her daughter. She was right! We had no right to have been acting like we knew so much more than her!

Karen then called the mother at home that evening, which she told the class "shocked" her colleagues. She wrote in her journal:

> I started rethinking what I thought of this mother. Now I started thinking how uneasy and scared and alone she must have felt when we had our first meeting. The meeting consisted of her and four white "professionals." I began thinking, "How horrible for her." I decided it was my responsibility to make her feel more of a team member with wanted input from the team. I called and asked her to meet with me. She was only available at 6:30 in the evening. Many people I knew would have said forget it, but I felt it was my duty as her child's teacher to talk with her. We decided to meet for coffee one evening.
> As scared as I was about the meeting (maybe because the numbers were even?), I thought it went well. We talked, and I told her I wanted her to feel comfortable

with me. She could ask me anything she wanted. I would try to help her as best I can. We met for forty-five minutes. I went home feeling pretty good about myself. But then I started thinking . . . What have I done but make myself feel good? I did make my first step, but now I have a lot to prove to the mother. Yes—me prove to her, basically by following through with her and her daughter. Now it's time for me to prove that I have taken the first of many steps that I need to take to knock down the wall of racism. To be continued . . .

Karen's reflections about realizing that she felt "good" about herself raises another concern. Many people expect "rewards" when they "go against the grain." If they don't see results or get noticed, they may become resentful or withdraw their support. In a speech to educators, antiracist educator Enid Lee[9] said something that I had often heard during the civil-rights movement: "Just remember—we do this work for our own self interest—we are trying to save ourselves so that we don't grow old in an impossible society. You are not doing anyone a favor, so don't expect applause."

TEACHER REFLECTIONS ON THE IMPACT OF THE ANTIRACIST STAFF-DEVELOPMENT CLASS

Many teachers reported in their journals or wrote in their class evaluations that our often controversial discussions had a "therapeutic" effect, even as the class was disturbing them, such as the following:

This class has made me go through a range of emotions (most of them not positive ones), but I have been thinking about this a great deal and talking about it with my husband and children every night after class. I am grateful that I had the opportunity to take this class because the discussions and the readings have helped me put together the "pieces of the puzzle." It has not been "enjoyable" to make the connections between our history and the problems we are having in education today, but it has helped me see the bigger picture and how it affects how we are treating our at-risk kids. It has been therapeutic for me in the sense that it has brought me closer to some of my colleagues and has made me feel more confident about beginning to talk about some of these problems in ———— School. (white female, high school teacher)

I'm glad I am taking this class. Wednesdays have become very long days, but I am at the point where I look forward to our discussions. When I leave the class, I usually feel weird, like something isn't right, like I'm upset or distressed about something. I know it's because we've been talking about "deep" stuff that matters. It makes me question what I do, say and think. I know this helps me to grow. This class puts racism on the table and says it exists here and now and I may (even unknowingly) be a part of it; even be perpetuating it. Those things are hard for me to hear, but I do feel that (like you said) if you are not part of the solution, you are part of the problem. (white female, middle school teacher)

When I first came to this class, I thought—what is this white woman going to teach me? Initially I did not think I would stay through the whole class. But now I've decided to sign up for the part two class. I have found that it is possible to learn from anyone who has the knowledge. Knowledge has no color. Your knowledge of history has helped me. It has been unusual for me to agree to share with people, as I am asked to do that constantly at school. But the class has been very good for me to sort out my thoughts and know that they will be understood. (Latina elementary school teacher)

I am amazed at how much I think about racism now, all the time. . . . With as much as I am questioning myself, I also become amazed at how many people absolutely do not think about these issues, particularly related to education. Teachers seem to have this attitude that by the mere virtue of being in such a caring profession as teaching, they are somehow above the regular human experiences of things like racism. I am also amazed at how unwilling teachers are to look at practices and attitudes and to admit that changes could be made. This class has helped me to deal with and handle racial problems in my school in a different way. (white female, elementary school teacher)

All of these discussions made me realize that my own upbringing, how I was taught, how I see and what I know of our history (or what I thought I knew) have a great effect on what kind of teacher I am and can become. I can only wonder, Why didn't we learn this before? The awareness of "institutional and individual racism" that I have learned about in this class has helped me see my role in teaching against racism, both to my white students as well as my African American and Hmong students. (white female, high school teacher)

Sometimes I have a hard time accepting the idea that there is institutionalized racism. It is not a tangible thing for me. It's also probably because I am in the majority—I don't experience racism very often. It's easier for me to relate to and accept concrete examples (such as calling pantyhose nude). I think that's also true for my kids. (white female, middle school teacher)

I have learned how to view what I read even more critically than what I already do. . . . This class has made me more aware of how racism shows up in schools. I think this class is the first step in sensitizing people to racism. Your incorporating of history was valuable for me. We can't change history, but we can change the interpretation of history by presenting true facts. Our social and economic problems didn't happen overnight. It will take time to change. Awareness can and will make a difference to reverse this path of injustice. I now feel more ready to be an "ambassador" for antiracist social change. (African American female, middle school teacher)

These vignettes and anecdotes indicate that there was a positive effect on most of the teachers who took my classes, in the sense that their sensitivity was heightened, their knowledge base was challenged and expanded, as was their sense of responsibility for dealing with racial issues in school. Most of these teachers had come into the class with little understanding of the multiple ways in which racism is manifested in their schools. The majority of the teachers said that they had a different sense of history now and were able to place their own "white" culture into some sort of context. That is why I have subtitled this chapter "Facing History *in* Ourselves," recalling Baldwin's admonition, "If I am not what I have been told I am, then it means that you're not what you thought you were either!"

From their anonymous evaluations of the class, a majority (usually 90 percent) said that the class had an impact on their relationships in other aspects of their life. Many said they were discussing these issues with family members and were now watching television and reading newspapers more critically. They reported becoming more aware of bias and inequities in the school culture and curriculum. They also reported that they were more conscious of how they were responding not only to their students of color, but also to the manifestations of racism among whites. Some teachers revealed that they had become more vocal about challenging racism in school, particularly when they heard remarks from staff. One teacher reported that she had put up an "antiracism bulletin board" in the staff lounge, on which she posted newspaper and magazine articles dealing with racial issues, in order to generate discussions among the staff. Many who had come into the class with the knee-jerk reaction of "blaming the victim" were beginning to reflect rather than simply react to the problems in a negative manner. The collaborative and group-centered pedagogical approach was important for helping people connect with other educators about common concerns. Often people maintained this connection by taking a "Part Two" class, where we conducted "action research" in which participants developed curricula and action plans to try out in their classrooms.

I am aware that not all experiences in multicultural education have a positive impact, however. For example, Haberman and Post's (1992) research in preservice teacher education points to cases where field experiences in "multicultural" settings may actually have the opposite effect than intended, when teacher-education students come out of the field experience with negative attitudes actually reinforced by the experience. Such reactions under certain circumstances may be anticipated if there has not been appropriate antiracist education before they are placed in the field. The experience of people who work in economically depressed or racially oppressed communities may actually reinforce their prejudices and beliefs that the problems people have are of their own doing. This perception may obtain despite the fact that they may spend many hours a week in those very communities. But to reiterate an earlier point, exposure or contact with diverse "others" does not necessarily mean that one becomes more empathetic to the people involved, or that members of the community are particularly thrilled to be "studied" or "served." Contact in itself is not enough to lead to positive cross-cultural interactions, particularly if social divisions and power differentials remain unchanged and unchallenged. Hence, it is not unusual for policemen, for example, or social workers or teachers to have very negative views about the people whom they are "serving." From their limited and specific interactions, they may *see* only pathologies. They may not understand the totality of the experience or the historical chain of causality that leads to certain problems, because they have not been given the cognitive tools with which to interpret problems that they encounter (if they do, in fact, encounter them). Furthermore, whites have rarely been required *to see who they are as white people in this society.* We should not assume that merely plopping teacher-education students or teachers (or anybody) into a "multicultural" context will sensitize them to the realities of diverse others if they are not conscious of the meaning of their own "whiteness."

Sleeter (1992) found that a multicultural in-service teacher-education course that she observed did not result in a transformation in attitudes or practices. She found, instead, that those who came into the program with initial prejudices about low-income people or people of color left the program with those perspectives reinforced. One would have to critically examine, however, whether such an outcome was not a reflection of the inadequacy of the program rather than the inability of the teachers to change. In any case, the program Sleeter described was along the lines of the more traditional multicultural courses that I critiqued earlier and did not appear to incorporate a critical antiracist perspective. While acknowledging that multicultural preservice experiences do not *necessarily* lead to progress, some teacher educators who have taught multicultural-education courses to preservice teachers stated that the experience of taking such courses has been reported by the students themselves to have had a profound and meaningful impact on them. These experiences have been written about, for example, by King and Ladson-Billings (1988) and Hollins (1992). This raises the critical question, "So what" if people who have taken such a course "feel" that they understand better? Will this truly help them interact and bond with marginalized communities in ways that are more egalitarian? Will this translate into better teaching? Will this actually lead to a more meaningful participation of parents and students of color in schools? Over time, does this make people better teachers?

As I mentioned earlier, this study was an examination of teachers' initial engagement with antiracist pedagogy. Becoming conscious about racism and white supremacy is only the first step in a process that must be reinforced in order to make people act on that consciousness. Regarding the long-range impact of the class on teachers' behavior, a systematic study of their incorporation of antiracist teaching on a long-term basis is currently in process. Preliminary results show that many teachers have continued to reflect on the problems of racism in their schools. However, there are a significant number who, unless this perspective is reinforced, will fall back on "automatic pilot" and continue with "business as usual." This underscores the necessity for schools of education and school districts to incorporate antiracist education into all aspects of educational policy and practice. Even though there were not systemic or structural changes in the district, I continually meet teachers who have taken my course over the years who tell me that the class did make a difference. For example, recently at a conference, a teacher from one of the more problematic schools that I had worked at told me, "I just want you to know that even though you probably thought we were never going to do anything, your class did make a difference. We are talking about things at meetings now, and some of our teachers are trying to introduce new materials and ideas." Others tell me that they have become more involved with the parents of students of color, and I have seen some of them attending community meetings. Still others have told me that they have been trying to get the union to take a more proactive stand. These are all necessary (though not by themselves sufficient) steps toward changing the racial climate in schools.

Regarding the question of whether antiracist education for teachers has a long-lasting impact, I think the more important question we should ask is, What is the long-lasting impact on teachers and students, if we *do not* provide them with such perspectives? I would argue, rather, that everything that we do and do not do will have a consequence, even though we may not be there to witness it. Therefore, it is problematic to assume that we can always measure the consequences directly. Learning and being are measurable only in the experience, which itself is mediated by others. Certain things may not necessarily be measured by numbers of incidents, and the effects of teaching from an antiracist perspective, or a perspective that educates toward justice, may be seen only in years to come. We must guard against the arrogance of believing that if we do something, the "results" will immediately follow. We should not be responsible for having to prove that it is good to do the right thing. What we can measure, however, is what we had intended with a particular approach or program, and whether we were able to get there. With that approach, we can see that if a certain strategy backfired, it is not because the ultimate goal of sensitizing students' thinking was faulty, but because our methodology was faulty.

The goals of antiracist education not only are to sensitize people to multiple realities and perspectives, but also provide an interpretive framework to help them understand the real causes of racial and economic inequality, so they may be better equipped to deal with the problems and tensions they are encountering in their professional life. It is also important to emphasize that the proactive element is an integral component of antiracist pedagogy—to help people develop a vision of possibility for working against injustices and inequities, and find ways of anchoring this vision in reality. This activist component—praxis— is essential to an antiracist approach. This perspective, which links theory to practice helps teachers understand that they are already taking a stand—consciously or not—and what they are doing or not doing is already political in the sense that it represents certain interests and may even be sabotaging other interests—often their own!

In this process of antiracist education, we are of necessity creating a new discourse—a set of rules and standards that can articulate the relational aspects of racism, which heretofore for many teachers were uncomfortably "felt" but not sufficiently understood and for many others were totally denied. It is important, also, that in the process of antiracism teaching, we do not replicate oppressive or dogmatic ways of teaching, for style can be as important as content, especially when one is teaching "against the grain" (Carrington and Troyna, 1988). Developing an antiracist consciousness requires a nonalienating, inclusive, and democratic process, where, in the activist tradition of Freire, Martin Luther King, Malcolm X, Fannie Lou Hamer, and many others, you must start from the experiences of the actor. In this case, the actors, predominantly white and female— but also a significant number of white males—have likely experienced a particular socialization that has been negatively affected by white supremacy, and this may mean a resistance to change. This is why it is extremely important that people be allowed to see the genesis of this behavior at an institutional level and helped to understand how that contributes to individual or personal manifestations of the problem. This is preferable, in my opinion, to many of the race awareness training approaches that start with the premise "All white people are racists," which tends to focus on individual guilt and leads to a circular and cynical reasoning that nothing will ever change no matter what we do. This does not mean that we deny our individual responsibility for racist reproduction, for we must also know that *we are all affected by racism.* Hence, we must "own up" to our responsibility before we can "disown" and replace it with an antiracist perspective.

Teaching or taking an antiracist class will not alter the fundamental power relations in our society, but I do believe that it can have far-reaching consequences by attempting to remove (or at least etch away at) one of the main obstacles to a major transformation of society—which is racism. In fact, I would go so far as to say that antiracist education for teachers, and for anyone who works with other humans, is a necessary precondition to any strategy and tactics of a movement that is attempting to change and democratize existing relations of gender, class, and race domination.

I hope that this study of antiracist education will help convince administrators, teachers, union activists, and educational planners, as it has convinced most who have taken the class, including many parents, that race-relations education is an essential part of the necessary retooling for the job of working in an educational institution. As an African American mother in Lakeview remarked to the schoolboard when arguing why she thought teachers should be required to have antiracist education: "Teachers need to be re-schooled and re-tooled, or re-moved!"

CONCLUSIONS

In this book, I have attempted to weave a path through an extraordinarily complex problem of racism in American education. I have focused here on the problem of counteracting the effects of the apartheid in the teaching force in America, which leaves children of color in many ways effectively "colonized." But I must also emphasize the need to seriously restructure teacher-education programs and the entire admissions and credentialing processes such that students going into and graduating out of teacher education programs are truly representative of the demographic makeup of the population, so that everybody is teaching everybody's children. An unbalanced teaching force leads to an unbalanced education.

In the beginning of this book, I alluded to the connections between racism and fascism and therefore between antifascism and antiracism. We must examine these connections especially now, when so many young people of color are being personally affected by what is called the "prison industrial complex." We must examine the chain of events that contributes to so many African American children being classified as learning disabled, or whatever current terminology is in vogue that ends up ascribing many to the margins of society. We must examine how this may lead further to young men and even boys ending up in the criminal justice system rather than the educational system. We must also examine the effects on the entire society when a society becomes militarized and forfeits democracy for fear. This must also be put into a global perspective, because we are living in a time of unprecedented capital accumulation, where transnational capital has penetrated to every area of the earth, and development becomes further distorted as boundaries are increasingly maintained by corporations rather than by nations. This new world, global capitalist order, which has been referred to as "globalization," has become so complex and confusing that the American worker may be more likely to feel hostility toward the worker in the poor, developing world than he or she does toward the giant corporation. As in the past, racism continues to obscure the relations of domination, whether we are talking about institutions like schools or the larger society in general.

In part 1, I examined some historical precedents to this obscurantism and mystification with regard to race relations in American education. This discussion examined some of the racist underpinnings of our history and culture, but it also examined the resistance to racism, particularly coming out of the democratic grass-roots movements of the civil-rights era. I also examined the kinds of responses that this resistance elicited, particularly from the predominant discourses of multiculturalism and antiracism that have informed the theoretical debates. Because of the way in which "multicultural" education has often been distorted and appropriated in the academy, in the schools, as well as in the dominant culture, the typical "liberal" multicultural approach has led not to emancipation, but to containment, giving some people the illusion of challenging the status quo, while never seriously challenging the relations of domination. These approaches rob multiculturalism of its revolutionary potential to challenge the causes of inequality and injustice. This is why it is essential that we adopt a truly critical multicultural or antiracist pedagogy. This approach must examine the intersections of race, class, and gender from a dialectical and historical perspective, placing them in the socioeconomic and historical context of capitalism and slavery.

In part 2, I focused on the practice of antiracist education. I constructed a curricular framework for an antiracist pedagogy, which is a work in progress. Not only is a critical curriculum that counteracts the lies of white supremacy required, but a new consciousness that examines the social construction of race, and particularly of "whiteness," also must be developed among teachers. At the same time, I stress that teachers are not the only actors in this drama, and we cannot blame them simplistically for the ills in education. They too are caught in a tangled web of interests that are increasingly imposing on teachers ridiculous demands to serve the corporate order. We certainly cannot ask teachers to change without respecting the real working conditions and stresses of their profession, one that has become increasingly "proletarianized." Yet teachers do make a difference and can play a key role in the sum total of race relations, for they are in the unique position of being charged specifically with engaging the life of the mind. To paraphrase Henry Adams, a teacher affects eternity; no one knows where his or her influence ends. But while teachers have the responsibility to name the problem, as they have traditionally been educated and socialized, they are not equipped to take on this responsibility, because they are also victims of a miseducation. The subtle and not-so-subtle ways in which this miseducation reinforces prejudices, low expectations, and misinformed judgments about "other people" contributes to stress and failure not only for children, but for teachers as well. The impact of this miseducation is discussed also in chapter 6, where I examined how white teachers perceive and interpret the problem of racism in their schools.

My purpose in writing this book in the first place was affected by what I have seen—or have not seen—happen in social-justice movements. Hard-won civil-rights laws *alone* have not changed and cannot change discriminatory behaviors. One simply cannot decree that people cannot be sexist or racist or homophobic or anti-Semitic or ethnocentric or ageist or ableist or any of the other intolerant attitudes that people may have learned. One must have the opportunity to unlearn these attitudes. To paraphrase Manning Marable, it requires more than an act of Congress to realize justice; it also requires an act of conscience to make antiracist social change. In this respect, antiracist education is our hope for developing such a new consciousness about racial and economic equality. It is not individuals, but collective resistance and people's movements that are essential for social change, but if racism and other "isms" keep us divided in the development of these movements, we will not have the ability to transcend our differences and protect our common interests. In order to begin to address the problem of racism in our schools, in-service and preservice teachers must be given a meaningful intervention—an education that will give them reasonable time and breadth of knowledge so that they can begin the long process of demystification. The urgency of antiracist conscientization has never been greater.

Notes

Preface

1. For a history of this period, see Patterson (1971).

2. Freire writes: "It was during my twenties that the verbal violence against blacks alerted my consciousness to the degree that I began not only to understand that Brazilian society was profoundly racist and unjust but this injustice provoked in me a sense of revolt and disgust. This awareness that began to take root, as I said, during my twenties, radicalized me to take a very critical position against all forms of discrimination and expressions of oppression, including the oppressive position to which Brazilian women, particularly women of color, were relegated." From Freire and Macedo (1993), p. 170.

3. Some years later, after the Freedom of Information Act was passed, my father requested the files that the FBI had on him, which revealed their "visits" to various unnamed persons and places. Though most of the information had been blocked out, making it difficult to know what it was the FBI had really done, certain things remained—things that the FBI figured would not incriminate them, I guess. One of them was something to the effect that "Mr. Kailin is a Jew but you would not know it because he is very quiet and well mannered and doesn't act like most Jews."

4. I discovered the details of this event nearly forty years later, when my daughter, Syovata Edari, then a senior in high school, resurrected the historical documents and wrote a history of this strike. Using my father's archives and the newspaper accounts, she wrote a paper that won first prize in the Wisconsin State Labor History essay contest, "African American Farm Workers Strike against Peonage in Wisconsin," published in *Wisconsin Labor History News* 7, no. 3 (September 1989).

Introduction

1. *New York Times*, February 26, 2000.

Chapter One

1. Lakeview is the pseudonym that I have given to the city and the school district where I did this work and where I collected the data for this research. In chapter 6, I provide a more detailed profile of the district.

2. All of these statistics were published in the mid-1990s in a major report on race-based inequities in the school district where I conducted my research. The study was conducted by a conservative public-policy think tank. The results of this study were published in one of Lakeview's major newspapers.

3. While the medical and educational communities' understanding and advances in the study and treatment of biochemical neurologically affected disorders have undoubtedly helped many children—particularly in this era, where there are so many chemical pollutants in the environment—this is also a field about which we must be very cautious. For such diagnoses of behavior may be influenced by cultural and class bias on the part of practitioners, who may be advancing and projecting their own racism or cultural or class bias on their interpretation of the behavior of children about whom they are culturally ignorant. For many children, especially those who are poor or children of color, or those who are simply nonconformist, their difficulty in school is often labeled attention deficit disorder (ADD). But sometimes this may be more appropriately seen as *interest* deficit disorder, where the student may be unconsciously or consciously reacting to his or her marginalized status or simply turning off to boring material. For a critical analysis, see G. Coles (1988).

4. All individuals and places in the ethnographic section of this study have been given pseudonyms to maintain participants' anonymity.

5. In conversations with Ladson-Billings, she told me that the white teachers in her study had transforming experiences that served as a linchpin—there seemed to be a central cohesive element in their background experiences that may have given them more insights on relating to and teaching children of color. For example, she said that one of them had been married to a member of the Black Panthers and that experience changed her outlook. Another teacher grew up in a Black neighborhood and her family had an antiracist consciousness.

6. See, for example, Becker, Geer, Hughes, and Strauss (1961); and Lofland and Lofland (1995).

7. National Center for Educational Statistics (1998), table 273, p. 174.

8. The figures are actually as follows: Of all professors, 86.8 percent are white, 0.5 percent are Native American, 5.3 percent are Asian, 4.9 percent are Black, and 2.5 percent are Hispanic. Whites constitute 90 percent of all full professors, 87.8 percent of associate professors, and 47.5 percent of assistant professors. Chronicle of Higher Education (1995), p. 22.

9. For a similar critique by a more "mainstream" educator, see also Goodlad (1984).

10. For informative analyses of globalization, see, for example, Chossudovsky (2000). See also Parenti (1998).

11. This expression is often erroneously attributed to the Italian communist Antonio Gramsci, who was fond of quoting this phrase, which was actually coined by the French writer Romain Rolland (1866–1944). See C. Boggs (1984).

Chapter Two

1. From the summer of 1919, which James Weldon Johnson called the "Red Summer," until December of that year, there were twenty-five major race riots across the

country, in places like Washington, D.C.; Omaha, Nebraska; Tulsa, Oklahoma; Long-view, Texas; Arkansas; Chicago; and elsewhere. Labor unrest was seen in the hundreds of strikes in the post–World War I period, such as the harbor strike of 1920, which stopped all ships from leaving New York, or the printers' strike, which stopped publications of most magazines in the country. Many strikes, such as the New York Garment Workers strike and the Great Steel strike of 1919, were carried out or influenced by recently arrived immigrants. See Franklin (1974).

2. See Roediger (1991). This "white" identity did not originate in the twentieth century and actually developed much earlier, after chattel slavery was firmly established.

3. The case of *Plessy v. Ferguson* (1896) involved the constitutionality of a Louisiana law that required separate accommodations for white and "colored" passengers on railroads in the state. Homer Plessy, an African American man from Louisiana, had been arrested for refusing to obey the order of the conductor of a train to sit in the car designated for Blacks. Mr. Plessy appealed to the Supreme Court, claiming that the statute was contrary to the Thirteenth and Fourteenth Amendments. Justice Brown upheld separate accommodations, declaring that "the object of the Amendment was undoubtedly to enforce the absolute equality of the two races before the law, but in the nature of things it could not have been intended to abolish distinctions based upon color, or to enforce social, as distinguished from political, equality, or a commingling of the two races upon terms unsatisfactory to either." In 1954, the case of *Brown v. Board of Education of Topeka, Kansas* barred the *de jure* segregation of students by race, ruling that separate schools were inherently unequal, effectively overturning the *Plessy* case. See Swisher (1969) and Woodward (1974).

4. See Caute (1978), who documents several cases of teachers driven to suicide after continual harassment by the FBI, which included threatening letters and planted "evidence" meant to implicate them as subversives.

5. According to Stolee (1993, p. 236): "'Intact busing' came to mean that the children would report to their original school; board buses with their regular teachers and ride to the receiving school; remain intact as classrooms with their regular teachers; remain under the supervision of their original principal; often be transported back to their original school for lunch and then returned to the receiving school; and usually have recess periods separate from the pupils regularly attending the receiving school." See Stolee in Rury and Cassell (1993).

6. Such a position was articulated in Banfield (1970). Banfield became part of Nixon's inner cabinet, along with Daniel Patrick Moynihan. The "culture of poverty" thesis was also argued by others in the 1980s, such as Nicholas Lehmann (June and July 1986). This theory, as well as the human capital theory had been criticized, for example by some, such as Valentin (1968) and Franklin and Resnick (1973). The above "culture of poverty" advocates distorted the original perspective articulated by Oscar Lewis, who first introduced the idea of a "culture of poverty" in such works as *Five Families: Mexican Case Studies in the Culture of Poverty* (1959) and *The Children of Sanchez* (1961). As Robin d. g. Kelley (1997) points out, Lewis "insisted that capitalism impoverished segments of the working class who were denied access to mainstream institutions. The culture they created to cope with poverty and disfranchisement was passed down through generations and thus led to passivity and undermined social organization. Lewis had no

intention of using the culture of poverty thesis to distinguish the 'deserving' from the 'undeserving poor'" (p. 181).

7. As Lewis M. Steel (2001) writes: "The Supreme Court's 1978 *University of California v. Bakke* decision . . . led the court slowly but surely to undermine the viability of Affirmative Action. In a split ruling the Bakke Court ruled that public educational institutions could not save a few spaces for qualified Blacks who for the most part had attended inferior inner-city schools in order to insure some African American presence, but instead could develop admissions criteria that might give minorities a helping hand. . . . I read it the same way Anthony Amsterdam and Jerome Bruner did: . . . as a decision that with 'its offspring [a series of ever more restrictive affirmative action rulings] turn[s] the Equal Protection Clause of the Fourteenth Amendment [under which *Brown* was decided] into a guarantee that white people will not be discriminatorily deprived of any of their traditional privileges'" (p. 30).

8. Such as Heatherly (1981). The Heritage Foundation was founded in 1973 by Brewer Joseph Coors and New Right activist Paul Weyrich. For an analysis of their influence on federal policy, see Pincus (1983).

9. For some of the conflicts and contradictions over how school desegregation impacted on children of color, see, for example, Schofield (1982); Ortiz (1988); and Meier, Stewart, and England (1989).

10. For a critique of the "contact hypothesis," or the assumption that contact in itself will automatically lead to positive intergroup relations, see Hewstone and Brown (1986).

11. *The Nation*, May 27, 1991. This figure does not necessarily reflect the actual number of incidents, only the sites where incidents were reported. Many campuses, such as the University of Wisconsin, reported numerous incidents.

12. Bob Peterson, editor of the journal *Rethinking Schools*, describes in a March 2001 email communication the dangerous impact of vouchers on public education: "Milwaukee has the largest publicly funded voucher program in the nation. In the current school year, 49 million public tax dollars will be diverted from the public schools of Wisconsin to pay for private voucher schools in Milwaukee. Nearly 10,000 children receive $5,326 to attend 103 private schools. Over 70 percent of those students attend religious schools, most of them are segregated by race and very few of them serve limited-English-speaking students or students with special needs. There are also about 2,500 students enrolled in 5 private schools chartered by the city and the local university. The city of Milwaukee is the only city governmental body in the country that has the authority to charter 'private' schools in which they receive nearly $6,500 per student.

"The state also gave the University of Wisconsin—Milwaukee power to charter schools, which it did—the one and only Edison School in the city. That school, which opened in September, has had one-third of its staff leave, is on its third principal and has had several hundred students leave. Despite all this, it just received the initial OK for $12.1 million in tax-free bonds from the city Redevelopment Authority. (The local Milwaukee Area Technical College also has authority to charter schools, but the strong AFT local has prevented it from doing so.) To round this out, Milwaukee is home of both the conservative Bradley Foundation (which has been a huge factor in the growth of vouchers in Wisconsin) and Howard Fuller. Fuller, a Bush education advisor and darling of right-wing think tanks and foundations, and husband of Deborah McGriff, president of Edison Colleges, recently started the Black Alliance for Educational Options. This national organization, according to the *Boston Globe*, has spent over $1.3 million for advertising in favor of vouchers in the Washington, D.C., area. One of their strategies is to convince Congress to bring vouchers to D.C. Fuller, who has remained silent on virtually all other social issues, calls the voucher effort the 'new civil rights movement' and, at a recent meeting of the BAEO in Milwaukee (with over six hundred attendees from over thirty-five states), called the struggle for vouchers a 'war.'"

Chapter Three

1. See Roediger (1991).

2. See, for example, Banfield (1970). See also Sowell (1975).

3. S. Rosenthal, communication from the Progressive Sociologists Network (PSN), July 11, 1998.

4. See, for example, Troyna (1984); Troyna and Williams (1986); Brandt (1986); and Gillborn (1995).

5. Such as the work of Brandt (1986); Troyna (1984); Sivanandan (1985); Carrington and Troyna (1988); Gillborn (1995); Mullard (1981); and Troyna and Williams, (1986).

6. Indeed, the usage of the terms *antiracist* or *antiracism* is rare in the educational establishment in the United States. The marginality of the antiracist terminology is reflected in the annual proceedings of the American Educational Research Association, the major educational research organization in the United States. A perusal through the program books from annual conferences from 1992 to 2000 does not show the terms *antiracism* or *antiracist* indexed among the approximately twelve hundred descriptors used.

7. It is important to note that the term "black" may have a different meaning outside of the United States. In Great Britain, for example, "black " refers not only to Africans, but also to Indians, Asians, or anyone else who is not white, whereas in the United States, the term refers specifically to people of African descent.

8. See, for example, Perlo (1975), as well as voluminous works by Herbert Aptheker and W. E. B. Du Bois. See also Lightfoot (1970); Patterson (1971); Winston (1977); and Davis (1981).

9. Such as the Black Nationalist perspective of Haki Madhubhuti.

10. Such as the Republic of New Africa, which advocated, among other things, the creation of a semiautonomous African American nation consisting of five southern states.

11. Some of the works in critical whiteness studies include Frankenberg (1993); Wellman (1993); and Lipsitz (1998), among many others.

12. Critical race theorists in education were influenced by the critical race theorists, such as in the work of Derrick Bell (1995). See also Harris (1993) and Crenshaw, Gotanda, et al. (1995).

Chapter Four

1. In 1990, Maurer reported that there were 609,690 African American males in prison and only 436,000 enrolled in college. By 1995, nearly one-third of African American males and 12 percent of Latino men between the ages of twenty and twenty-nine were in prison or jail, or on probation or parole, compared with 6.7 percent of their white counterparts. See also Barsamian, "Interview with Angela Davis" (*Progressive Magazine* 65, no. 2 [2001, February]).

2. By 1996, 86.6 percent of public elementary and secondary teachers were white; 7.34 percent were Black; and 4.25 percent Hispanic. National Center for Educational Statistics (1998), table 273, p. 174.

3. See, for example, Thomas, Dove, and Hodge (1986). The authors point out that in Florida, for example, non-Hispanic Black students constituted 38 percent of the student population in classes for the "educably mentally retarded" (EMR); 35 percent in classes for the "mentally disturbed"; and 27 percent in "learning disability" (LD) classes.

4. These are 1996 figures. See National Center for Educational Statistics (1998), table 273, p. 174. These figures show an increase in female teachers from the total reported in Spencer (1986), who noted that 83 percent of elementary teachers were women and 46 percent of secondary school teachers were women, with a total of 66 percent of all teachers being women in 1986. See also Rury (1989).

Chapter Five

1. Du Bois wrote a more insightful biography, titled *John Brown* (1974).

2. For a critique of the traditional teacher education programs, see Haberman (1987); see also, Haberman (1993).

Chapter Six

1. Parts of this chapter were previously printed in Kailin (1999), copyright © Blackwell Publishers. Reprinted with permission.

2. These surveys were conducted by the major Lakeview newspaper and television media in the fall of 1995.

3. *Merriam-Webster's Collegiate Dictionary*, 10th ed., s.v. "racism."

4. While the vast majority of the participants were classroom teachers, there were also several other staff members, such as school nurses, social workers, and other support staff, who attended the in-services. Additionally, there were also two parent liaisons who attended. Other staff, such as custodial or food-service workers, were not given or offered this in-service by the district.

5. These mandatory workshops were required by the district at the beginning of each semester. While these in-services rarely focused on issues like race relations, occasionally, because of the influence of certain individuals on the schools' "multicultural" committee, a school chose to discuss race or multiculturalism for the in-service day. This was often after there had been a racial incident in the school. More typically, the in-services focused on less controversial topics.

6. The high school staff consisted of 102 teachers, including 2 teachers of color, in a school in which 13.4 percent of the students were students of color. At the middle school, at which 30 percent of the students were students of color, there were 65 staff members, including 3 teachers of color. At the elementary school, which had 41.5 percent students of color, there were 2 support staff and 1 teacher of color in a staff of 55. At all three schools, the majority of the students of color were African American, although there were also significant numbers of Hmong and Latino students.

7. Jacqueline Jordan Irvine made these remarks in a speech at the University of Wisconsin—Milwaukee School of Education "Urban Forum" on October 20, 1997.

8. Ibid.

9. The number could actually be higher, since those who reported may not have been the only ones who heard this language, but were the ones who cited it as problematic.

10. This image of the working-class bigot or ignorant Southern "redneck" is itself an elitist stereotype that places the blame on the ignorance of the lower classes, while ignoring the role perpetrated from above in the corporate suites.

11. Forty-six of the total number of 281 examples given were about hearing racist remarks from white teachers. This number actually represents a higher percentage, because the examples were given by 46 people of the total number of 189 respondents.

Chapter Seven

1. Similar perceptions and beliefs by white teachers are cited, for example, in Murrell (1993).

2. The twenty-one African American teachers were 6 percent of the total number of teachers who took my class. Nearly half (46 percent) of the total number of forty-six African American teachers in the district took my class. The ten Latina teachers comprised 3 percent of the total, and seven teachers (2 percent) were Asian. There were usually ten to fifteen people per class.

3. Of course, there are those who will never "see the light," and for such people, I can only urge that they not be placed in positions where they are working with other people. That is why it is imperative that this kind of pedagogy is implemented before people are allowed to receive teaching credentials.

4. There were exceptions to the influence of this white hegemony in the experiences of some of the African American teachers who had been educated in the segregated South of the forties and early fifties. Many of them had been consciously educated against racism and reported receiving a strong "Afrocentric" perspective from their Black teachers in segregated Southern schools.

Chapter Eight

1. Such as Brown (1867); Higgenson (1870); Du Bois (1903); or Du Bois (1964).

2. Certain governmental agencies, like the FBI, working in collaboration with various universities, also attempted to discredit his scholarship. There were even assassination attempts by right-wing paramilitary organizations to silence him. See Kailin (1998).

3. Quoted from Bob Marley's song "Buffalo Soldiers."

4. Some examples are Woodson (1922) and also Woodson's classic, *The Mis-education of the Negro* (1933/1990); Wesley (1927); Du Bois (1903); and Du Bois (1964).

5. Rethinking Schools Ltd. is located in Milwaukee and publishes *Rethinking Schools, An Urban Educational Journal.* Some of their other publications include *Rethinking Columbus* (1991); *Rethinking Our Classrooms: Teaching for Equity and Justice* (1994); *The Real Ebonics Debate: Power, Language and the Education of African American Children* (1997).

6. This was an audiotape of a lecture by Manning Marable on "The Impact of Columbus on African American History," originally given at the University of Wisconsin—Madison, October 1992.

7. In most of my classes, only two or three participants reported that they had ever heard of these publications. Rarely did anyone report that they were subscribers to *Rethinking Schools*.

8. *Color Adjustment*, produced by California Newsreel, San Francisco, 1992.

9. Enid Lee, speaking at the annual meeting of the National Coalition of Education Activists in Milwaukee, summer 1992.

References

Alba, R. (1990). *Ethnic identity: The transformation of white America*. New Haven, CT: Yale University Press.

Allport, G. W. (1954, 1979). *The nature of prejudice*. Reading, MA: Addison-Wesley.

Althusser, L. (1971). *Lenin and philosophy and other essays* (B. Brewster, Trans.). London: New Left Books.

American Council on Education. (1988). *One third of a nation*. Washington, DC: Author.

Apple, M. (1982). *Education and power*. Boston: Routledge & Kegan Paul.

———. (1988). *Teachers and texts: A political economy of class and gender relations in education*. New York: Routledge & Kegan Paul.

Aptheker, B. (1966). *Big business and the American university*. New York: New Outlook Publishers.

———. (1969). *The educational system in the United States*. New York: New Outlook Publishers.

Aptheker, H. (1938). *The Negro in the Civil War*. New York: International Publishers.

———. (1943). *American Negro slave revolts*. New York: Columbia University Press.

———. (1959). *The colonial era*. New York: International Publishers.

———. (1951–74). *A documentary history of the Negro people in the United States: From the colonial period to the establishment of the NAACP*. 3 vols., with a preface by W. E. B. Du Bois. New York: Citadel Press.

———. (1978). The American historical profession. In B. Aptheker (Ed.), *The unfolding drama: Studies in U.S. history* (pp. 31–42). New York: International Publishers.

———. (1992). *Anti-racism in the U.S.: A history of the first 200 years*. New York: Greenwood Press.

Arends, R., Hersh, R., and Turner, J. (1978). Inservice education and the six o'clock news. *Theory into Practice* 17, 196–205.

Aronowitz, S., and Giroux, H. (1985). *Education under siege: The conservative, liberal and radical debate over schooling*. South Hadley, MA: Bergin & Garvey Publishers.

Asante, M. (1987). *The Afrocentric idea*. Philadelphia: Temple University Press.

Baldwin, J. (1963/1988). A talk to teachers. In R. Simonson and S. Walker (Eds.), *The Graywolf annual five: Multicultural literacy* (pp. 3–12). St Paul, MN: Graywolf Press.

(Originally published as "The Negro Child—His Self-Image" in *Saturday Review*, December 21, 1963, and later published in a collection of essays, *The Price of the Ticket*, St. Martin's Press, 1986.)

Ballard, A. B. (1973). *The education of Black folk: The Afro-American struggle for knowledge in white America.* New York: Harper & Row.

Banfield, E. C. (1970). *The unheavenly city: The nature and the future of our urban crisis.* Boston: Little, Brown.

Banks, J. A. (1981). *Multiethnic education: Theory and practice.* Boston: Allyn & Bacon.

———. (1995). Multicultural education: Its effects on students' racial and gender role attitudes. In J. A. Banks and C. A. McGee Banks (Eds.), *Handbook of research on multicultural education.* New York: Macmillan Publishing.

Banks, J. A., and McGee Banks, C. A. (Eds.). (1995). *Handbook of research on multicultural education.* New York: Macmillan Publishing.

Barndt, M., and McNally, J. (2001). *The return to separate and unequal: Metropolitan Milwaukee school funding through a racial lens.* Milwaukee: Rethinking Schools.

Barsamian, D. (2001, February). Interview with Angela Davis. *Progressive Magazine* 65(2).

Beauboeuf-Lafontant, T. (1999). A movement against and beyond boundaries: Politically relevant teaching among African American teachers. *Teachers College Record* 100(4), 702–23.

Becker, G. S. (1964). *Human capital: A theoretical and empirical analysis, with special reference to education.* New York: National Bureau of Economic Research, Columbia University Press.

Becker, H. S., Geer, B., Hughes, E., and Strauss, A. (1961). *Boys in white: Student culture in medical school.* Chicago: University of Chicago Press.

Bell, D. (1995). Racial realism—after we're gone: Prudent speculations on America in a post-racial epoch. In R. Delgado (Ed.), *Critical race theory: The cutting edge* (pp. 2–8). Philadelphia: Temple University Press.

Bennett, C. (1986). *Comprehensive multicultural education: Theory and practice.* Boston: Allyn & Bacon.

Berger, P. L., and Luckmann, T. (1966). *The social construction of reality: A treatise on the sociology of knowledge.* New York: Doubleday.

Berlowitz, M. J., and Chapman, F. E., Jr. (Eds.). (1980). *The United States educational system: Marxist approaches.* Minneapolis: Marxist Educational Press.

Berlowitz, M. J., and Edari, R. S. (Eds.). (1984). *Racism and the denial of human rights: Beyond ethnicity.* Minneapolis: Marxist Educational Press.

Bernal, M. (1987). *Black Athena: The Afroasiatic roots of classical civilization.* New Brunswick, N.J: Rutgers University Press.

Bidol, P. M. (1971). *From racism to pluralism.* New York: Council on Interracial Books for Children.

Bigelow, W., et al. (1992/1997). *Rethinking Columbus: Teaching about the 500th anniversary of Columbus's arrival in America.* Milwaukee: Rethinking Schools.

Bigelow, W., and Christenson, L., et al. (Eds.). (1994). *Rethinking our classrooms: Teaching for equity and justice.* Milwaukee: Rethinking Schools.

Boggs, C. (1984). *Two revolutions: Gramsci and the dilemmas of Western Marxism.* Boston: South End.

Boggs, G. L. (1970). Towards a new system of education. In N. Wright, Jr. (Ed.), *What Black educators are saying* (pp. 31–38). New York: Hawthorne Books.

Boggs, J. (1970). *Racism and the class struggle: Further pages from a Black worker's notebook.* New York: Monthly Review Press.

Boggs, J., and Boggs, G. L. (1970). *Uprooting racism and racists in the USA.* Detroit: Radical Education Project.

Bowles, S., and Gintis, H. (1976). *Schooling in capitalist America: Educational reform and the contradictions of economic life.* New York: Basic Books.

Bowser, B. P., and Hunt, R. G. (Eds.). (1981). *Impact of racism on white Americans.* Beverly Hills, CA: Sage Publications.

Boyer, R. O., and Morais, H. M. (1975). *Labor's untold story* (3rd ed.). New York: United Electrical, Radio and Machine Workers of America.

Braden, A. (1980). Brown to Bakke: The crisis of public education. In M. J. Berlowitz and F. E. Chapman, Jr. (Eds.), *The United States educational system: Marxist approaches* (pp. 5–19). Minneapolis: Marxist Educational Press.

Brandt, G. L. (1986). *The realization of anti-racist teaching.* London: Falmer Press.

Brown, W. W. (1867). *The Negro in the American rebellion: His heroism and his fidelity.* Boston: Lee & Shepard.

Carrington, B., and Troyna, B. (1988). Combating racism through political education. In B. Carrington and B. Troyna (Eds.), *Children and controversial issues: Strategies for the early and middle years of schooling* (pp. 205–22). London: Falmer Press.

Castells, M., et al. (1999). *Critical education in the information age.* New York: Rowman & Littlefield Publishers.

Caute, D. (1978). *The great fear: The anti-Communist purge under Truman and Eisenhower.* New York: Simon & Schuster.

Chossudovsky, M. (2000). *The globalization of poverty: Impacts of the IMF and World Bank reforms.* New York: Common Courage Press.

Chronicle of Higher Education. (1995). *Almanac* 17(1) (September 1, 1995).

Churchville, J. A. (1970). On correct Black education. In Nathan Wright, Jr. (Ed.), *What Black educators are saying* (pp. 121–29). New York: Hawthorne Books.

Citron, A. (1969). *The rightness of whiteness: The world of the white child in a segregated society.* (Pamphlet.) Detroit: Ohio Regional Educational Lab.

Clarke, J. H. (1970). Black power and Black history. In N. Wright, Jr. (Ed.), *What Black educators are saying* (pp. 217–27). New York: Hawthorne Books.

Coles, G. (1988). *The learning mystique: A critical look at "learning disabilities."* New York: Pantheon Books.

Collins, J. L., and Lutz, C. A. (1993). *Reading National Geographic.* Chicago: University of Chicago Press.

Color Adjustment. (1992). (Video recording.) San Francisco: California Newsreel.

Crenshaw, K., Gotanda, N., et al. (1995). *Critical race theory: The key writings that formed the movement.* New York: New Press.

Davis, A. Y. (1981). *Women, race and class.* New York: Random House.

————. (1998). Race and criminalization: Black Americans and the punishment industry. In W. Lubiano (Ed.), *The house that race built* (pp. 264–79). New York: Random
House.

Dei, G. J. (1996). *Anti-racism education: Theory and practice.* Halifax, NS: Fernwood
Publishing.

Delgado, R. (Ed.). (1995). *Critical race theory: The cutting edge.* Philadelphia: Temple
University Press.

Delpit, L. (1988). The silenced dialogue: Power and pedagogy in educating other people's children. *Harvard Educational Review* 58: 280–98.

Diop, C. A. (1974). *The African origins of civilization: Myth or reality?* (M. Cook, Trans.).
New York: L. Hill.

D'Sousa, D. (1995). *The end of racism: Principles of a multiracial society.* New York: Free
Press.

Du Bois, W. E. B. (1903). *The souls of Black folk: Essays and sketches.* London: Archibald
Constable.

————. (1964). *Black reconstruction in the United States, 1860–1880.* New York: Merid-
ian.

————. (1973). *The education of Black people: Ten critiques 1906–1960.* (Herbert Aptheker, Ed.). Amherst: University of Massachusetts Press.

————. (1974). *John Brown.* New York: International Publishers.

————. (1980). *Selections from the Brownies books.* (Herbert Aptheker, Ed.). New York:
Kraus-Thomson Organization Limited.

Dunning, W. A. (1897/1931). *Essays on the Civil War and Reconstruction and related topics.* New York: Macmillan.

Edari, R. S. (1984). Racial minorities and forms of ideological mystification. In M. J.
Berlowitz and R. S. Edari (Eds.), *Racism and the denial of human rights: Beyond ethnicity* (pp. 6–15). Minneapolis: Marxist Educational Press.

Edari, S. K. (1989). African American farm workers strike against peonage in Wisconsin.
Wisconsin Labor History News 7: 4–6.

Figueroa, P. M. (1984). Race relations and cultural differences: Some ideas on a racial
frame of reference. In G. K. Verma and C. Bagley (Eds.), *Race relations and cultural
differences: Educational and interpersonal perspectives* (pp. 15–28). New York: St. Martin's Press.

Fine, M. (1986). Why urban adolescents drop into and out of public high school. In G.
Natriello (Ed.), *School dropouts: Patterns and policies.* New York: Teachers College
Press.

Fine, M., Weis, L., Powell, C., and Mun Wong, L. (Eds.). (1997). *Off white: Readings on
race, power, and society.* New York: Routledge.

Fish, S. (1993). Reverse racism; or, How the pot got to call the kettle black. *Atlantic
Monthly* 11: 135.

Fleming, W. L. (1905). *The Civil War and Reconstruction in Alabama.* New York: Columbia University Press.

Foner, P. S. (1947). *History of the labor movement in the United States.* New York: International Publishers.

Foner, P. S. (Ed.). (1975). *The life and writings of Frederick Douglass.* 4 vols. New York: International Publishers.

Fordham, S., and Ogbu, J. (1986). Black students' school success: Coping with the burden of "acting white." *Urban Review* 18: 176–206.

Foster, W. Z. (1970). *The Negro people in American history.* New York: New World Publishers.

Frankenberg, R. (1993). *White women, race matters: The social construction of whiteness.* Minneapolis: University of Minnesota Press.

Franklin, J. H. (1974). *From slavery to freedom: A history of Negro Americans* (4th ed.). New York: Alfred A. Knopf.

Franklin, R. S., and Resnick, S. (1973). *The political economy of racism.* New York: Holt, Rinehart & Winston.

Freedman, S., and Baynes, M. (1984). Sexism and multicultural education in elementary schools: A discussion. *Radical Teacher* 27(11): 12–15.

Freire, P. (1970). *Pedagogy of the oppressed.* (Myra Bergman, Trans.). New York: Herder & Herder.

Freire, P., and Macedo, D. (1993). A dialogue with Paulo Freire. In P. McLaren and P. Leonard (Eds.), *Paulo Freire: A critical encounter.* New York: Routledge.

Gillborn, D. (1995). *Racism and anti-racism in real schools: Theory, policy, practice.* Buckingham, UK: Open University Press.

Giroux, H. (1994). Insurgent multiculturalism and the promise of pedagogy. In D. T. Goldberg (Ed.), *Multiculturalism: A critical reader.* Malden, MA: Blackwell Publishers.

Glazer, N., and Moynihan, D. P. (1963). *Beyond the melting pot; The Negroes, Puerto Ricans, Jews, Italians, and Irish of New York City.* Cambridge, MA: MIT Press.

Goodlad, J. (1984). *A place called school.* New York: McGraw-Hill.

Gordon, B. M. (1985). Towards emancipation in citizenship education: The case of African American cultural knowledge. *Theory and Research in Social Education* 12(4): 1–23.

Gossett, T. F. (1975). *Race: The history of an idea in America.* Dallas: Southern Methodist University Press.

Gould, S. J. (1996). *The mismeasure of man,* rev. ed. New York: W. W. Norton.

Haberman, M. (1987). *Recruiting and selecting teachers for urban schools.* New York: ERIC Clearing House on Urban Education, Institute for Minority Education.

———. (1991). Can cultural awareness be taught in teacher education programs? *Teaching Education* 4(1): 25–31.

———. (1993). Teaching in multicultural schools: Implications for teacher selection and training. In L. Kremer-Hayon, H. Vonk, and R. Fessler (Eds.), *Teacher professional development* (pp. 267–94). Amsterdam: Swets & Zeitlinger.

Haberman, M., and Post, L. (1992). Does direct experience change preservice students' perceptions of low income minority children? *Midwestern Educational Researcher* 5(2): 29–31.

Hacker, A. (1992). *Two nations: Black and white, separate, hostile, unequal.* New York: Scribners.

Hall, S. (1981). Teaching race. In A. James and R. Jeffcoate (Eds.), *The school in the multicultural society.* London: Harper & Row.

Hamilton, C., and Carmichael, S. (1967). *Black power: The politics of liberation in America.* New York: Random House.

Harris, C. I. (1993). Whiteness as property. *Harvard Law Review* 106(8): 707–91.

Heatherly, C. L. (Ed). (1981). *Mandate for leadership: Policy management in a conservative administration.* Washington DC: Heritage Foundation.

Herrnstein, R. J., and Murray, C. (1994). *The bell curve: Intelligence and class structure in American life.* New York: Free Press.

Hewstone, M., and Brown, R. (Eds.). (1986). *Contact and conflict in intergroup encounters.* Oxford: Basil Bleakly.

Higgenson, T. W. (1870). *Army life in a Black regiment.* Boston.

Hofstadter, R. (1963). *Anti-intellectualism in American life.* New York: Knopf.

Hollins, E. (1992). Debunking the myth of a monolithic white American culture; or, moving toward cultural inclusion. *American Behavioral Scientist* 34: 201–9.

Hurtado, A., and Stewart, A. (1997). Through the looking glass: Implications of studying whiteness for feminist methods. In M. Fine, L. Weis, L. Powell, and L. Mun Wong (Eds.), *Off white: Readings on race, power and society* (pp. 297–311). New York: Routledge.

Jacobson, M. F. (1998). *Whiteness of a different color: European immigrants and the alchemy of race.* Cambridge, MA: Harvard University Press.

Jones, J. M. (1981). The concept of racism and its changing reality. In B. P. Bowers and R. G. Hunt (Eds.), *Impacts of racism on white Americans.* Beverly Hills, CA: Sage Publications.

Joyce, B., et al. (1976). *In-service teacher education.* Palo Alto, CA: Stanford Center for Research and Development in Teaching.

Kagarlitsky, B. (1999). *New realism, new barbarism: Socialist theory in the era of globalization.* (Reunifier Clarke, Trans.). London: Pluto Press.

Kailin, C. S. (1991). *Black chronicle: An American history textbook supplement* (3rd ed.). Madison: Wisconsin Department of Public Instruction.

Kailin, J. (1994). Anti-racist staff development for teachers: Considerations of race, class and gender. *Teaching and Teacher Education* 10: 169–84.

———. (1998). Toward nonracist historiography: The early work of Herbert Aptheker. In H. Shapiro (Ed.), *African American history and radical historiography: Essays in honor of Herbert Aptheker* (pp. 19–38). Minneapolis: Marxist Educational Press.

———. (1999). How white teachers perceive the problem of racism in their schools: A case study in "liberal" Lakeview. *Teachers College Record* 100(4): 724–50.

Karliner, J. (1997). *The corporate planet: Ecology and politics in the age of globalization.* San Francisco: Sierra Club Books.

Katz, J. H. (1978). *White awareness: Handbook for anti-racism training.* Norman: University of Oklahoma Press.

Kelley, R. d. g. (1997). *Yo' mama's disfunktional!: Fighting the culture wars in urban America.* Boston: Beacon Press.

Kerner Commission. *National advisory commission on civil rights.* New York: Bantam, 1968.

King, J., and Ladson-Billings, G. (1988). The teacher education challenge in elite university settings: Developing critical perspectives for teaching in a democratic and multicultural society. *European Journal of Intercultural Studies* 1: 15–23.

King, J. E. (1991). Dysconscious racism: Ideology, identity, and the miseducation of teachers. *Journal of Negro Education* 60: 133–45.

Kohl, H. (1994a). I won't learn from you!: Confronting student resistance. In W. Bigelow and L. Christenson, et al. (Eds.), *Rethinking our classrooms: Teaching for equity and justice* (pp. 134–35). Milwaukee: Rethinking Schools.

———. (1994b). *I won't learn from you and other thoughts on creative maladjustment.* New York: New Press.

Kozol, J. (1991). *Savage inequalities: Children in America's schools.* New York: Crown Publishers.

Kunjufu, J. (1985). *Countering the conspiracy to destroy Black boys.* Chicago: African American Images.

Ladson-Billings, G. (1994). *The dream keepers: Successful teachers of African American children.* San Francisco: Jossey-Bass.

———. (1995). Multicultural teacher education: Research, practice and policy. In J. A. Banks and C. M. Banks (Eds.), *Handbook of research on multicultural education* (pp. 747–59). New York: Simon & Schuster.

Ladson-Billings, G., and Tate, W. F. (1995). Toward a critical race theory of education. *Teachers College Record* 97(1): 47–68.

Lehmann, N. (1986, June). The origins of the underclass, part I. *Atlantic Monthly* 257.

———. (1986, July). The origins of the underclass, part II. *Atlantic Monthly* 258.

Lerner, G. (1979). *The majority finds its past: Placing women in history.* New York: Oxford University Press.

Lewis, O. (1959). *Five families: Mexican case studies in the culture of poverty.* New York: New American Library.

———. (1961). *The children of Sanchez.* New York: Random House.

Lightfoot, C. (1970). *Black America and world revolution.* New York: New Outlook Publishers.

———. (1977, September). On the centrality of the struggle for African American liberation. *Political Affairs* 30–52.

Lipsitz, G. (1998). *The possessive investment in whiteness: How white people profit from identity politics.* Philadelphia: Temple University Press.

Liston, D. P., and Zeichner, K. (1991). *Teacher education and the social conditions of schooling.* New York: Routledge.

Loewen, J. W. (1995). *Lies my teacher told me: Everything your American history textbook got wrong.* New York: Simon & Schuster.

Lofland, J., and Lofland, L. H. (1995). *Analyzing social settings: A guide to qualitative observation and analysis* (3rd ed.). Belmont, CA: Wadsworth Publishing Company.

Lumpkin, B. (1988). Ancient Egypt for children: Facts, fiction, lies. In B. Bacon (Ed.), *How much truth do we tell the children?: The politics of children's literature* (pp. 185–95). Minneapolis: MEP Publications.

Majors, R., and Billson, J. M. (1993). *Cool pose: The dilemma of Black manhood in America.* New York: Simon & Schuster.

Mann, K. (1942). *The turning point, thirty-five years in this century.* New York: L. B. Fischer.

Marable, M. (1983). *How capitalism underdeveloped Black America: Problems in race, political economy, and society.* Boston: South End Press.

———. (1995). *Beyond Black and white: Transforming African-American politics.* London: Verso.

Martinez, E. (1990, July–August). The politics of "cultural diversity": Old poison in new bottles. *Z Magazine* 35–39.

Marx, K. (1967). *Capital: A critique of political economy.* Vol. 1, *The process of capitalist production* (Samuel Moore and Edward Aveling, Trans., Frederick Engels, Ed.). New York; International Publishers.

Massey, G. C., Scott, M. V., and Dornbusch, S. M. (1975, November). Racism without racists: Institutional racism in urban schools. *Black Scholar* 10–19.

Maurer, M. (1990). *Young Black men and the criminal justice system: A growing national problem.* Washington, DC: Sentencing Project.

Mazrui, A. A. (1986). *The Africans: A triple heritage.* Boston: Little, Brown.

McCarthy, C. (1993). After the canon: Knowledge and ideological representation in the multicultural discourse on curriculum reform. In C. McCarthy and W. Crichlow (Eds.), *Race, identity, and representation in education.* New York: Routledge.

McCarthy, C., and Crichlow, W. (Eds.). (1993). *Race, identity, and representation in education.* New York: Routledge.

McChesney, R. W. (1997). The global media giants: Nine firms that dominate the world. *Extra!* 10: 11–18.

McDermott, R. (1982). Achieving school failure: An anthropological approach to literacy and social stratification. In G. Spindler (Ed.), *Doing the ethnography of schooling: Educational anthropology in action.* New York: Holt, Rinehart & Winston.

McIntosh, P. (1989, July–August). White privilege: Unpacking the invisible knapsack. *Peace and Freedom* 21–26.

McLaren, P. (1997). *Revolutionary multiculturalism: Pedagogies of dissent for the new millennium.* Boulder, CO: Westview Press.

McLaughlin, M. W., and Marsh, D. D. (1979). Staff development and school change. In A. Lieberman and L. Miller (Eds.), *Staff development: New demands, new realities, new perspectives.* New York: Teachers College Press.

McNeil, L. M. (2000). *Contradictions of school reform: The educational costs of standardized testing.* London: Falmer Press.

Meier, K. J., Stewart, J., Jr., and England, R. E. (1989). *Race, class and education: The politics of second-generation discrimination.* Madison: University of Wisconsin Press.

Miller, A. (1994, November). New York forum about "the bell curve": Footnotes from hell. *Newsday* A42.

Montagu, A. (1974). *Man's most dangerous myth: The fallacy of race* (5th ed.). New York: Oxford University Press.

Moore, R. (1985). *Racism in the English language.* New York: Council on Interracial Books for Children.

Moultry, M. (1989). Multicultural education among seniors in the College of Education at Ohio State University. Paper presented at the American Educational Research Association, San Francisco (ED 296634).

Mullard, C. (1981). The social context and meaning of multicultural education. In B. Davies (Ed.), *Educational analysis*. Oxford: Carfax Publishing.

Murray, C., and Clark, R. M. (1990, June). Targets of racism. *American School Board Journal* 30–39.

Murrell, P. (1993). Afrocentric immersion: Academic and personal development of African American males in public schools. In T. Perry and J. W. Fraser (Eds.), *Freedom's plow: Teaching in the multicultural classroom* (pp. 231–59). New York: Routledge.

National Center for Educational Statistics. (1998). *Statistical abstracts of the United States* (118th ed.). Washington, DC: U.S. Government Printing Office.

National Education Association. (1973). *Education and racism: An action manual*. Washington DC: Author.

Nieto, S. (1996). *Affirming diversity: The sociopolitical context of multicultural education*. New York: Longman Publishers.

Novak, M. (1972). *The rise of the unmeltable ethnics: Politics and culture in the seventies*. New York: Macmillan.

Ogbu, J. (1978). *Minority education and caste*. New York: Academic Press.

———. (1994). Racial stratification and education in the United States: Why inequality persists. *Teachers College Record* 96(2): 264–98.

Omi, M., and Winant, H. (1986). *Racial formation in the United States: From the 1960's to the 1980's*. New York: Routledge.

O'Reilly, K. (1989). *"Racial matters": The FBI's secret file on Black America, 1960–1972*. New York: Free Press.

Ortiz, F. I. (1988). Hispanic-American children's experiences in classrooms: A comparison between Hispanic and non-Hispanic children. In L. Weis (Ed.), *Class, race, and gender in American education*. Albany: SUNY Press.

Pallas, A., Natriello, G., and McGill, E. (1989). The changing nature of the disadvantaged population. *Educational Researcher* 18(5): 16–22.

Parenti, M. (1978). *Power and the powerless*. New York: St. Martin's Press.

———. (1995). *Against empire: A brilliant exposé of the brutal realities of U.S. global domination*. San Francisco: City Lights Books.

———. (1998). *America besieged*. San Francisco: City Lights Books.

Patterson, W. L. (1971). *The man who cried genocide*. New York: International Publishers.

Patton, M. Q. (1980). *Qualitative evaluation methods*. Beverly Hills, CA: Sage Publications.

Perkins, L. (1989). The history of Blacks in teaching. In D. Warren (Ed.), *American teachers: Histories of a profession at work* (pp. 344–69). New York: Macmillan.

Perlo, V. (1975). *The economics of racism USA: The roots of Black inequality*. New York: International Publishers.

Perlo, V., and Welty, G. (1984). The political economy of racism and the current scene. In M. J. Berlowitz and R. S. Edari (Eds.), *Racism and the denial of human rights: Beyond ethnicity* (pp. 68–75). Minneapolis: Marxist Educational Press.

Perry, T. (1993). *Toward a theory of African American school achievement.* Report No. 16. Center on Families, Communities, Schools, and Children's Learning. U.S. Department of Education (R117Q 00031).

Perry, T., and Delpit, L. (Eds.). (1997). *The real ebonics debate: Power, language, and the education of African American children.* Milwaukee: Rethinking Schools.

Perry, T., and Fraser, J. W. (1993). *Freedom's plow: Teaching in the multicultural classroom.* New York: Routledge.

Pewewardy, C. (1999). "I" is NOT for Indian: Reclaiming tribal identity by deconstructing American hegemony and education. Unpublished paper.

Pfaff, T. (1993). *Paths of the people: The Ojibwe in the Chippewa Valley.* Eau Claire, WI: Chippewa Valley Museum Press.

Phillips, U. B. (1929). *Life and labor in the Old South.* Boston: Little, Brown.

Pincus, F. L. (1983). The Heritage Foundation and federal educational policy. *Radical Teacher* 25: 1–6.

Pollack, C. (1990). Urban schools: Program for failure. In M. J. Berlowitz and F. E. Chapman, Jr. (Eds.), *The United States educational system: Marxist approaches.* Minneapolis: Marxist Educational Press.

Popkewitz, T. (1987, November–December). Organization and power: Teacher education reforms. *Social Education.*

Record, W. (1971). *The Negro and the communist party.* New York: Atheneum.

Roediger, D. R. (1991). *The wages of whiteness: Race and the making of the American working class.* New York: Verso.

———. (1994). *Towards the abolition of whiteness: Essays on race, politics, and working-class history.* New York: Verso.

Rury, J. L. (1989). Who became teachers? In D. Warren (Ed.), *American teachers: Histories of a profession at work* (pp. 370–92). New York: Macmillan.

Rury, J. L., and Cassell, F. A. (Eds.). (1993). *Seeds of crisis: Public schooling in Milwaukee since 1920.* Madison: University of Wisconsin Press.

Ryan, W. (1971). *Blaming the victim.* New York: Pantheon Books.

Sarason, S. (1971). *The culture of the school and the problem of change.* Boston: Allyn & Bacon.

Schofield, J. W. (1982). *Black and white in school: Trust, tension, or tolerance?* New York: Praeger Publishers.

Sheets, R. H. (2000). Advancing the field or taking center stage: The white movement in multicultural education. *Educational Researcher* 29(9): 15–21.

Sikula, J., Buttery, T., and Guyton, E. (Eds.). (1996). *Handbook of research on teacher education* (2nd ed.). New York: Macmillan.

Sivanandan, A. (1985). RAT and the degradation of Black struggle. *Race and Class* 26(4): 1–33.

Sleeter, C. E. (1992). *Keepers of the American dream: A study of staff development and multicultural education.* Washington, DC: Falmer Press.

Sleeter, C. E., and Grant, C. A. (1988). *Making choices for multicultural education: Five approaches to race, class, and gender.* Columbus, OH: Merrill Publishing.

Solorzano, D. G. (1997). Images and words that wound: Critical race theory, racial stereotyping, and teacher education. *Teacher Education Quarterly* 24(3): 5–19.

Sowell, T. (1975). *Race and economics in Black education: Myths and tragedies*. New York: Longman.

Spencer, D. A. (1986). *Contemporary women teachers: Balancing school and home*. New York: Longman.

Spring, J. (1994). *American education* (6th ed.). New York: McGraw-Hill.

Steel, L. M. (2001, February 5). Separate and unequal, by design. *Nation* 27–32.

Steinberg, S. (1995). *Turning back: The retreat from racial justice in American thought and policy*. Boston: Beacon Press.

Stolee, M. (1993). The Milwaukee desegregation case. In J. L. Rury and F. A. Cassell (Eds.), *Seeds of crisis: Public schooling in Milwaukee since 1920* (pp. 229–68). Madison: University of Wisconsin Press.

Stratman, D. (1991). *We CAN change the world: The real meaning of everyday life*. New Democracy Books.

———. (1998, September–October). You'll never be good enough: Schooling and social control. *New Democracy*.

Swisher, C. B. (1969). *Historic decisions of the Supreme Court* (2d ed.). New York: Van Nostrand Reinhold.

Tate, W. F. (1996). Critical race theory and education: History, theory, and implications. *Review of Research in Education* 22: 195–247.

Tatum, B. D. (1992). Talking about race, learning about racism: The application of racial identity development theory in the classroom. *Harvard Educational Review* 62: 1–24.

Terkel, S. (1992). *Race: How Blacks and whites think and feel*. New York: New Press.

Thomas, S., Dove, T., and Hodge, W. (1986). Black students in special education: Issues and implications for community involvement. *Negro Educational Review* 37: 17–26.

Thompson, A. (1999). *Education Review*. (On-line journal.) Review of M. Fine, et al. (Eds.), *Off white: Readings on race, power, and society*. <http://coe.asu.edu/ednev/reviews/rev76.htm>.

Torres, C. A. (1998). *Democracy, education, and multiculturalism: Dilemmas of citizenship in a global world*. Lanham, MD: Rowman & Littlefield Publishers.

Troyna, B. (1984). Multicultural education: Emancipation or containment? In L. Barton and S. Walker (Eds.), *Social crisis and educational research* (pp. 75–97). London: Croom Helm.

Troyna, B., and Williams, J. (1986). *Racism, education and the state*. Beckenham, UK: Croom Helm.

University of Wisconsin. (1989). *It does happen here*. (Video recording.) Madison, WI: University of Wisconsin.

Valentin, C. (1968). *Culture and poverty: A critique and counter-proposals*. Chicago: University of Chicago Press.

Vanfossen, B. E. (1979). *The structure of social inequality*. Boston: Little, Brown.

Wallace, M. (1993). Multiculturalism and oppositionality. In C. McCarthy and W. Crichlow (Eds.), *Race, identity, and representation in education*. New York: Routledge.

Warren, D. (Ed.). (1989). *American teachers: Histories of a profession at work*. New York: Macmillan.

Weatherford, J. (1988). *The Indian givers: How the Indians of the Americas transformed the world*. New York: Fawcett Columbine.

Wellman, D. (1993). *Portraits of white racism.* Cambridge: Cambridge University Press.

Wesley, C. H. (1927). *Negro labor in the United States, 1850–1925: A study in American economic history.* New York: Russell & Russell.

Wilayto, P. (1997). *The Feeding trough, the Bradley foundation, "the bell curve," and the real story behind W-2, Wisconsin's national model for welfare reform: An investigative report by Phil Wilayto and a job is a right campaign* (2nd ed.). Milwaukee: The Campaign.

Williams, E. (1966). *Capitalism and slavery.* New York: Capricorn Books.

Williams, G. W. (1883). *The history of the Negro race in America.* New York: Bergman Publishers.

Wilson, C. E. (1970). Racism in education. In B. N. Schwartz and R. Disch (Eds.), *White racism: Its history, pathology, and practice.* New York: Dell Publishers.

Winston, H. (1977). *Class, race and Black liberation.* New York: International Publishers.

Woodson, C. G. (1922). *The Negro in our history.* Washington, DC: Association for the Study of Negro Life and History.

———. (1933/1990). *The mis-education of the Negro.* Trenton, NJ: Africa World Press.

Woodward, C. V. (1974). *The strange career of Jim Crow* (3rd rev. ed.). New York: Oxford University Press.

Zeichner, K. M. (1983). Alternative paradigms on teacher education. *Journal of Teacher Education* 34(3): 3–9.

Zeichner, K. M., and Hoeft, K. (1996). Teacher socialization for cultural diversity. In J. Sikula, T. Buttery, and E. Guyton (Eds.), *Handbook of research on teacher education* (2nd ed.) (pp. 525–47). New York: Macmillan.

Zepezauer, M., and Naiman, A. (1996). *Take the rich off welfare.* Tucson, AZ: Odonian Press.

Zinn, H. (1980/1999). *A people's history of the United States: 1492 to the present.* New York: Perennial Classics. (Originally published in 1980 by HarperCollins.)

Index

About the Author

JULIE KAILIN is an assistant professor in the Department of Educational Policy and Community Studies at the University of Wisconsin—Milwaukee. She has worked for many years in the civil-rights and trade-union movements, including as an AFT organizer. Since the late 1980s, she has also worked as an educational consultant to school districts in the areas of race relations and cultural diversity.